The Integration of
Baseball in Philadelphia

The Integration of Baseball in Philadelphia

CHRISTOPHER THRESTON

McFarland & Company, Inc., Publishers
Jefferson, North Carolina, and London

Library of Congress Cataloguing-in-Publication Data

Threston, Christopher, 1967–
 The integration of baseball in Philadelphia / Christopher Threston.
  p.   cm.
 Includes bibliographical references and index.

 ISBN 0-7864-1423-5 (softcover : 50# alkaline paper)

 1. Baseball—Pennsylvania—Philadelphia—History. 2. African American baseball players—Pennsylvania—Philadelphia—History. 3. Discrimination in sports—Pennsylvania—Philadelphia—History. 4. Racism in sports—Pennsylvania—Philadelphia—History. I. Title.
 GV863.P372P558   2003
 796.357'09748'11—dc21   2002153761

British Library cataloguing data are available

©2003 Christopher Threston. All rights reserved

No part of this book may be reproduced or transmitted in any form or by any means, electronic or mechanical, including photocopying or recording, or by any information storage and retrieval system, without permission in writing from the publisher.

Cover photograph: Tony Gonzalez of the Philadelphia Phillies
(Baseball Hall of Fame Library, Cooperstown, NY)

Manufactured in the United States of America

McFarland & Company, Inc., Publishers
 Box 611, Jefferson, North Carolina 28640
  www.mcfarlandpub.com

This work is dedicated to
Denise and Megan. Two great students
who never got *their* opportunity.

Acknowledgments

The inspiration for this project came during two distinct eras in my life. First, my love of organized sports, forged during my childhood, encouraged me to find its historical significance in American culture. For young people, team sports offer the opportunity to learn many lessons, especially the importance of character in our competitive world. Secondly, the realization that the issue of race has long been a neglected historical topic inspired me to try to break new ground. Furthermore, work on what became this book began during a time when I searched for meaning in my own life. The information gained taught me that through maintaining integrity and values, one tends to reap the historical benefits. Because of the lessons learned from this work, I choose to hold on to my ideals rather than submit to the temptations of selfishness, egocentrism, and discrimination.

This book began as my master's thesis for Rutgers University (Camden) during the spring of 1997. In its early form, it began as a history of the Negro Leagues in Philadelphia. But during my preliminary research, I discovered that this relatively ignored topic was addressed quite effectively in Neil Lanctot's *Fair Dealing and Clean Playing* (1994). After discussing this issue with both my colleagues in the Graduate History program at Rutgers and Mr. Lanctot himself, I found that an adjustment of my topic became necessary. This adjustment accounts for my decision to focus on the integration of Philadelphia baseball.

The topic of the integration of major league baseball has become a well-covered issue over the years. This issue receives recognition on a more national level or as part of some other type of work. As far as the city of Philadelphia goes, no previous extensive work exists. Therefore, this work relies on a tapestry of vastly different sources. Researching this topic required the assistance of other groups and individuals. In other words, while only one author's name is on the title page, this work relied on the contributions of many individuals.

First and foremost, the people probably most responsible for the completion of this work come from the graduate program at Rutgers University (Camden). I would to thank the instructors within the program, most especially Dr. Janet Golden, who taught me truly how to write a historical work. She combed over many of the early drafts of this project. Thanks also go to Dr. Rodney Carlisle, who taught me how to research effectively, and to Dr. Allen Woll, who emphasized the value of looking at issues through a variety of perspectives. Finally, special thanks go to Ms. Loretta Carlisle, for keeping all of us graduate students in line.

Also important are my former colleagues from the Graduate School of History at Rutgers. I am grateful to the founding members of "Under the Bridge Productions." (Let us hope that we are on a merely lengthy hiatus rather than becoming defunct.) Much gratitude goes to fellow graduate student Jeff Anderson, who found many research possibilities for me and was quite supportive during the formative years of this work.

The most guidance I received came from Neil Lanctot. He provided me with much advice in the direction of this work. He also became someone I could ask questions of at any time. Another author who was quite helpful was Bill Kashatus. Although he submitted a similar idea to the same publisher, he graciously stepped aside until the completion of my project. Like Mr. Lanctot, Mr. Kashatus also provided me with much needed advice. Many other authors of baseball history (too numerous to name) also communicated their knowledge to me. For their selfless contributions, I send my thanks. I would also like to thank all those who failed to have confidence in me, refused to give me an opportunity, or believed I would not succeed. You filled me with the necessary resolve.

I would also like to acknowledge the following organizations: the Hagley Museum of Wilmington, Delaware, for the Carpenter collection; the Research Library at the Baseball Hall of Fame for their clipping files; the Free Library of Philadelphia, for their newspaper morgues; and the Paul Robeson Library of Rutgers University (Camden). These institutions provided unique and much needed information that proved essential to the survival of this project. In addition, the Society of American Baseball Research (SABR) and the Philadelphia Athletics Historical Society provided me with a wealth of information that proved helpful. In particular, I am grateful to Len Levin from the SABR Research Library for his prompt responses to my research queries. Finally, I would also like to thank W.C. Burdick at the National Baseball Hall of Fame photo department. Mr. Burdick provided most of the photographs used in this work.

Most of all, I would like to express my gratitude towards my family and friends for their love and support. Whether it was giving me baseball books as Christmas or birthday presents or finding interesting articles in the newspaper, they have proved quite supportive in times of need. I would especially like to thank my father, Joseph, my mother, Jean, my sister, Anne, and my brother, Joe, for all they have done for me.

Contents

Acknowledgments   vii

    Preface   1
1. The Early Days   7
2. Hilldale   24
3. Ed Bolden   30
4. Here Come the Stars   37
5. Attempted Integration of Philadelphia Baseball   46
6. The Demise of Black Baseball   59
7. Intolerance   70
8. Integration of Philadelphia Baseball   82
9. Integration in the 1960s and 1970s   100
    Epilogue   115

Appendix A: Former Philadelphia Stars Who Played in the Major Leagues   121
Appendix B: Black Players with the Philadelphia Athletics   125

*Appendix C: African American and Latin American
    Phillies, 1957–1979* 127
Notes 165
Bibliography 173
Index 181

Preface

The 1997 commemoration of the fiftieth anniversary of Jackie Robinson's debut in Major League baseball, together with the release of Ken Burns' 1994 documentary film *Baseball*, increased attention to the collective institution known as the Negro Leagues. Negro League baseball, first created in the 1920s, developed because owners of major league clubs informally agreed to exclude black baseball players from their rosters. The symbol of segregation, Jim Crow, invaded practically every American institution during the late 1800s, including professional baseball. As a result, blacks were forced out of organized white baseball. Thus, excluded blacks formed their own teams and leagues. These institutions existed until the integration of major league baseball in 1947. Despite Robinson's achievement that year with the Brooklyn Dodgers, integration was met with scorn and resistance.

Popular portrayals of both the history of the Negro Leagues and Jackie Robinson's story present both Philadelphia teams and fans negatively. In his film, Burns referred to Philadelphia as a place renowned for its "hostility toward its black players."[1] Further study reveals that this reputation exists throughout the Philadelphia baseball community, as evidenced by the failure of the community to support African American Philadelphia superstars such as Dick Allen. Indeed, Philadelphia teams and fans resisted integration of the major leagues.

A glaring example of this resistance occurred when Robinson's Dodgers first played the Phillies. Ben Chapman, the Phillies' manager at the time, instructed his players to verbally abuse Jackie Robinson. The severe criticism that Chapman received for his actions eventually cost him his job. This incident, which recently resurfaced during the celebration of this fiftieth anniversary, serves as a reminder of the difficulty the city had with the integration of its baseball teams.

The damaged reputation of the city is further marred by the hiring policies exhibited by Philadelphia teams. The city's two major league teams, the Phillies and the Athletics, were quite slow in acquiring black players. While in Philadelphia, the Athletics did not integrate their team until late in the 1953 season. In 1957, the Phillies became the last National League team to integrate its roster.[2] It was not until 1964 that Philadelphia had its first black superstar, Dick Allen. Moreover, Allen was booed often and he failed to become the cherished hero of Phillies fans. Former St. Louis Cardinals center fielder Curt Flood, when traded to Philadelphia for Allen in 1969, chose to embark on a fight against baseball's hated reserve clause rather than reporting to the Phillies. This reserve clause bound a player to the team that owned his contract rights. Flood, an African American, justified his legal fight by admitting his belief that the Phillies were the worst organization in baseball for a member of his race.[3] All of these factors contribute to Philadelphia's reputation as a city that puts little stock in the tradition of black baseball. This work examines how Philadelphia acquired that reputation as a tough place for black players.

In order to understand this work fully, one must possess a clear understanding of the terminology. The players of the Negro Leagues were not only African American but also dark-skinned Latin Americans from countries such as Cuba, Puerto Rico, and the Dominican Republic. Therefore, the use of "African American" is not always correct and the term "black" is used. The distinctions between physical appearance, origin, and race remained even after the breaking of baseball's color barrier. Many major league teams first integrated not with African Americans but with players of other nationalities or ethnic backgrounds, such as Cubans or Dominicans. More often than not, teams (including the Phillies) chose to integrate by employing Latin Americans rather than African Americans. In fact, of the seven black players on the Phillies' roster in 1960, none were African American.[4] This example indicates that the issue of integration not only affects African Americans but all people of color. Thus, the inexact term "black," used by the teams themselves, becomes necessary when describing the integration of major league baseball.

The first steps towards integration began in the 1920s. When African Americans poured into Northern cities as part of the Great Black Migration of the early 20th century, it marked the beginning of change. These individuals left the South, an area that offered few or no job prospects, and moved North seeking a better life. During World War I, blacks proved that they could provide a positive contribution to the war effort by assisting the nation both militarily and in the manufacturing of war materials. After proving their worth it seemed to some only a matter of time before all American institutions would become integrated.

Throughout the first half of the 20th century, most instances of defeating the stigma of race took place in sport or during war. Because of their performance as either soldiers or employees in factories constructing war materials, blacks proved themselves worthy of gaining equality in American life. Their contributions proved crucial to American success in both world wars. It was organized sports, however, that truly eliminated or minimized the effects of prejudice. Sports allowed blacks to receive more of a fair and equal opportunity. Robinson, like heavyweight champion Joe Louis and Olympic gold medalist track star Jesse Owens before him, proved that sports could "vanquish the stigma of race."[5]

This desire for racial equality also touched baseball, at first through the creation of the Negro Leagues. The creation of black professional baseball leagues occurred as a result of the fierce segregation that prevailed in America even after World War I. Despite evidence to the contrary, major league owners felt that their teams would not continue to flourish if integrated. They did not believe that fans would want to see their teams play if they were integrated. Through baseball, however, blacks showed that integration was possible. Negro League stars would consistently prove, in various ways, that they could compete on the same level as major league ballplayers. Nevertheless, the major leagues resisted integration. Professional baseball was no different than any other American institution, just one of the more visible. Despite calls for change, major league team owners still refused to include black players on their rosters. Because of the long delay in the integration of professional baseball, it became more difficult to do so in institutions like schools, public facilities, and public transportation.

This resistance to integration appears to create the clouded past for Philadelphia baseball history. From the post–World War I period to the present, the history of black baseball in Philadelphia suffered from instances of missed opportunities to embrace equality, active resistance from management, and intolerance from fans. Again, as this delay lengthened, integration naturally became more difficult. When Philadelphia teams finally integrated, it became a subject of controversy in the city. The problems that surrounded the integration of Philadelphia baseball appear to dominate the city's baseball history.

Not of issue was the quality and persistence of black baseball in Philadelphia. Until recently, these teams were largely neglected by baseball historians and, even today, remain less renowned than Negro League teams in other cities. Many younger baseball fans remain unaware of the fact that Philadelphia possessed successful Negro League teams. Through the high quality of their play, these Philadelphia teams contributed to the overall success of the Negro Leagues. Having star quality players, successful teams, and well-respected owners allowed the Philadelphia teams to enjoy a long-lasting presence within the Negro Leagues.

The two best known Philadelphia teams during the post–World War I period are the Hilldale Club, of Darby, and the Philadelphia Stars. Although other Philadelphia teams (particularly in the 1920s) participated in the Negro Leagues, they did not enjoy the longevity or success of Hilldale or the Stars. Many great players plied their trade on these teams as both gained sizable followings. Among the Hall of Fame players that toiled for Philadelphia Negro League teams were Judy Johnson, Satchel Paige, Oscar Charleston, and Martin Dihigo.[6] Negro League baseball held a strong place in the Philadelphia community and, during segregation, gained the respect of the city's African American baseball fans. The Hilldale club won the league championship three times and the Stars won once.[7] Negro League baseball in Philadelphia proved quite successful and enjoyed a loyal following. This success lasted until the integration of the major leagues when the Negro Leagues lost importance in the black community.

This work argues that Philadelphia's reputed racial intolerance of black players resulted not from segregation but from integration. As professional baseball began to move towards integration, more resistance than acceptance existed among fans and owners. When compared to other organizations such as the Brooklyn Dodgers, Cleveland Indians, and New York Giants, the Philadelphia teams lagged far behind. Then, once the rosters of the Phillies and Athletics became integrated, opposition remained within team management, the press, and the fans. The reluctance to integrate the city's teams created a legacy of intolerance in many other institutions. Because major league baseball holds a secure place in American culture, there remains little doubt that it reflects the historical developments of the nation.

Does baseball have a role in American history? As historian John Thorn said, "I am most proud to be a baseball fan when baseball has led America rather than followed it." Thorn was referring to Jackie Robinson's breaking of the color barrier in major league baseball.[8] This achievement occurred in 1947, seven years before the *Brown v. Board of Education* decision, fostering an increased movement towards civil rights. Robinson biographer Jules Tygiel states, "the forces that led to Robinson's hiring, the reaction among both blacks and whites, the institutional response of the baseball establishment, and the resulting decline of the Jim Crow leagues reveals much about the United States in the 1940s and 1950s."[9] Tygiel's quote indicates that once major league baseball became integrated, other American institutions followed suit. Examples of this changing racial policy include schools, all forms of transportation, restaurants, gas stations, bathrooms, and other public facilities. Like it or not, baseball does play a role in influencing American history. Therefore, it is conceivable that many could consider Philadelphia racially intolerant merely because of the reputation that surrounds its baseball history.

This work examines the very slow and difficult process of the integration of major league baseball in Philadelphia. As far back as the 1860s, there were attempts to integrate professional baseball in Philadelphia. Until September 1953, all of these efforts proved futile. This work examines these attempts and the reason for their failure. While Philadelphia remained segregated, other teams managed to integrate their teams. The city's reaction to these integrated teams often reflected the intolerance of both the Athletics and the Phillies. Many of the great black players of the time went to other clubs, which eventually hindered the play of the city's major league teams. Furthermore, this intolerance acted as a barrier to the integration of Philadelphia baseball and created a division between the white and the African American communities. An examination of this division and the barriers of integration are provided in this work.

When Philadelphia baseball finally became integrated, it was anything but a smooth transition. In many ways, integration created new problems that often reflected continued intolerance. These difficulties are chronicled here. Baseball serves as an excellent vehicle for this study of the difficult process of integration.

In writing this book, I have used numerous primary and secondary resources. Sometimes, these resources may only tell one side of a story or have problems with complete accuracy. Also, some secondary sources should be read with caution since some may be poorly documented and factually dubious. This work attempts to provide the most reliable information and tries to approach issues by using all available accounts. Of the sources used to complete this work, some failed to fully investigate events or anecdotes. I have tried to acquire as many accounts of an issue as possible before making any judgment or asserting any argument. The primary goal of this work is to shed light on a segment of history not previously reported. To accomplish this goal, it needs to bring together different accounts from a variety of sources. While this work focuses on

Philadelphia, it often is necessary to mention national issues to understand local occurrences. In historians' lingo, this work emerges as a "top-down" effort by taking national events and showing them from a smaller perspective: in this case, the issues of integration of baseball and civil rights as applied to the city of Philadelphia.

1

The Early Days

> *Baseball is the most popular sport in this country. In every hamlet, town, and city, may be the future Rube Fosters; romping over corner lots, batting, pitching, and learning how to play the game. Organize your team.*
>
> —W.E.B. Du Bois[1]

Segregation and Jim Crow laws denied African Americans many opportunities but also forced them to create institutions of their own. This situation proved especially true of baseball, easily America's most popular sport of the late 1800s and early 1900s. With the exception of Moses Fleetwood Walker of the Toledo Blue Stockings in 1884, major league baseball excluded blacks.[2] African American players, therefore, created their own teams. For the most part, these teams were barnstorming clubs that traveled around the country looking for opponents for exhibition games. The forming of these independent teams ultimately led to the creation of the collective institution known as the Negro Leagues.

The Negro Leagues not only served as an alternative to the major leagues but also as a form of cultural identity. African Americans rallied around the best players and teams of the time. Teams such as the Kansas City Monarchs, Pittsburgh Crawfords, and Homestead Grays maintained large followings among the African American community. Players such as Andrew "Rube" Foster, Leroy "Satchel" Paige, and Josh Gibson received recognition as heroes. As these and other Negro League players excelled, many major league players who saw them play respected and even praised their abilities. White all-star teams would play black barnstorming teams in exhibition games and come away impressed with the advanced level of play of the black teams.

Despite the abilities displayed by the black players, major league baseball, like many other institutions in America, remained segregated. Thousands of fans attended Negro League games each year or followed their favorite teams. African American newspapers such as the *Pittsburgh Courier* and the *Philadelphia Tribune* would cover Negro League baseball. Negro League teams eventually became the most profitable and influential of African American businesses.

The organization of black baseball teams in the Philadelphia area began as far back as the 1860s. Among the earliest teams were the Excelsiors of Philadelphia and the Philadelphia Pythians, who played most of their games in Camden, New Jersey. Members of these teams included former African American officers of the Union army during the Civil War. These teams played white teams in the area, but experienced much difficulty obtaining permits to play in fields in the city. This situation would force these teams to play each other in Camden or in other places outside the city. Compared to the fields used by the white clubs, the ones used by the black teams often proved quite inferior. Despite this persistent problem, black teams from New York and Washington, D.C., would come into the area to play the Pythians and Excelsiors. More often than not, the Philadelphia teams emerged victorious. In fact, when the Pythians defeated the Uniques of Chicago in a game billed as the "World's Colored Championship," they earned the billing of "Black Champions." With the success of the Pythians, Philadelphia briefly became known as the capital of black baseball.[3]

The organizer and promoter of the Pythians, Octavius V. Catto, was quite an interesting figure in the African American history of Philadelphia. A schoolteacher by trade, Catto also organized and participated in many mass meetings for Philadelphia blacks during the 1860s. His main cause was the integration of the city's streetcars. He served as a member of a committee that succeeded in integrating several lines of streetcars.[4] Later in the decade, Catto became principal of the Quaker-sponsored high school for blacks: the Institute of Colored Youth. He also organized a movement to encourage blacks to vote in the general elections. As a result of these activities, Catto emerged "as the most magnetic and perhaps the most promising leader the Philadelphia black community had yet produced."[5] To Catto, the Pythians became more than just a baseball team. They symbolized another attempt by Catto to end the massive segregation prevalent throughout American society.

Catto's involvement in professional baseball proves two points. First, the fact that Catto became well known as an early crusader for civil rights demonstrates the importance of baseball in American society. To Catto, the Pythians served as another vehicle for the integration of all facets of society. Catto, therefore, fails to embody the stereotypical baseball entrepreneur because he set his goals far higher than mere profits. To black civil rights leaders, the integration of professional baseball meant the possible creation of opportunities in other institutions. Furthermore, since the Pythians enjoyed a degree of success and maintained a strong following, Catto proved that blacks could run their own businesses effectively. Unfortunately, due to unforeseen circumstances, the Pythians' success eventually dissipated.

As baseball became more of a business, white organizers became threatened by both the athletic and financial prowess of black teams. This success provided the incentive for black teams to seek entrance into white professional baseball. In 1867, Catto attempted to enter the Pythians in the National Association of Base Ball Players (NABBP), then the ruling body of professional baseball. Catto sought to eliminate race as an issue in order to allow the Pythians to enter this association. Unfortunately, the nominating committee of the NABBP rejected Catto's proposal by voting to bar any club "composed of one or more colored persons."[6] Moreover, the association membership ruled that if "colored clubs were admitted there would be in all probability some division of feeling, whereas, by excluding them no injury could result to anybody and the possibility of any rupture being created on political bounds would be avoided." On the surface, this ruling was not the result of racial intolerance but of a desire to steer clear of political issues such as civil rights. The Association's position, however, began a policy of formal segregation that, for the most part, existed for eighty years.[7]

What made matters worse for the Pythians was the death of Catto. While attempting a movement to register African Americans to vote, Catto was murdered by rioters trying to keep blacks from the polls on Election Day 1870. Despite Catto's standing in the city's African American community, no individual was ever brought to trial for his murder. Catto's death meant the loss of an early crusader for civil rights in Philadelphia.[8] Left without their leader, the Pythians quickly disbanded. After their demise, a dearth of black professional teams existed.

With the Association's rejection of the Pythians, blacks needed to find other methods to integrate baseball. If a black team could not compete on its own in the major leagues, then two options existed: (1) integrate white teams or (2) play exhibition games against white teams. After the Pythians' failed attempt to integrate the National Association, blacks pursued both options. During the 1870s and 1880s, many black players managed to belong to white professional teams, with varying degrees of success. While many of these players became renowned for their skills, their appearance often created controversy. Usually such controversy manifested when a star player from another team refused to play against an integrated club.

The turmoil surrounding games between an all-white team and an integrated club remains best exemplified by the virulent racial attitudes of baseball superstar Cap Anson. An Iowa native, Anson was the star first baseman and manager of the Chicago White Stockings (later known as the Cubs) of the National League in the late 1800s. During this time, Anson became arguably the first big-money superstar in professional baseball. He accumulated 3,041 hits and possessed a gaudy .333 batting average during his Hall-of-Fame playing career. Furthermore, while serving as manager, Anson led the Chicago team to five league championships. Born in the Midwest and educated at Notre Dame University, Anson served as the clean-cut leader of major league baseball at a time when it received the reputation as a rough-and-tumble profession.[9] But Anson steadfastly refused to play against any teams with black players.

Because of Anson's place in professional baseball, league officials and team owners were greatly influenced by his opinions. As baseball gained momentum in American society during the late 1800s, owners hoped to continue to cash in on the reputations of players such as Anson. Therefore, league members would do whatever necessary to appease the league's best players in order to ensure continued success. For instance, the "World Champion" St. Louis Browns refused to play the era's best black team, the Cuban Giants.[10] Unfortunately, three years later, Anson issued a similar threat that was taken seriously.

This was on July 17, 1887, prior to an exhibition game between Anson's White Stockings and a team from Newark. The Newark club belonged to the International League, a minor league, and played the major league White Stockings. Newark planned to use their ace pitcher, African American George Stovey, against Chicago. Anson stated that his team would refuse to play against Newark unless another pitcher took the mound. On the day of the game, Newark announced that Stovey took ill and could not pitch against Chicago. At the end of the season, Newark dropped Stovey from the roster.[11] As a result of Anson's actions, concerned team owners began to reject the possibility of retaining black players. More importantly, teams around the league refused to hire any qualified black players.

Although Anson's background fails to provide any inclination that accounts for his prejudice, this refusal to compete against blacks set in motion the future segregationist policies of major league baseball. Owners believed that the inclusion of black players might decrease the number of fans attending each game, thereby reducing club profits. Therefore, worried owners merely avoided the hiring of black players. This attitude originates with the star power possessed by Anson and those who followed him.

Rejected by the National League, promising black players toured the country looking for opportunities to play in smaller, lesser-known professional leagues. For much of the 1870s and 1880s, black baseball teams were something of a rarity. Philadelphia, however, still offered high quality black baseball. Two stellar semipro teams, the Mutuals and the Orions, formed in the 1870s and 1880s as Philadelphia maintained its hold as the "capital of black baseball." This distinction allowed for the rise of the first black professional team, the Keystone Athletics, formed in May of 1885. In only two months, however, the club relocated to Long Island, merged with the Manhattans of Washington, D.C., and the Philadelphia Orions, and became known as the Cuban Giants. The Cuban Giants traveled the country year-round playing both white and black professional teams. The success of the Cuban Giants led to the formation of other black professional teams around the country. Philadelphia, unfortunately, lacked a team of its own and relied on local black amateur teams.[12]

Meanwhile, "Fleet" Walker was forced to leave the Toledo club and could only play with teams in smaller leagues. Before the turn of the century, Walker abandoned his attempt to re-enter the major leagues when it became apparent that integration was impossible. The well-educated Walker first began to publish his own black, issue-oriented newspaper and later wrote his own book, *Our Home Colony: The Past, Present, and Future of the Negro Race in America*. His frustration as a result of his inability to fully integrate baseball (as well as his own legal problems) became evident when he wrote that African Americans should emigrate back to Africa because America offered nothing but failure and disappointment.[13] Other black players persisted in their attempts to play major league baseball.

By the turn of the 20th century, many African American baseball players excelled throughout the country, such as "Bud" Fowler, "Fleet" Walker, and Charlie Grant.[14] It was Grant who, in 1901, presented himself as a Cherokee Indian in order to try out for the Baltimore Orioles of the new American League as a second baseman. This tryout was the idea of Orioles manager John McGraw, who always secretly wished to include the best black baseball players on his roster. In fact, after his death, McGraw's wife found a list of black players that her husband secretly wished to acquire when he managed the New York Giants.[15] Grant's effort exposed some of the prejudiced opinions of major league owners. An example of the feelings of team owners was expressed by Chicago White Sox president Charles Comiskey:

> I'm not going to stand for McGraw bringing in an Indian on the Baltimore team. If Muggsy really keeps this Indian, I will get a Chinaman of my acquaintance and put him on third. Somebody told me that the Cherokee of McGraw's is really Grant, the crack Negro second baseman from Cincinnati, fixed up in war paint and a bunch of feathers.[16]

Grant's bid eventually failed when friends who cheered him on revealed his true identity. Despite his feelings to the contrary, McGraw abandoned any future attempts to admit black players to his roster. It would be another forty-five years before the next attempt to integrate the major leagues.

Grant's unsuccessful attempt reflects not only the prejudice prevalent in the major leagues at the time, but also the contradicting racial perceptions in the United States. While Grant was known as an African American, he suffered exclusion from the major leagues. When masquerading as a Native American, Grant nearly received an opportunity to play big league baseball. Although criticism existed, it failed to prevent a Native American from playing professional baseball. This situation reflects the virulent racism exhibited towards African Americans at the turn of the century. While both Native Americans and African Americans were perceived as inferior, often blacks suffered greater exclusion from traditional "white" culture. Native Americans often received less racism and slightly more opportunities within American culture. This problem affected other ethnic groups as well.

Although known as the tempestuous, no-nonsense leader of the New York Giants, John McGraw often dreamt of including some of the finest black players on his team. His attempts to integrate, however, were futile. (Courtesy of the National Baseball Hall of Fame)

Throughout the early part of the twentieth century, the inequities of the racial views of Americans became most visible in professional baseball. After the turn of the century, major league organizations began to explore the possibilities of hiring "light-skinned" Latin Americans to play on their teams. Until the post–World War II era, any Latin Americans considered good enough to play in the major leagues often became the subject of ethnic scrutiny. Forced to prove their ethnic background, many Latinos suffered exclusion from big league baseball merely because they were viewed as too "dark-skinned" to play in the major leagues. Many quality Latin Americans played in alternate leagues or were forced to remain in their native country because of the color of their skin.

Ironically, the Philadelphia Athletics became one of the first clubs to venture into this tenuous ethnic situation. In 1902, they acquired a Colombian infielder named Luis "Jud" Castro, who played that season for a team that won the American League pennant. Apparently, Castro had light skin, which afforded him the opportunity to play with the Athletics. Despite his ethnicity, Castro came from a relatively wealthy background and attended school in the United States, allowing him to assimilate with the rest of his teammates.[17]

Unfortunately, Castro arrived as a member of the Athletics during an unusual and difficult period for the franchise. Prior to Castro's arrival in Philadelphia, the regular second baseman for the Athletics was the legendary Napoleon Lajoie, a future member of baseball's Hall of Fame. In fact, Lajoie hit an astounding .422 during the 1901 season, one of the highest batting averages in major league history. Unfortunately, Lajoie's previous club, the Phillies, challenged the validity of his Athletics contract. Early in the 1902 season, the Pennsylvania Supreme Court ruled that Lajoie's Athletics contract was invalid. The ruling forced Lajoie to leave the Athletics and he ended up playing with the Cleveland Indians. This situation left the Athletics without a regular second baseman. Therefore, Castro filled the position under these unusual circumstances.[18]

Handed the position in desperation, Castro appeared overmatched as the starting second baseman. In particular, his relative inability to hit major league pitching forced Athletics' owner and manager Connie Mack to search elsewhere for an answer. Eventually, Mack found one-time New York Giants second baseman Danny Murphy to take over the position. Murphy played admirably and Castro became relegated to the bench. Despite this apparent instability, the Athletics won the American League pennant by six games over the St. Louis Browns.[19]

Castro's presence did little to generate enthusiasm for signing Latin

Although he used the first Hispanic player in American League history, Connie Mack never explored the possibility of using black players. (Courtesy of the National Baseball Hall of Fame)

American players. During the 1902 season, Castro hit only .245 in 42 games while serving as a backup infielder. He did not return to the Athletics for the following season.[20] Castro's presence on the Athletics differed from future club policies towards minorities, as the team avoided integration of any kind. Furthermore, no Latin American players existed in the majors until 1911, when the Cincinnati Reds signed two Cubans to play on its club. Although the Reds received some criticism for this move, they insisted that both players were white.[21]

While there appeared to be a disregard of Latin American players, African Americans remained completely excluded from professional baseball. Despite the grim prospects for the integration, many of the best African American athletes still played baseball. At this time, baseball remained the dream job for African Americans because all other employment options appeared dreary and without promise. Such jobs included migrant farming, delivery "boys," stock hands, and other menial jobs. Since most major colleges excluded blacks, few opportunities existed for any type of upward mobility through an advanced education. For many, baseball offered the opportunity to leave the hot fields of the South or the slums of the cities and travel the country playing a game. As Jackie Robinson would later write in his autobiography, "Athletics, both school and professional, comes nearer to offering an American Negro equality of opportunity than does any other field of social and economic activity." Nevertheless, in comparison to major league players, the best black players remained underpaid and underappreciated.[22] Without integration, it was difficult to compare the most talented blacks to the top major league players.

Therefore, the only way that the best black players faced the best white players on the field was through exhibition games.

In order to supplement their salaries during the off-season, major league players often went on exhibition tours playing against semi-pro teams or other professional teams. These touring groups were either an entire team, such as the Detroit Tigers or the Philadelphia Phillies, or a group of major leaguers, such as the Earl Mack All-Stars. The Mack All-Stars, created by Athletics' owner-manager Connie Mack's son, consisted of major leaguers from several East Coast teams. In either case, these touring teams played whomever and wherever they could draw a large crowd. With attendance and profits as the main goals of such tours, race became less of an issue. Either way, these games against touring clubs provided black players the only opportunities to play against major leaguers. Black players made the most of these chances and often defeated the star-laden major league All-Star teams.

For the black professional baseball player, the opportunity to play against major leaguers was more than a mere exhibition. These players took it upon themselves to attempt to show that they could play on a major league level. For the major league players, these games only represented a chance to make a little extra cash. But often, professional pride took over and many league players were disappointed with their results versus black players. Former Philadelphia Athletics pitching legend Lefty Grove once said he refused to play against Negro League teams. He claimed he "never played against blacks in my life." As truth would have it, Grove did in fact play against black players. Grove, who often displayed a terrible temper whenever he lost (which was quite seldom), would rather claim that he did not play against blacks than admit he lost to them.[23]

Despite the abundance of quality African American baseball players, major league teams still refused to even consider integration. Although Cap Anson left baseball for good by 1900, the tradition of segregation in major league baseball continued. In fact, it became enhanced by the views and actions of Detroit Tigers superstar outfielder Ty Cobb. He became well known for his violent behavior towards blacks. Cobb once assaulted a black groundskeeper and his wife because the groundskeeper wanted to shake the outfielder's hand. Cobb, raised in the post–Civil War South, often publicly stated his racist views. When asked about the possibility of integration in major league baseball, Cobb responded, "There will never be a darky in the majors.... Darkies' place is in the stands or as clubhouse help." In 1909, many of the Tigers players traveled to Cuba to play exhibition games against a team composed of Hispanic and black players. They did so without Cobb, who swore that he would never step onto a

Although Lefty Grove actually was on barnstorming All-Star teams that played against black teams, he refused to admit doing so. (Courtesy of the National Baseball Hall of Fame)

field against non-whites. The Tigers lost eight of twelve games of that exhibition tour.[24]

In November of 1910, Cobb finally agreed to take part in a similar exhibition tour. Cobb, however, only went to Cuba after he was offered paid travel expenses and a substantial bonus. He played against the finest black player of the time, Shortstop John "Pop" Lloyd. Although the Tigers won more of the games, Lloyd outplayed Cobb. Lloyd's performance proved that playing ability had nothing to do with skin color.[25] Nevertheless, Lloyd's skin color kept him from admittance to the big leagues. More importantly, Cobb's views encouraged continued segregation in the major leagues because he was regarded as the best player in baseball. Since Cobb could attract fans to the ballpark, owners followed his opposition to the integration of the major leagues. In the early 1900s, the prospect of black players in major league baseball seemed practically impossible.

These apparently dim prospects, however, did not force African Americans to give up their dream of playing in the major leagues or from forming their own teams. Professional teams formed in different cities throughout the country, including New York and Chicago. Although another fifteen years would pass before Philadelphia would experience the Great Black Migration during the post–World War I era, other cities experienced an increase in black population. This migration occurred in most large Northern cities during the early part of the twentieth century. It signified the increased employment opportunities available in the cities as opposed to the rural areas of the South. For blacks, the South also represented potential crop failures and the fear of lynching.

A labor shortage encouraged many to move to the North. As a result of this migration, more people (immigrants as well as blacks) lived in the cities.[26] This higher population expanded the audience for professional baseball. Therefore, baseball became big business and many hoped to cash in on the craze. Soon, Philadelphia would join these cities when a newspaperman organized what eventually became the finest team in black baseball.

In order to corner the Philadelphia market, Walter "Slick" Schlichter sought to organize a team of his own. A white sports editor for the *Philadelphia Item*, Schlichter formed his team with the help of Sol White, former captain of the Cuban X Giants, and Harry Smith of the *Philadelphia Tribune*, the city's African American newspaper.[27] The Philadelphia Giants serve as a typical example of an all-black baseball team controlled by a white owner. Individuals such as Nat Strong, J.L. Wilkinson, and Eddie Gottlieb either controlled their own teams or entire leagues. These men often controlled the rights to negotiate where black teams could play. Such individuals, however, often needed experienced black players or managers to actually form the teams. For Schlichter, Sol White filled that role as he enticed many excellent players to the Philadelphia Giants. White also played first base and served as captain on what would become one of the most successful black professional baseball teams of the early twentieth century.[28]

Schlichter and White succeeded in recruiting some of black base-

Although considered one of the greatest players in major league history, Ty Cobb was a virulent racist who became well known for his violent behavior towards blacks. He also held negative views towards playing against black All-Star teams. Cobb finished his career with Connie Mack's Philadelphia Athletics. (Courtesy of the National Baseball Hall of Fame)

Charlie Grant was the star second baseman of the Philadelphia Giants at the beginning of the 20th cnetury. New York Giants manager John McGraw attempted to sneak Grant onto his roster by saying Grant was a Native American. The ploy failed when Grant's true identity was revealed. (Courtesy of the National Baseball Hall of Fame)

ball's best players, including Charlie Grant, "Pop" Lloyd, and pitchers Andrew "Rube" Foster and Danny McClellan. Foster would become black baseball's most accomplished player of the era and later received the moniker "Father of the Negro Leagues."[29] Grant had already become known for his attempt to play for the American League's Baltimore Orioles. Lloyd earned the reputation as the "Black Wagner" for his fine play at shortstop and considered on par with the best major league players. Honus Wagner of the Pittsburgh Pirates received recognition as the best player in the National League. Wagner felt honored by the comparison. Philadelphia Athletics manager Connie Mack said of Lloyd, "You could put Wagner and Lloyd in a bag together and whatever one you pulled out, you wouldn't go wrong."[30] McClellan also received mention as a quality pitcher who, along with Foster, gave the Giants an almost invincible pitching staff.

Legend has it that Foster received the nickname "Rube" after he defeated the Philadelphia Athletics famed left-handed pitcher Rube Waddell in a 1902 exhibition game.[31] In 1904, Foster joined the Philadelphia Giants after a successful stint as a pitcher with the Cuban X Giants. Also based in Philadelphia, the Cuban X Giants became renowned as a touring team. As the Philadelphia Giants claimed themselves as the "Champions" of black baseball, the Cuban X Giants challenged them to a best-of-seven series. In fact, Foster jumped to the Philadelphia team after his Cuban X Giants defeated them in this seven game series. The Cuban X Giants defeated Philadelphia and then became known as the "World's Colored Champions." In that series, Foster became the winning pitcher in four of the five Cuban X Giants victories. The next season, Foster jumped to the Philadelphia Giants and they defeated the Cuban

X Giants in a best-out-of-three series. Besides winning two games as a pitcher, Foster also contributed with some clutch hitting. This victory allowed the Philadelphia Giants to reclaim the "world" title.[32]

Aside from his pitching brilliance, Foster was also an accomplished hitter who often batted cleanup on the lineup of some of his championship teams. He would often play the field on days that he did not pitch. Known for his power hitting during the "dead ball" era, Foster once hit a ball so hard that he broke it two. Because of his ability to both pitch and hit, Foster did what Babe Ruth did two decades later.[33] Needless to say, Foster was a dynamic star who would have dominated major league baseball if given the opportunity.

Star pitcher and creator of Negro League baseball, Rube Foster was the top player and main attraction of the Philadelphia Giants. He later jumped the team in search of better opportunities. (Courtesy of the National Baseball Hall of Fame)

Although Danny McClellan remains less known than Foster, his pitching earned the respect of both white and black players. McClellan received recognition as the first black player to pitch a perfect game, doing so for the Philadelphia Giants in 1903. Since statistics of black baseball in those days prove quite spotty, some may question whether McClellan really was the first to pitch a perfect game. Such an achievement, however, rarely occurs and, without a doubt, serves as a testament to McClellan's abilities. Furthermore, the presence of McClellan indicates the strength of the Philadelphia Giants pitching staff.[34]

Known as "the Champions of Black Baseball," the Philadelphia Giants received challenges from several other black teams. These challenges often led to showdowns amongst the best teams black baseball had to offer, generating large crowds. One of the championship contests against the Cuban X Giants drew approximately 10,000 people, on par with the attendance figures of the Phillies and Athletics. More often than not, the highly skilled Philadelphia Giants emerged victorious. Because of the high quality of their play and a strong following, the Philadelphia

Giants dominated black baseball between 1902 and 1907.[35] For example, the Giants team of 1905 possessed an outstanding record of 134 wins, 21 losses, and 2 ties.[36] No major league team can ever boast such an accomplished record.

As the Giants succeeded on the field, the team became profitable but the parsimonious Schlichter paid his players poorly. When Foster asked for a raise, Schlichter claimed that his club could not afford it and, as a result, Foster left Philadelphia. By 1908, the best players jumped to other teams. Many followed Foster to the Chicago American Giants, which then became the nation's leading black baseball club. At first, Sol White managed to recruit quality players to replace those who left his team and the Giants remained quite competitive. For instance, after several players left the Philadelphia Giants and followed Foster to Chicago, White managed to sign superstar shortstop "Pop" Lloyd for his team. But by 1910, Lloyd had enough of the Philadelphia Giants and left for the Leland Giants of Chicago. Then White managed to attract speedy outfielder Spotswood Poles, whose play earned him the interesting nickname "the black Cobb." Poles spent the 1911 season with the Philadelphia Giants, making them a competitive team but far from championship caliber. In fact, Poles hit an incredible .610 against white big leaguers. After the 1911 season, Poles bolted for a team in Lincoln, Nebraska. At the same time, White had a falling out with Schlichter and left with Poles for the team in Nebraska. Unfortunately, White had difficulty booking his new team for games and it folded in July 1912. Meanwhile, without White, the Philadelphia Giants collapsed as well.[37] The demise of the Giants led to the formation of many amateur and semipro teams competing for the supremacy of the Philadelphia area. Eventually, the lack of black professional baseball led to the creation of new teams, such as the Hilldale Club of Darby and the Philadelphia Stars, both of which joined the newly formed Negro Leagues.

The Philadelphia Giants were only one of several professional black baseball teams traveling around the country in search of competition from other black teams and white semipro teams. Furthermore, while the white press largely ignored the accomplishments of these teams, major league players knew of these teams and some respected them. Some of these barnstorming teams proved somewhat successful, both in record and finances, but it was difficult to find games against worthy opponents. Therefore, an organized league became necessary.

Keeping track of the first Negro Leagues is an extremely daunting task. As noted baseball author Robert Peterson states, "Tracing the course of the organized Negro Leagues is rather like trying to follow a single black strand through a ton of spaghetti. The footing is infirm, and the strand has a tendency to break off in one's hand and slither back into the amorphous mass." Early leagues were created and disbanded in the very same year. Franchises changed locations quite often and players jumped leagues and teams with alarming regularity. Early professional Negro League baseball proved a very insecure business. Therefore, only barnstorming teams achieved sustaining success after the turn of the century.[38]

The most telling achievements of black barnstorming teams came when they met major league competition. Often, white barnstorming teams composed of major league players would play against the black teams. While the white players considered these games just exhibitions, black players took them as an opportunity to demonstrate their abilities. Other games between the black teams and actual major league clubs also proved quite interesting. Future Negro League star outfielder Gene Benson said that black players "played harder when we played major leaguers because we were trying to prove something to them—that we could play." Because of their determination, black teams often defeated the white clubs. Yet, most white professionals continued to show little regard for black players as individuals, often exercising their prejudice towards blacks.[39]

Other major league players, however, decided to play against touring black teams. Either with the formation of all-star teams or the major league teams themselves, black teams often played the big leaguers in exhibition games. For instance, the 1915 National League champion Philadelphia Phillies played a touring group of black players. Unfortunately for the Phillies, the barnstorming team, led by the pitching of famed hurler Joe Williams, shut them out.[40]

Although largely unknown to white audiences, Williams' brilliance earned him election to the Hall of Fame in 1999. Known for throwing hard, Williams worked his way up to the Leland Giants in 1910 after an excellent career pitching for teams in San Antonio and Austin, Texas. In addition to his fine play against other black professional teams, Williams achieved a reputation as a pitcher who saved his best performances for the exhibitions against white teams. In addition to defeating the Phillies on several occasions, Williams also pitched exceptionally well against the Earl Mack All-Stars. He defeated such Hall-of-Fame pitchers as Grover Alexander, Chief Bender, Walter Johnson, Waite Hoyt, Satchel Paige, and Rube Marquard. In thirty recorded starts against top-level major league competition, Williams won twenty-two games, while losing seven and tying one. Of his seven losses, two came when he was still pitching at age 45. But even in his forties in the early 1930s, Williams had enough on the ball to impress the greatest pitcher of the era, Dizzy Dean of the St. Louis Cardinals. While believing that Satchel Paige was the best pitcher he ever saw, Dean complimented Williams on the speed of his fastball.[41]

While such accomplishments from black players occurred often, they lacked a degree of credibility because these players did not have a league of their own and remained excluded from the majors. Furthermore, black teams were not considered part of "organized baseball" and still failed to gain respect from the rest of the baseball community. Also, statistics from barnstorming tours, exhibitions, and most black professional teams were seldom kept and those that do exist prove incomplete and insufficient. Lacking credibility from the professional baseball community, black players felt that their talents went ignored. Therefore, blacks attempted to create a successful league of their own.

Among the early attempts to organize a professional league of black teams were: the League of Colored Base Ball Clubs, which lasted a week in 1887; the International League of Independent Professional Base Ball Clubs, which also included white teams and only lasted during the 1906 season.[42] The demise of the latter indicates that baseball fans were not yet receptive to an integrated league. The failure of these leagues substantiated the arguments of those who believed that blacks could not organize a successful league of their own. On the other hand, there appeared a potentially lucrative market in the cities with African American communities.[43] Unfortunately, no one stepped forward with a well-organized professional league to capitalize on these potential new fans for black baseball.

For the most part, the League of Colored Base Ball Clubs failed for one major reason: it could not entice the best independent black professional teams to join. For instance, the best independent black team of the 1880s was the Cuban Giants, based in New York City. The league hoped the Cuban Giants would join their fledging organization and give it instant credibility. Unfortunately, the Cuban Giants refused to join the league and chose to continue to play minor and major league teams in profitable exhibitions. Without a serious drawing card, the League of Colored Base Ball Clubs could not hope to survive and disappeared.[44]

The International League of Independent Professional Base Ball Clubs managed to last a whole season, but not without experiencing problems. The East Coast League included two white teams from the Philadelphia area: the Philadelphia Professionals and a team from Riverton-Palmyra (N.J.). Otherwise, the balance of the league included black professional teams such as the Cuban X Giants, Quaker Giants of New York, the Cuban

Stars, and the Havana Stars. When the Quaker Giants and Havana Stars dropped out of the league in July, the Philadelphia Giants and the Wilmington Giants replaced them. According to its manager Sol White, the Philadelphia Giants, still a formidable team, won the only league championship that season. Unfortunately, since the baseball world was not ready for an integrated league, the International League folded and the Philadelphia Giants continued as an independent team.[45] At this time, it appeared almost impossible for a professional league of black baseball players to become successful.

It would take the participation of the era's most successful player, Andrew "Rube" Foster, to create the first successful Negro League. Foster, once the star pitcher of the old Philadelphia Giants, became so accomplished that he received compliments from one of the era's best major league players, Pittsburgh Pirates shortstop Honus Wagner. Wagner once called Foster "the smoothest pitcher I've ever seen." Furthermore, in 1903, Foster also received the ultimate compliment from the era's finest manager, John McGraw of the New York Giants of the National League, when he asked Foster to instruct his pitchers. McGraw's best pitcher, the legendary Christy Mathewson, learned his screwball from these sessions with Foster.[46] After finishing his playing career, Foster, then manager of the barnstorming Chicago American Giants, proposed in the *Chicago Defender* that black players form an association modeled after the major leagues. Despite many previous failures by other promoters, Foster managed to put his plan in effect. The plan called for two leagues: one in the East and one in the Midwest. Owners of the top Negro teams gathered in Kansas City early in 1920 to organize the new league. With Foster acting as president, the Negro National League began operations the following spring. The creation of this new league eventually presented Philadelphia with the opportunity to enter the world of professional Negro League baseball.

2

Hilldale

The rise of the semipro and amateur Negro baseball scene in Philadelphia occurred with official disbanding of the once powerful Philadelphia Giants in 1911. Once the Giants disbanded, many area sandlot and semipro teams were formed and competed for supremacy in Philadelphia amateur baseball. The most prominent of these teams was the Hilldale Club of Philadelphia, which actually operated out of Darby in Delaware County. Formed in 1910, the Hilldale Club first ruled amateur and semipro baseball within the city and then graduated into the professional ranks. Eventually, Hilldale became a major force in the Negro Leagues in the 1920s and 1930s.[1]

Before reaching national prominence in the 1920s, Hilldale needed to conquer the Philadelphia Negro baseball scene. Around the time of decline of the Philadelphia Giants, many teams were formed throughout the area. The disappearance of the Giants did not dampen the enthusiasm that area African Americans felt towards baseball. According to baseball historian Neil Lanctot, "The Philadelphia area literally swarmed with black baseball clubs, all aspiring to reach the heights of the famous Philadelphia Giants." Aside from the many teams within the city, outlying areas such as Norristown, Ambler, Chester, Camden, and Wilmington had their own teams. Porters and post office employees created their own clubs. Local African American organizations and businesses, including the *Philadelphia Tribune* and the Southwest branch of the YMCA, created their own teams. The problem was not the opportunity to belong to a team, but finding a place to play. These teams consistently faced difficulties finding a suitable playground or park because area facilities proved inadequate, inaccessible, or segregated.[2]

Like most other institutions, major league baseball became a whites-only enterprise. Blacks did not have the opportunity or the desire to attend games at Shibe Park or Baker Bowl. Instead, blacks became resigned to attend the sandlots in order to watch the local semipro team. The local players became, in a small way, well-known figures and even role models for the community. As a result, Philadelphia became a city teeming with black semipro baseball teams that, more often than not, became popular and important enterprises.[3]

The presence of this vast number of teams occurred because of the expanded black population in the Philadelphia area. Coinciding with the Great Black Migration beginning in the World War I era, baseball teams became more than recreational devices. Now baseball teams began to become businesses whose owners hoped to cash in on the nation's most popular sport. Therefore, many blacks that hoped for a career in professional baseball received their start by playing for local semipro teams. Because of baseball's popularity, even semipro teams began to attract and maintain strong followings. While many of these clubs existed in the city, blacks began to move out to the Philadelphia suburbs. This occurred because of overcrowding and the fact that only certain sections of the city became available to blacks.

The creation of the Hilldale club resulted from the fact that a small number of African Americans, seeking to distance themselves from the congestion of the city, moved to a "satellite community" in what was then Darby Borough of Delaware County. The local white real estate agents refused to sell much of the township's property to African Americans. Therefore, a section known as "the Hill" became home to Darby's black residents, who comprised 10 percent of the town's population.[4]

In 1910, area residents created the Hilldale club as a team for 14 to 17 year olds. Their first manager, A.D. Thompson, was only 19 years old and most of the players worked in the area. Little is known of that first season and by 1911, Thompson left the team. Thompson's replacement, Ed Bolden, immediately brought stability to the young, undisciplined team. Bolden possessed a keen business sense, allowing Hilldale to gradually become quite well known around the Philadelphia area. Beginning in 1911, the Hilldale club grew in stature and rose to the forefront of semipro baseball in the Philadelphia area.

Bolden saw to it that Hilldale games were reported in the weekly newspaper for African Americans, the *Philadelphia Tribune*. He also used the paper to attract quality opponents for his team and to advertise his own team as one that exuded class and fair play. According to historian Neil Lanctot, "To Bolden, 'clean baseball' meant the difference between success and failure, and he demanded that his players be 'gentlemen in uniform as well as off the battlefield.'" In a relatively brief period of time, Bolden elevated Hilldale to a baseball team of major significance.[5]

Bolden elevated the Hilldale club through his ability to attract top quality black players to his team. Throughout the 1920s, Bolden amassed some of the best black baseball players onto his team. They included third baseman Judy Johnson, pitcher Phil Cockrell, and catcher Biz Mackey. These players served as the core of the best Hilldale teams of the decade and led the team from a semipro organization to the pinnacle of black professional baseball.

Judy Johnson originally suited up for Hilldale in 1920. Johnson first played professional baseball with the Bacharach Giants as a teenager, a team that often played in Philadelphia. Johnson received this opportunity because World War I called many of the top black players into the service. His time with Bacharach proved temporary as the inexperienced Johnson went on to playing semipro baseball with the Madison Giants of Philadelphia. Finally, by 1920, both Johnson's abilities and Hilldale's standing progressed enough for them to join forces. Hilldale owner Ed Bolden bought Johnson's services for only $100. Once with Hilldale, Johnson soon became the club's starting third baseman. Coming to Darby as a light hitter blessed with excellent fielding abilities, Johnson eventually developed into a quality offensive player. In Johnson's words, "I was no great hitter, but I would try almost anything to get on base." Johnson played for Hilldale for a decade until the club faltered during the Great Depression.[6] Johnson eventually enjoyed a lengthy career in baseball as a player, coach, and scout.

As Hilldale became one of the best black teams of the 1920s, Johnson was viewed as the team's leader. He improved his hitting to a steady .300. Johnson also was a regular in the Cuban winter league, which helped hone his skills and allowed him to play against big league players. By 1929, Johnson had enough skill and experience to lead the Negro National League in hitting and garner league Most Valuable Player honors. As Hilldale began unravel, Johnson jumped to the Pittsburgh Crawfords, who were putting together quite a team under black mobster Gus Greenlee. Johnson played for the Crawfords for several seasons before becoming a coach. Because of his legendary fielding and contributions to baseball, Johnson eventually received admission in the baseball Hall of Fame.[7]

Phil Cockrell became an important addition to the Hilldale club as it advanced into black professional baseball. He joined Hilldale in 1918 and soon garnered a reputation as a top quality pitcher. Known as the ace of Hilldale's staff in those days, Cockrell became renowned as a spitball pitcher who baffled the opposition. As his career progressed, Cockrell received enough recognition to face major league competition on several occasions. More often than not, Cockrell conquered the big league hitters. Cockrell served as the anchor of Hilldale's fine pitching staff.[8]

Like Judy Johnson, catcher Biz Mackey also became known for his fine defense. As future Negro League and Brooklyn Dodger great Roy Campanella said, "In my opinion, Biz Mackey was the master of defense of all catchers. When I was a kid in Philadelphia, I saw both Mackey and Mickey Cochrane in their primes, but for catching skills, I didn't think Cochrane was the master of defense that Mackey was." This was high praise from Campanella because many baseball experts claim Cochrane was the best catcher in major league history. Originally from Texas, Mackey smartly handled any pitching staff that he served. Negro League pitchers often preferred throwing to Mackey than any other catcher, and that included the great Josh Gibson. Mackey guided Hilldale pitchers to their best seasons of their careers and provided great clutch hitting throughout his career. Mackey joined Hilldale in 1923 and played in the Philadelphia area for the better part of the next twelve years. Mackey remains quite a prominent figure in the history of black baseball in Philadelphia.[9] Mackey's arrival in Philadelphia is closely tied to the success of the black professional teams in town.

Judy Johnson was a Hall of Fame third baseman for the Hilldale Club for several years. He later served in the Athletics organization and as a spring training instructor for the Phillies. (Courtesy of the National Baseball Hall of Fame)

By the 1920s, the Hilldale club won the respect of the organizers of the Negro National League. After its initial season in 1920, the league experienced a fair degree of success and survived into 1921. The league did have its difficulties though, as several franchises struggled financially and two franchises were forced to relocate to new cities.[10] Movement of this kind, unfortunately, became normal operating procedure for the league. A symptom of this instability is the fact that most of the teams of the Negro National League (NNL) did not own their own ballparks. For the most part, these parks were owned and operated by white promoters who either excluded the Negro League teams or charged them heavily for the privilege of playing on their field. Therefore, this unsteadiness created difficulties in scheduling games with other league members. In response to this problem, the National Association of Colored Professional Baseball Clubs, which ran the NNL, accepted two Eastern clubs—Atlantic City's Bacharach Giants and the Hilldale club—as "associate members" of the league. This status allowed regular league members to operate with a more expanded schedule. With this move, the Hilldale club now became a national professional organization.[11]

Hilldale agreed to join the association with one provision: that league teams must refrain from raiding their roster. Successful teams like Hilldale were always at risk while other professional teams attempted to lure their best players away with relatively lucrative contracts. This agreement meant that the drawing card of having star players on its roster would remain for the Hilldale club. Therefore, the team rose to prominence not only in Philadelphia, but also throughout the East Coast. The result of this success created a movement for a professional Negro league in the East.[12]

Players from the Hilldale club also became renowned for playing in exhibition games against major league All-Star teams. While players augmented their income through these games, it afforded Negro Leaguers a chance to prove themselves at the highest level. In fact, in 1926, a team composed of players from both the Hilldale club and the Homestead Grays played against an American League team composed of Athletics pitcher Lefty Grove and Detroit Tigers batting champ Heinie Manush, among others. In a six-game tour, the black team defeated the white team in five of those games. Hilldale pitcher Phil Cockrell shut out Grove in the final game.[13] These games only added to the prestige of the Hilldale club.

What further assisted Hilldale's rise in Philadelphia were the dismal performances of the city's two major league teams, the Athletics and the Phillies. The once powerful Athletics sank to the bottom of the American League in 1915 when owner-manager Connie Mack sold off his best players to other teams in order to pay his own debts. Such players included second baseman Eddie Collins, third baseman Frank "Home Run" Baker, and first baseman Stuffy McInnis. Furthermore, the team's best pitchers,

Eddie Plank and Chief Bender, bolted the Athletics in order to play in the new Federal League, an all-white major league formed in 1915. As the Athletics dropped in the standings, their attendance figures went with them.[14]

The Phillies' story seems quite similar. Led by star pitcher Grover Cleveland Alexander, the Phillies won their first ever National League pennant in 1915 and finished second in 1916 and 1917. In addition to being the team's star pitcher, Alexander became the drawing card that brought fans to Baker Bowl. But after serving in World War I, Alexander had difficulty dealing with the horrors of combat and began to drink heavily. Therefore in 1918, the Phillies traded the alcoholic Alexander to the Chicago Cubs and the Phillies quickly fell to the bottom of the league.[15] As a result, the Phillies were no longer a quality baseball attraction either. By the early 1920s, neither the Athletics nor the Phillies could draw greater than 400,000 fans per season.[16]

Because of the ineptitude of the city's major league teams, white fans would bypass them and search for other baseball alternatives, such as semipro teams or even Hilldale. According to Neil Lanctot, Hilldale did have something of a white following in the early 1920s and even sold "white tickets" at their games. Furthermore, many of Hilldale's away games were played against white semipro teams before predominantly white audiences.[17] According to Hilldale's star third baseman Judy Johnson, the crowds at Hilldale Park grew so large that additional seating became necessary. These seats were not just for the "Negroes," but for white fans too. The team even offered season tickets to their fans, something previously unheard of in local black baseball.[18] As a result, the Hilldale club capitalized on this popularity by maintaining their strong following and, therefore, had the resources to attempt to create their own Negro baseball league.[19]

3

Ed Bolden

Whether as a manager, general manager, or owner, racial thinking suggested that African Americans were incapable of leading a major league club. This issue came into the nation's attention with Ted Koppel's 1987 *Nightline* interview with Dodgers vice president Al Campanis. When asked if racial prejudice still existed in baseball, Campanis responded, "No, I don't believe it's prejudice. I truly believe that (blacks) may not have some of the necessities to be a ... let's say, a field manager, or perhaps a general manager."[1] Campanis evidently forgot that throughout the history of the Negro Leagues, African Americans ran successful franchises as owners, general managers, and managers. An example of such an executive is Philadelphia's own Ed Bolden.

When considering the development of black baseball in Philadelphia during the 20th century, the name of Ed Bolden should dominate the discussion. Diminutive yet ambitious, Bolden would lead both of the city's most successful Negro League teams, the Hilldale club and the Philadelphia Stars. Bolden made sure he procured the best players for his roster and always took initiative in publicizing his teams. He saw to it that the newspapers, particularly the *Philadelphia Tribune*, covered both Hilldale and the Stars. Bolden also vaulted to a leadership position within the Negro League baseball by becoming head of the newly formed American Negro League in 1929. He would go on to form a lucrative partnership with noted Philadelphia sports entrepreneur Eddie Gottlieb with the creation of the Stars. Bolden clearly deserves recognition as the king of Philadelphia black baseball.

During the 1920s, individuals like Bolden now could own and operate their baseball clubs. To paraphrase Sol White, blacks continued to play baseball despite the major league color barrier in order to show that they could successfully organize their own teams. Professional baseball provided the opportunity for blacks to run their own businesses, something that white society of the early 20th century could not fathom. The Negro Leagues provided an opportunity for African Americans like Ed Bolden to successfully operate their own professional sports franchises.[2]

Ed Bolden emerged from humble beginnings. Standing 5'7" tall and weighing 145 pounds, Bolden was no athlete but, since 1904, he worked at the Central Post Office in Philadelphia. At first sight, the bespectacled Bolden appeared as a quiet, dignified man. His appearance, however, belied his ambitious nature. The Hilldale club served as the vehicle for his desire as he moved immediately to improve the team. Because of his ability to move Hilldale from little-known amateur team to the zenith of professional black baseball, Bolden earned the nationwide respect of the Negro League community.[3]

The patriarch of Negro League baseball in Philadelphia, Ed Bolden brought two different teams (the Hilldale Club and Philadelphia Stars) to the forefront of professional black baseball. (Courtesy of the National Baseball Hall of Fame)

Bolden would become a prominent national figure in black baseball in 1923. In twelve years, he took the Hilldale club from a modest sandlot organization to the top semipro team in Philadelphia and finally to membership of the National Association of Professional Colored Base Ball Clubs. On the surface, this membership seems like the break that Bolden and Hilldale wanted. But this arrangement was only a limited membership as Rube Foster's league dominated the Midwest and had no interest in increasing travel costs by scheduling more games on the East Coast.[4] The extra travel costs associated with admitting a team such as Hilldale did not excite the NNL owners. Therefore, expanding an already unstable league was not considered an option and NNL owners chose to keep

Hilldale only as an "associate member." Bolden, however, became frustrated that Foster and the other leaders of the NNL would not allow Hilldale to participate as a full member.[5]

Bolden wanted to take advantage of the Eastern market and created the Eastern Colored League (ECL). It was a six-team league that, at first, served as competition to the NNL. Aside from Hilldale and Bacharach of Atlantic City, there were teams from New York, Brooklyn, and Baltimore. Bolden served as chairman of the new league, but Nat C. Strong, owner of the Brooklyn Royal Giants, possessed the real power.[6] Strong served as the booking agent for Colored Baseball Clubs for many years and was clearly in control of the ballparks in the new league.[7] In fact, Strong served as the agent for five of the six teams of the league and demanded each of the teams give him 10 percent of the gate receipts. The white Strong clearly signified the businessman-type that a pioneer like Rube Foster would detest.[8]

It is likely that Foster enjoyed the almighty dollar as much as anyone else, but he also wanted to further his race through baseball. Therefore, he saw the ECL as threat not only to his league, but also to his principles. Since only two (including Bolden) of the six ECL owners were African American, Foster bristled at the competition. "Calling the Eastern loop 'black', Rube sneered, was like calling a 'a streetcar a steamship'." Foster also became angered at the raids of his players by those representing the upstart league.[9] He did not respect Bolden for his participation in the ECL and became frustrated with his own failure to completely control professional black baseball. The pressure between the two leagues intensified, but each league also fought for its own survival. But Foster had considerable financial difficulties and, in anger, attacked Bolden by suggesting that the ECL would harm black baseball. Eventually, there would be a truce, of sorts.[10]

While Foster attacked the competition, fellow NNL owners took a different stance. In 1924, Bolden's Hilldale club won the ECL championship with an impressive 47–22 record.[11] With this strong showing, the debate was on: which league is better? The NNL champion in 1924 was the Kansas City Monarchs, owned by J.L. Wilkinson. Wilkinson, a white owner that Foster turned to when the Monarchs struggled financially, decided that criticizing the ECL was not in his best interests. Instead, Wilkinson offered a compromise by offering to play Hilldale in the first ever Colored World Series.[12] Bolden eagerly accepted this opportunity and the two teams met for Game 1 on October 3, 1924, in Phillies Park in Philadelphia. Hilldale lost the first game in front of an impressive crowd of 5,366. The second game, also in Philadelphia seen by 8,661, was won by Hilldale 11–0.[13] After that, the series moved to Baltimore, Chicago, and finally Kansas City. The best-of-nine series used different sites so that more black people could see the event. As the series shifted to these other sites, the fans followed. Hilldale eventually lost to the Monarchs in a well-played series, but there was no doubt black baseball was an economic force.[14] These attendance figures demonstrate that the Hilldale club, as well as black baseball in general, had won the respect of baseball fans.

In a relatively short period of time, Hilldale rose to great heights in professional black baseball. How did this popularity occur? First, Bolden publicized his team extremely well. The Hilldale club appeared in the *Tribune* more than any other semipro team. Then, once Hilldale entered the ECL, Bolden saw to it that he controlled professional black baseball in Philadelphia. He maintained this control by having good relationships with white booking agents such as New York's Nat Strong and Philadelphia's Eddie Gottlieb. These men controlled the playing fields and scheduled the games. This arrangement allowed Negro League games to take place at Baker Bowl, home of the Phillies. Whenever competitors attempted to challenge his control of the Philadelphia market, Bolden would see to it that Hilldale dominated the scene and would call on Strong and Gottlieb to force other teams out of town. For instance, this strategy prevented the competing Philadelphia Tigers from playing at Passon Field (a.k.a. Elks Park) in 1928, which might have endangered Hilldale's position in city baseball.[15] Instead, the Tigers soon disappeared but so did the ECL due to the failure of other teams in the league. As a result of the folding of the ECL, Hilldale returned to an independent schedule.[16] Bolden and Hilldale continued to survive and, for a while, thrive.

Although Hilldale continued to schedule games against other black teams and maintain a successful record as an independent, attendance dropped off significantly. The sharp economic recession of 1928–1929 adversely affected Philadelphia's black community, creating vacant stores once owned by blacks and mass unemployment. With economic disaster imminent, going to baseball games appeared less important. Despite the economic difficulties, the blame for Hilldale's falling attendance was on the failure of the ECL. Many sportswriters suggested that a new league would revitalize interest in black baseball. They felt that fans tended to follow league play more closely.[17]

Feeling the pressure from the media and believing that the criticisms made sense, Bolden helped organize another league, the American Negro League (ANL). Like the ECL, it was composed only of teams from the East. Unlike the ECL, it included the Homestead Grays of Pittsburgh, which would later become a powerful force in the Negro Leagues. Also, the ANL sought to eliminate the powerful white booking agents such as Nat Strong, now seen as detrimental and exploitative by much of black baseball. Although these agents were previously his bread-and-butter, Bolden accepted this provision and left Strong out of the league. Bolden's role in the creation of the ANL earned him the presidency of the new, six-team league.[18]

As president, Bolden sought to eliminate the problems that riddled the ECL. He created strict penalties against on-field violence against umpires and other players. Bolden also set policies that sought to eradicate the jumping to different teams and leagues by players. To accomplish this goal, Bolden provided league franchises with a "reserve clause," similar to that of the major leagues. This meant that a player was bound to his team for life or until he was traded or released. Players hated the clause for it forbade free player movement to different teams, which is what most employees of ordinary occupations enjoyed. In 1929, however, baseball experts who believed that the new league was an improvement praised the policies. Longtime black baseball expert Sol White praised the ANL by saying it is the "best we have had in the East." [19] Unfortunately, it did not last long.

The league suffered from economic problems brought on by the Depression. Also, the owners could not agree on league policy or the enforcement of one. Players accepted more lucrative offers to jump to Nat Strong's own independent team. In particular, Bolden experienced difficulties with the manager of the Homestead Grays, Cumberland Posey. Often times, Posey refused to follow league policy. In addition, because of Posey's power within the league, Bolden placated rather than disciplined him. As a result, Bolden received most of the blame for the eventual failure of the league. Therefore, no league existed in 1930 and Hilldale again operated independently. After trying again the following season, the ANL completely disappeared after 1930.[20]

With the failure of the ANL, the mantle of leadership of Eastern professional black baseball shifted from Bolden and Philadelphia to Pittsburgh. This shift began decline in Bolden's career in black baseball. Bolden's failure to confront Posey allowed the Grays' owner to control the Eastern baseball scene. Furthermore, the creation of the soon-to-be-successful Pittsburgh Crawfords during the 1930s made Pittsburgh the premier city of black baseball. The Crawfords were owned by wealthy numbers-runner Gus Greenlee, who enticed the most talented players to his team. Unable to compete with these formidable rivals and saddled with financial problems, Bolden became an increasingly unpopular figure. He also tended to trade or release many of the favorite players of the team and make many concessions with white promoters and backers. By 1930, Bolden had enough and sought to disband his team, starting a new one in the city. This move failed because new backers preserved the Hilldale club and kept it in Darby. Bolden also struggled with his job at the post office and it appeared in serious jeopardy. By the early 1930s, Ed Bolden was left without a team in black professional baseball and his career in the sport appeared over.[21]

Hilldale continued on with its participation in the new "East-West" league of 1932. It comprised many of the professional black teams of the era and a few new teams in the Midwest.[22] Hilldale, however, struggled mightily under the new leadership of Lloyd Thompson. Thompson, a well-known local figure in amateur baseball in Darby, did not have the money or the backing that Bolden maintained. Also, he did not have the connections or the power and by 1930, Thompson's Hilldale managing career ended and he was replaced by John Drew. In 1931, the last year of ANL, Hilldale had its last great season. But 1932 was different story as the club experienced a poor season. A terrible record compounded by poor attendance hastened the departure of many key players. Hilldale's best player, Judy Johnson, left the club in mid-season and joined the Pittsburgh Crawfords. By the end of July, the team folded before the league season ended.[23]

Meanwhile, Ed Bolden sought to make a comeback. He squared away his job situation at the post office and looked for a new team to lead. He went back to his baseball roots by becoming the director of the amateur Darby Phantoms in 1932.[24] This new team competed against area teams and actually received a fair degree of coverage from the *Tribune*. Unfortunately, while the Hilldale club floundered, the Phantoms did not fare much better. Bolden, unable to accept a mediocre team, kept hiring and firing players with the hope that the Phantoms could become a winner. Due to Bolden's involvement, the Phantoms maintained a decent following but were unable to field a strong team and soon folded.[25] Bolden's days as a controlling force within black professional baseball appeared gone forever.

As both the East-West League and Hilldale faltered, there was no black professional team in the Philadelphia area in 1933. What once served as a huge market for Negro League baseball now became vacant. Enter Eddie Gottlieb, a true Philadelphia sports personality, to turn failure into opportunity. Gottlieb realized that a void existed in the Philadelphia sports market that needed filling. With this vacancy in mind, Gottlieb founded the Philadelphia Stars. The Stars were a new professional black baseball team that joined the Negro National League in 1934.

Gottlieb, more renowned for his involvement in the world of professional basketball with the Philadelphia Warriors in the National Basketball Association, knew little of black baseball. While Gottlieb certainly sympathized with the plight of black baseball players, cashing in on a financial opportunity became his primary goal in the founding of the Stars. Above everything else, Gottlieb proved himself as a good businessman who relished any opportunity to make money in professional athletics. Therefore, he joined forces with the preeminent force of black baseball in the Philadelphia area, Ed Bolden. Gottlieb's connections in professional sports combined with Bolden's experiences through his previous success with the Hilldale club engendered high expectations. This combination could prove a prosperous venture into professional baseball. Most noteable of all, Ed Bolden returned to the Negro Leagues.

4

Here Come the Stars

In 1933, Eddie Gottlieb and Ed Bolden created the Philadelphia Stars. The Stars existed almost twenty years and, although they did not have as successful a record as Hilldale, the club became an integral part of Philadelphia baseball history.[1] In the 1930s, Gottlieb became renowned for his work with the Hebrew All-Stars, a very successful touring basketball team (there was no National Basketball Association in the 1930s). Gottlieb saw the light when he noticed the potential that black baseball possessed in the Philadelphia area. He held great influence in the Philadelphia sports scene and, for years, booked many black teams into the city. He could guarantee that Negro League baseball would receive exposure in town by booking games at major league stadiums such as Baker Bowl and Shibe Park.[2] His lack of knowledge of Negro League baseball, however, created the need for a partnership with someone possessing experience in running a professional team. This necessity led to the inclusion of Bolden, whose connections within the Negro Leagues allowed for the potential of financial and athletic success.

Another factor for expansion into Philadelphia was the choice for Commissioner of the National Negro League, nationally known black newspaperman W. Rollo Wilson. Wilson, who lived in Philadelphia, earned the interesting moniker "The Colored Landis" when he became the commissioner. He became the final arbiter of any disputes involving trades, player conduct, or disciplinary action. With Wilson in office, the survival of the Stars benefited because of his ties to the city.[3] After his days in office, Wilson became the sports columnist for the *Philadelphia Tribune*. He wrote in great detail of his opinions for the integration of major league baseball in 1945–1946. But in the 1930s, Wilson served as the head of the Negro National League, which proved a difficult position. Like all professional sports league commissioners, Wilson had to deal with powerful and opinionated team owners. But as far as the formation of the Stars was concerned, the presence of Wilson certainly did not hurt. The interesting mix of Bolden, Gottlieb, and Wilson allowed the Stars to flourish for many seasons.

As soon as Bolden accepted the position of co-owner and general manager, he went to work forming a team. He hired many of his old Hilldale veterans to play on the Stars, such as pitcher Phil Cockrell, catcher Raleigh "Biz" Mackey, pitcher Webster McDonald, shortstop Paul "Jake" Stephens, and outfielder Chaney White.[4] These were proven Negro League players who immediately made the Stars a contending team. McDonald, for instance, later out-pitched St. Louis Cardinals star Dizzy Dean in a 1935 exhibition game. Afterward, Athletics owner Connie Mack told McDonald, "I'd give half of my ball club for a man like you." Needless to say, Mack did not seriously entertain the thought of adding McDonald to his roster, but it demonstrates the talent available on the Stars' roster.[5]

Bolden selected these players because he already knew of their abilities and felt the hometown connection would immediately draw fans to the fledgling franchise. He supplemented this nucleus with some young yet talented players, such as pitcher Stuart "Slim" Jones, who won 22 games in the 1934 season.[6] Although this was technically an "expansion" team, it was a very talented group that immediately challenged for a league title.

Aside from acquiring players, Bolden needed a place to play. For most of the home games, the Stars played at Passon Field, located at 48th and Spruce Streets. Gottlieb's connections afforded the playing of an occasional game at one of Philadelphia's major league parks. Despite receiving far less press coverage than the Phillies or Athletics, the 1934 Stars drew an estimated average of 4,000 fans per game.[7] The explanation behind these relatively impressive first season attendance figures comes from the fine play of the Stars.

The Negro National League season was split into two halves. Also, games were scheduled against "associate" members who could contend for the league title. For instance, the Bacharachs, once based in Atlantic City, relocated to Philadelphia despite the objections of Bolden and Gottlieb. Because of this controversy, the Bacharachs endured the first half of the 1934 season as an "associate" member. They officially joined the league in the second half of that season. The league games were played on the weekends and most teams played local semi-pro teams during the week.

Therefore, seasons lasted as long as those of other professional baseball leagues but the standings only consisted of a fraction of the amount of games of the major leagues. The Negro National League created this schedule in order to reduce expenses. These reduced seasons accentuated the importance of each league game and, therefore, made the race for each half-season quite intense.[8]

Cole's American Giants from Chicago won the first half of the 1934 season while the Stars won the second half. This created a best-of-seven playoff between the two teams. It was a series that proved both tedious and controversial. The series opened September 11th in Philadelphia with the Stars losing heartbreaker to the Giants by the score of 4–3, as a Stars rally fell short. Five days later, the series then shifted to Chicago for a doubleheader between the two clubs. The teams split two very well played games. The next day, the Stars lost another heartbreaker to fall behind three games to one. Due to booking difficulties, the next game was not played until September 27th in Philadelphia. In that contest, the Stars prevailed 1–0 behind the strong pitching of Rocky Ellis. Two days later, the Stars prevailed again 4–1 to tie the series at three games apiece.[9]

The score of this game, however, was dwarfed by the controversy surrounding it. In the eighth inning of Game Six, two Stars, catcher Emile Brooks and first baseman Jud Wilson, were guilty of violently laying their hands on an umpire while disputing a call. Such an act usually means, at the very least, the ejection and probable suspension of such players.[10] Both players, however, remained in the game despite the protests of Giants' manager David Malarcher. Commissioner Rollo Wilson wanted to suspend both players for Game Seven but Bolden refused to accept the punishment. He threatened to boycott the game unless both players were reinstated. Faced with the prospect of canceling the championship series, the commissioner relented. Both players were in the lineup as the Stars won Game Seven and the series, four games to three.[11]

The success of the "Boldenboys" (as the Stars were often called) during the 1934 season became sullied by the disputable series victory. It provided proof to those critics who claimed that the Negro Leagues were lawless and out of control. A weak commissioner in the Negro National League contrasted with the iron-fisted regime of Major League Commissioner Kenesaw Mountain Landis. The very fact that two players in separate incidents could remain in a game after physically abusing umpires brought much skepticism. It added fuel to the fire of those who believed that the major leagues could not integrate because black players could not control themselves. It also underscored the fact that the commissioner was under the spell of the owners who ultimately controlled the playing facilities.

The conduct of the Stars, the umpires, and commissioner Wilson received strong criticism from *Tribune* sports columnist Ed R. Harris, who believed that strong fines and suspensions were in order. His column truly represented the dismay that most Negro League baseball fans felt by saying that the Negro National League "took a kick in the pants."[12] Many fans shared the same opinion and only 2,000 fans attended Game Seven, about half of the usual attendance.[13] Nevertheless, it became the only title won by the Stars and it was not until 1980 that Philadelphia had another champion in professional baseball.

The 1934 season proved the high point of the Stars. Most of the leaders of that championship team became too old to continue their excellent play and soon faded away. While some quality replacements toiled for the Stars, the club never again repeated their early success. Although the Stars never again approached championship level, they remained a competitive and respected franchise within the Negro Leagues. Furthermore, the team continued to draw fairly sizeable crowds for the next decade. In fact, as the Phillies struggled with their attendance, the Stars often drew more fans. The team accomplished this feat while playing in a smaller venue than the home field of the Phillies, Baker Bowl.[14] Therefore, although the Stars failed to win another championship, their play still earned them a loyal following. Some of the team leaders during this time included infielder Marvin Williams, outfielder Gene Benson, and catcher Bill Cash.

Although Williams never actually played in the major leagues, his name remains a footnote in the history of the breaking of baseball's color barrier. During World War II, many writers of black newspapers stepped up their demands for the major leagues to consider integration. This movement began with the establishment of the Fair Employment Practices Commission by President Franklin Delano Roosevelt in 1941. Independent black sportswriter Wendell Smith attempted to convince major league teams to bring in the best Negro League players for a tryout. A white Boston city councilman by the name of Isadore Muchnick began to support the movement to integrate. Muchnick, who represented a predominantly black district, pressured the city's two major league teams, the Red Sox and Braves, to consider integration. Smith contacted Muchnick and promised that he could bring in three players to try out for the Boston's two teams. Finally, in April of 1945, infielder Jackie Robinson of the Kansas City Monarchs, outfielder Sam Jethroe of the Cleveland Buckeyes, and Williams arrived in Boston ready to try out. The question remained whether one of the teams would actually provide such an opportunity. Finally, in response to public pressure, the Red Sox agreed to bring the three players into Fenway Park for a tryout.[15]

Prior to this time, Robinson already gained notoriety for his athletic exploits at UCLA. Robinson received All-American honors in both football and basketball during his career at UCLA. He also lettered in track and baseball. For Robinson, baseball was his least effective sport. But baseball was the only sport that offered him a professional career. Because of his overall athletic ability, Robinson received this opportunity with the Red Sox. As for Jethroe, he led the Negro Leagues in hitting in 1944 and truly earned this tryout. Jethroe later signed with the Brooklyn Dodgers organization and eventually entered the big leagues with the Boston Braves. Although Williams remains the least known of these players historically, he definitely earned the right to try out. In 1944, Williams hit .338 for the Stars. At the tryout, all three players performed well and were told that the Red Sox would contact them in the future. No word came from the Red Sox organization and instead of becoming the first team to integrate, they became the last in 1959.[16] As for Williams, his Negro League career continued but he never again received the opportunity to play big league baseball. Injuries plagued Williams and although he never played in the majors, he played several seasons in the Triple-A Pacific Coast League. Williams continued to play in the minor leagues until 1961.[17]

Unlike Williams, Gene Benson never got that close to integrating the major leagues. Benson was a consistent .300 hitter who served as a fixture in the Stars lineup throughout the 1930s and 1940s. He was also known for his flashy glove in center field and his mannerisms were later copied by Hall-of-Famer Willie Mays. Benson is also known as having a steadying influence on Jackie Robinson when they played together in the Venezuelan Winter League. Robinson expressed doubts to Benson about his ability to play at the major league level. Benson, knowing of the importance of this opportunity, calmed Robinson and assured him that he could make it in the big leagues. Unfortunately, Benson never received the opportunity to play big league baseball himself. Benson's age did not fit the desires of major league organizations. By the time the major leagues were integrated, major league organizations preferred younger players.[18]

Bill Cash was a fundamentally sound catcher with a strong arm capable of throwing out many base runners. He was part of a long line of catching greats who played for the Stars. Although he could not hit like Benson, Cash typified the steady leader that most clubs desire behind the plate. Because of players like these, the Stars maintained a strong fan base and existed into the 1950s. Although Cash managed to play two years in the Chicago White Sox farm system in the 1950s, neither Cash nor Benson received an opportunity to play in the major leagues. Cash's quest for the opportunity to play for the White Sox became derailed due to

Gene Benson was probably the best player in the history of the Philadelphia Stars. Not only was Benson known for his fine play, he proved a great influence on Jackie Robinson when both played together on an All-Star team. (Courtesy of the National Baseball Hall of Fame)

suffering a broken leg while in the minor leagues.[19] Nevertheless, players such as Williams, Benson, and Cash provided inspiration for black athletes in the area.

Aside from providing Philadelphia with a baseball alternative, the Stars also inspired many black youngsters to pursue the sport as a career. In the 1930s and 1940s, few opportunities existed in professional athletics. The creation of the National Football League (NFL) initially was integrated when it began in 1920. But with the onset of the Great Depression, the NFL became segregated during the 1930s and remained so until after the war. No Negro League alternative existed for professional football. Therefore, baseball became the only option for black athletes in professional sports. In Philadelphia, the Stars served as the one option for young black athletes to gain a career in professional sports. Some examples of players from the city who played in the Negro Leagues are infielder Mahlon Duckett, catcher Stanley Glenn, and pitcher Jimmy Dean.

Duckett, who ran track at Philadelphia's Overbrook High School, played semi-pro baseball in the Main Line League before trying out for the Stars. In those days, Negro League teams did not have farm systems or minor leagues. Therefore, players such as Duckett were often discovered during informal tryouts. After a successful tryout, the 17 year old Duckett immediately became a member of the Stars in 1940. Like Jackie Robinson, Duckett's advanced athleticism impressed his teammates and allowed him to become a superb second baseman. Duckett played ten seasons with the

Stars and one more with the Homestead Grays before signing with the New York Giants organization in 1951. Unfortunately, a bout with rheumatic fever prevented him from reaching the major leagues.[20]

Stanley Glenn, originally from Virginia, became well known in Philadelphia for his fine play for the John Bartram High School baseball team. Stars player-coach and future Hall-of-Famer Oscar Charleston signed Glenn to play for the Stars. While Glenn was thrilled with the opportunity to play for the hometown team, the Stars already had an established catcher in Bill "Ready" Cash. While Glenn originally did not play regularly, he learned quite a bit of the proper techniques of catching. This knowledge became useful for Glenn as he received quite a reputation as a skilled defensive catcher. This status helped Glenn to get the opportunity to play several seasons of minor league baseball, but he never received the opportunity to play in the major leagues.[21]

Jimmy Dean, born in Ambler, played on a team known as the Norristown Colored Elks. Prior to then, baseball served as Dean's inspiration since he was eight years old. Dean often attended major league games at Shibe Park, where he once saw a Cleveland Indians pitcher strike out sixteen batters in a game against the Athletics. After serving in World War II, Dean played for the other local teams until being signed by the Stars in 1946. The Stars signed the pitcher after they became informed of the New York Cubans' interest in Dean. Not eager to lose a local player to another team, Stars manager brought Dean on a Stars road trip and had him pitch for the club. Dean spent four of his five Negro League seasons with the Stars. When he noticed the declining crowds

Shown near the end of his playing days, Oscar Charleston was another Hall of Fame Negro League player who performed in Philadelphia. He also brought other blacks to play Negro League baseball in Philadelphia. (Courtesy of the National Baseball Hall of Fame)

at Stars games, Dean chose to attend college. Upon graduation, Dean became a successful chemist, never playing in the major leagues.[22]

The plights of Duckett, Glenn, and Dean reflect the impact that the integration of the major leagues had on the Stars. As the crowds increased for major league baseball, the following for the Stars dissipated. During the early 1950s, the Stars neared extinction. The Stars' players scrambled for new career options, whether it was the major leagues or a more sedate profession. Some of the younger and more accomplished Stars' players received opportunities to sign with major league organizations. Others ended their baseball careers and went elsewhere.

Some of the players who left the Stars and went on to major league organizations include pitcher "Satchel" Paige, outfielder Harry Simpson, infielders Buzz Clarkson and Milt Smith, and catcher Charlie White. Paige was only with the Stars briefly during the 1947 and 1950 seasons. The long time star pitcher was well past his prime when he finally got his chance with the Cleveland Indians in 1948. Although Paige had some respectable moments pitching in the majors, his advanced age prevented him from enjoying a lengthy major league career.[23]

Harry Simpson did not exactly burn up the record books during his three year stay with the Stars. Simpson failed to hit over .250 in any of this seasons in Philadelphia. The then-youthful Simpson, however, was praised for his talent and many major league organizations were willing to develop the athletic outfielder. After some negotiations, the Cleveland Indians won Simpson's services and sent him to their Wilkes-Barre farm club. By 1951, Simpson became a regular outfielder for the Indians.[24]

"Buzz" Clarkson played for the Stars throughout much of the 1940s. As a burly power-hitter, he often brought fear to opposing pitchers. Once, Satchel Paige decided to walk Clarkson with the bases already loaded in order to avoid more runs scoring. Although Clarkson could play third base and the outfield, he was best known for playing shortstop, an uncommon position for power hitters in those days. Clarkson's best years for the Stars came in 1946 when he hit .308 with 34 RBIs in just 38 games and 1949 when he hit .313. Clarkson left the Stars after the 1950 season to try his hand in the Boston Braves organization. With their top farm team, the Milwaukee Brewers of the American Association, Clarkson's fine season helped them win the pennant. In early May of 1952, the Braves called up 34 year old Clarkson, who was described as "ancient" and of "indeterminable" age. This reputation adversely affected Clarkson's stay in the big leagues because it was rare for major league teams to use older black players. After only 5 hits in 25 at-bats, Clarkson was sent back to Milwaukee to finish out the 1952 season. Clarkson never returned to the major leagues.[25]

Second baseman Milt Smith played for the Stars from 1949 to 1951.[26] Although quite young when he played for the Stars, Smith was a highly regarded infield prospect. He attracted the attention of several major league teams who craved young black players to develop in their organization. The Cincinnati Reds won Smith's services and sent him to their minor league system. After hitting .338 at San Diego in the Pacific Coast League, Smith was called up to the Reds at the end of the 1955 season. Unfortunately, after hitting only .196, Smith was traded to the St. Louis Cardinals, but never made their major league roster.[27]

Catcher Charles White also played for the Stars in 1950. He was another in a long line of good catchers who played for this club. White fit right in with such players as Biz Mackey, Bill Cash, and Stanley Glenn. Only 22 years old when he played for the Stars, White was the type of highly regarded catching prospect that major league teams hoped they could find in the Negro Leagues. Due to the presence of Cash and Glenn, White also played third base in his short stay in Philadelphia. Soon after his stay in Philadelphia, White was signed by the St. Louis Browns organization and stayed with them through their move to Baltimore, but never made their major league roster. However, the Orioles traded White to the Milwaukee Braves, where he served as their backup catcher for the 1954 and 1955 seasons. Unfortunately, the Braves sent White back to the minors during the 1955 season. He never made it back to the major leagues.[28]

The decline of the Stars is attributed to the success of Jackie Robinson in 1947. As he excelled with the Brooklyn Dodgers, other black players chose to experiment with entering the majors as opposed to toiling in the less-publicized Negro Leagues. By 1950, most of the best players on the Stars attempted to work their way into the major leagues. That year also became an end to an era as Ed Bolden died on September 27. The Stars lost their most recognizable figure and became a less organized franchise. The club also lost their right to play at Passon Field by 1940 and spent their remaining days playing mostly road games, save for the rare appearances at Shibe Park.[29] Once Jackie Robinson broke the color barrier, fans of the Negro Leagues abandoned their local loyalties and chose to attend major league games whenever black players were on the field. Newspapers such as the *Tribune* largely neglected the Stars and instead followed the progress of black major leaguers. Under different management, the Stars continued to operate until a last-place finish in the 1952 season.[30] The club ceased operations before the 1953 season. As the Stars disbanded, neither of the city's major league franchises had yet to integrate.

5

Attempted Integration of Philadelphia Baseball

The history of the integration of Philadelphia baseball provides many answers to the question as to why relatively little support of the Phillies emanates from the African American neighborhoods. The move from segregation to integration in Philadelphia baseball was anything but a smooth process. Both the Athletics and Phillies were extremely slow in integrating their rosters. Not until late in the 1953 season did the Athletics, shortly before their move to Kansas City, hire a black player. The Phillies did not have a black player on their roster until 1957, becoming the last National League team to do so.[1] Furthermore, the failure for the city's fans to embrace integration of its baseball clubs haunts Philadelphia to this day. This difficult process also says much about racial relations in the city itself.

As many Negro Leaguers became well known for their abilities, many progressive thinking baseball men began to make movements toward breaking the major league color barrier. Attempts to break the barrier were in themselves nothing new. The Philadelphia Pythians tried to break into white baseball in 1870, but were denied by the white ruling majority.[2] In 1901, there was Philadelphia Giants star Charlie Grant's failure to integrate John McGraw's American League Baltimore Orioles.[3] For years afterward, such baseball luminaries as McGraw and Branch Rickey secretly wished they could integrate their rosters. Grant's effort, however, represents the last official attempt to integrate any major league team until 1945.[4] But this forty-four-year gap did not mean that any individual or organization failed to seriously consider the integration of the major leagues.

Actually, several opportunities existed for Philadelphia to become the first major league city to integrate its teams. The first target of integration was the financially troubled Phillies franchise. In 1942, Eddie Gottlieb convinced two Jewish businessmen, Ike and Leon Levy, to make an offer to purchase the Phillies. Prior to this time, Dr. Leon Levy owned the Philadelphia radio station WCAU and later built the Atlantic City Race Track.[5] The idea was that the Levys would own the team and that Gottlieb would serve as the general manager. In that position, Gottlieb could acquire black players if he chose to do so through his experience controlling the Philadelphia Stars. Furthermore, if successful, the Levys would become the first-ever Jewish owners of a major league franchise. That too posed a problem for the seemingly prejudiced major leagues, which would frown at the prospect of Jewish owners for one of their clubs.[6]

Before following through with the offer to buy the Phillies, the Levys wanted assurances from National League President Ford Frick that no rule existed against Jews owning big league franchises. When asked about this possibility, Frick said that he knew of no rule preventing Jewish ownership of a major league team. But when it came time for Frick to meet with the Levys, the National League President refused to do so. Instead, Frick chose to stonewall the sale to the Levys. Frick said that he could not "discuss anything about the sale of the Phillies." Therefore, he refused to meet with the Levys or any of their representatives. This obstruction discouraged the Levys from becoming further interested in purchasing the Phillies and Gottlieb never became part of Phillies management.[7]

Frick's actions made it clear that he wanted neither Jewish owners nor black players in the majors. The Levys never purchased the Phillies or any other major league team. Also, Gottlieb never became the general manager of the Phillies or any other major league team.[8] Later, Gottlieb became general manager of the Philadelphia Warriors of the fledgling National Basketball Association. Under his tutelage, the Warriors won the first NBA Championship in 1947. Meanwhile, the Phillies continued to struggle throughout the 1940s.

If the Levys purchased the Phillies, would integration have taken place? With the involvement of Gottlieb, arguments existed for both integration and continued segregation. While Gottlieb maintained many connections with the Philadelphia Stars and the Negro Leagues, it is unknown whether he would integrate the Phillies. Gottlieb certainly knew of the most talented Negro League players and probably could have easily

Ford Frick stonewalled an attempt by Jewish businessman to purchase the Phillies while serving as President of the National League. (Courtesy of the National Baseball Hall of Fame)

acquired them to play for the Phillies. But Gottlieb also proved himself as a shrewd businessman who knew the best way to make a profit in professional sports. He knew that integration of the major leagues would adversely affect the profits of black baseball in Philadelphia. Gottlieb would potentially lose money as a result of integration. Nevertheless, one may argue that if this purchase succeeded, integration was a possibility. It appeared that the lure of breaking into major league management proved too strong for Gottlieb. But it was not the last attempt of any businessman to purchase the Phillies and offering the prospect of integration.

By 1943, the club was close to bankruptcy and Frick put the pressure on Phillies owner and president Gerry Nugent to find a buyer for his financially strapped team. Any failure to find a suitable owner would result in the League's takeover of the club operations. Therefore, Nugent entertained offers from all types of prospective owners, including one group that sought to move the Phillies to Baltimore. The most memorable individual that showed interest in the Phillies was a minor league team owner named Bill Veeck.[9] Veeck, who later owned the Cleveland Indians, St. Louis Browns (now the Baltimore Orioles), and Chicago White Sox, will forever be considered baseball's ultimate showman and an innovator. In the early 1940s, however, Veeck had yet to establish himself as a major league baseball entrepreneur. He was quite eager to follow in the footsteps of his father, a one-time president of the Chicago Cubs,[10] and the flagging Phillies seemed like an ideal opportunity to do so. Conceivably, he could acquire the Phillies rather cheaply, which would provide Veeck the opportunity to own a major league team. Therefore, Veeck pursued the matter of purchasing the Phillies from the seemingly desperate Nugent.[11]

Prior to 1943, Veeck owned the successful Milwaukee Brewers minor league franchise. He became noteworthy for not only his team's play but for the innovative promotions scheduled along with the games. His later career in the major leagues included such wild promotions as sending a midget to bat as a pinch-hitter, destruction of disco records in the 1970s, and exploding scoreboards that went off whenever one of his players hit a home run.[12] Therefore, a man of Veeck's potential methods would probably become a welcome sight to the dismal Phillies. But according to Veeck, if he owned the Phillies, he would attempt a then-radical concept: integration.[13]

In his autobiography, Veeck claimed that if he owned the Phillies that he would staff the team with the best players that the Negro Leagues offered. Veeck mentioned such players as Satchel Paige, Roy Campanella, Luke Easter, and Monte Irvin. Paige was a Hall of Fame talent who had yet to receive a chance to pitch in the big leagues. Philadelphia native Campanella, too, later became a member of the Hall of Fame. Easter was a power-hitting first baseman who later succeeded with the Veeck-owned Cleveland Indians.[14] Irvin became a star outfielder for the pennant-winning teams of the New York Giants in the 1950s. Veeck argued that the Phillies would become instant pennant contenders with these players on the roster. He wrote that, in effect, the Phillies would become all-black team because the existing white players were not good enough to play ahead of those that Veeck hoped to acquire.[15]

While all team owners want to make money, Veeck felt that this plan made sense because of World War II. As many of baseball's best players were inducted into the armed forces, major league teams scrambled to field competitive squads. Many teams resorted to signing players who retired years before, those who somehow became classified as 4-F (unsuited for service) cases and not drafted, and those too young to serve in the military. The rosters of major league franchises became littered with players either in their forties or teens. Obviously, the brand of "major league" baseball displayed during the war proved inferior. Some examples of the desperate situation surrounding professional baseball at this time was the formation of the All-America Girls Professional Baseball League and the hiring of Pete Gray, a one-armed outfielder, by the St. Louis Browns. With the drafting of African Americans possible but less likely, Veeck believed that the high quality of baseball could be maintained by breaking the color barrier. Also, since a large number of blacks served in the armed forces, there was no reason for their continued exclusion from major league baseball. He believed that the lily-white major league owners and Baseball Commissioner Kenesaw Mountain Landis could not effectively argue for maintaining segregation.[16]

A common perception exists that Commissioner Landis proved the most significant barrier to the integration of major league baseball. Landis, a Southerner, consistently maintained that no rule existed which prevented the integration of major league baseball, yet he privately saw to it that no major league owner integrated his team. It did not, however, take much effort for Landis to accomplish segregation because the owners unanimously supported him.[17] Landis' feelings towards integration became evident as he imposed limitations on major leaguers from playing barnstorming exhibitions against Negro League All-Star teams. Landis' actions came cryptically and without explanation. According to star Negro League first baseman Buck Leonard, "I don't know why he stopped us from playing the major-leaguers. Somebody said that the major-leaguers weren't organized and didn't want an unorganized major-league team playing."[18] In his explanation, Leonard obviously took great care in not jumping to any conclusions. The same cannot be said of former Brooklyn Dodgers manager Leo Durocher, who claimed that Landis' opposition prevented him from acquiring black players. In response, Landis "ludicrously insisted" that blacks were not banned from the major leagues: "Negroes are not banned from organized baseball by the commissioner.... There is no rule in organized baseball prohibiting their participation."[19] Despite that denial, segregation continued in organized baseball.

Bill Veeck showed no

Long-time Commissioner of Major League Baseball, Kenesaw Mountain Landis is viewed as the great opponent of integration. His allowance of the "gentlemen's agreement" in major league baseball kept it an all-white sport for decades. (Courtesy of the National Baseball Hall of Fame)

diplomacy at all when he claimed that Landis blocked his effort to purchase the Phillies. In his autobiography, Veeck asserts that when he informed Landis of his intentions to integrate the Phillies, the commissioner blocked the sale. Veeck wrote that he possessed the necessary financial backing and successfully gained the approval of Phillies President Gerry Nugent. Despite all of this apparent evidence, the franchise was inexplicably turned over to the league, which promptly sold the Phillies to another buyer for less money.[20] The new owner, William Cox, bought the team for half of what Veeck supposedly offered and, subsequently, maintained the major leagues' policy of segregation. This same owner would later suffer banishment for being linked to gamblers.[21] Veeck never owned the Phillies and it would be fourteen more years before the team became integrated.

While Veeck's story appears convincing, it does not have any type of confirmation. According to Veeck, he had the financial backing from the Phillies Cigar Company. This claim proves questionable because it never received any corroboration. Also, this story defies good business sense because the desperate Nugent would eagerly accept Veeck's offer. It is conceivable to argue that Veeck did not have this financial backing and, therefore, could not create an acceptable offer. While Veeck met with Nugent, talks broke off because the two could not reach a compromise over price and the meeting proved unproductive. This meeting was the only known recorded session between the two men.[22]

Did Veeck manufacture this story? And if so, why would he do so? Veeck would later become the owner of the Cleveland Indians, which became the second major league franchise to integrate its roster and the first American League team to do so. Veeck accomplished this feat by signing future Hall-of-Fame outfielder Larry Doby from the Newark Eagles during the 1947. It remains a possibility that Veeck regrets not breaking the color barrier first. Also, his ill feelings towards Brooklyn Dodgers president Branch Rickey (who first integrated the major leagues) and Commissioner Landis were evident in this story. He considered Rickey a self-centered manipulator and Landis a dictatorial commissioner.[23] Veeck probably wanted to exercise some of his disgust towards the two men by making his Phillies venture part of the public record.

Could Veeck's story merely an unintentional misrepresentation of the facts? When Veeck made his move to buy the Cleveland Indians in 1946, he hired Louis Jones to handle the public relations associated with the move towards integration. Veeck said he wanted to prepare the "black segment of Cleveland" for the arrival of black ballplayers. Veeck mentioned that he "was presumptuous" that integration would become acceptable for both black and white baseball fans in Philadelphia. This revelation indicates that he learned a lesson of some sort with a previous unsuccessful effort, such as an attempt to buy the Phillies.[24] But again, no public documentation of this effort exists anywhere. Furthermore, with the deaths of many of the principle actors of this drama, it is impossible to determine whether Veeck's claim maintains any validity.

If successful in his attempts to purchase the Phillies, would Veeck have integrated its roster? Again, he became the first owner to integrate the American League, which eventually proved helpful to the Indians' World Championship team of 1948. But prior to his ownership of the Indians, he never successfully integrated his minor league club, the Milwaukee Brewers. Veeck claimed to make an effort to integrate the Brewers in 1940, only to face expulsion from professional baseball by Commissioner Landis if he did.[25] Therefore, the Brewers never integrated during Veeck's tenure as owner.

Furthermore, Veeck only integrated the Indians gradually. Larry Doby became the first black player in the American League when he first suited up for the Veeck-owned Indians in August 1947. The following season, the Indians acquired pitcher Satchel Paige midway through the 1948 season. The next year, first baseman Luke Easter and outfielder Minnie Minoso further integrated the Indians.[26] His claim to buy the Phillies included the provision that the team would almost be entirely black. Therefore, such a dramatic maneuver does not coincide with Veeck's later actions.[27] Nevertheless, because of those subsequent actions, one may perceive that if he actually bought the Phillies, the roster would probably become integrated soon after. Furthermore, one cannot deny the fact that Veeck proved instrumental in the eventual full-scale integration of major league baseball.

After Veeck's apparent effort to buy the Phillies, a player attempted to break the color barrier himself. The player was Philadelphia native Roy Campanella, then the star catcher of the Negro League Baltimore Elites. It was 1945 and, because of the war, major league rosters continued to display a lack of quality talent. On a day off from the Elites, Campanella traveled home to spend time with his pregnant wife and to attend a Phillies game. He showed up an hour before game time and, in a moment of inspiration, went down to the field to talk to Phillies manager Hans Lobert. Lobert knew Campanella from watching him play for the Elites and was aware of his abilities. At this time, the Phillies were still floundering and desperately needed, among other things, a quality starting catcher.[28]

In his conversation with Lobert, Campanella received the satisfaction that the manager thought highly of his abilities. Lobert admitted that

Campanella would help his troubled team and he would, under ordinary circumstances, enjoy having him on the Phillies. Careful not to make a controversial decision, however, Lobert suggested that Campanella talk to Phillies president Gerry Nugent. Nugent held that same position when he had met with Veeck and now was on the hot seat with integration again. When Campanella spoke to Nugent on the phone, all that he asked of the Phillies was a tryout. Unfortunately, the sweet-talking Nugent explained that the "unwritten rule" barring the integration of major leagues still existed. Essentially, Nugent and the Phillies refused to give Campanella a tryout. Although the Phillies used the very capable Andy Seminick behind the plate after World War II, Campanella still possessed Hall-of-Fame ability. The next season, the Brooklyn Dodgers signed Campanella to their Nashua, New Hampshire farm club. But it was another four years before Campanella played in the majors for the Dodgers.[29] "I also know," former Phillies centerfielder Richie Ashburn once said, "that Campanella always said he wanted to play with the Phillies. He didn't want to play for the Dodgers."[30] Meanwhile, the hapless Phillies continued to struggle near the bottom of the standings and remained segregated.

While this conversation probably took place, Campanella's account of Lobert was incorrect. According to Campanella's autobiography, he spoke to Lobert. He described Lobert as the "Phillies manager." If this meeting took place in 1945, Lobert was not the manager. Lobert's final season as manager of the Phillies came with the club's last place finish in 1942. When this meeting supposedly took place, the racially intolerant Ben Chapman was then the manager of the Phillies. Lobert, however, did serve as a coach for the Phillies for a couple of years after his managing tenure ended.[31] Campanella's account, no matter how he describes Lobert, does emphasize that major league owners would put out an inferior product rather than integrate their teams.

What did the Phillies use as alternatives to acquiring black ballplayers? By the 1944 and 1945 seasons, the Phillies roster included several players between the ages 16 and 18. Two of those teenagers were infielders Granny Hamner and Putsy Caballero. Both players were later members of the Phillies 1950 National League Pennant winning team. Hamner served as the club's starting shortstop and Caballero as a reserve infielder. But even Hamner was forced into the war effort when he turned eighteen during the 1945 season. Because of the apparent instability of the club, the Phillies finished in last place in 1945.[32] The use of teenage players existed with other major league clubs as well. Yet, big league teams refused to consider the use of black players in order to raise the quality of play during the war years. Therefore, professional baseball suffered greatly during World War II as mediocre play reigned in the big leagues.

Philadelphia's other major league team, the Athletics, also refused to even consider integration. For most of their history in Philadelphia, the Athletics were owned and managed by Connie Mack. During his extensive tenure with the Athletics, Mack managed some of the best teams of major league history. Unfortunately, he also had a legacy of refusal to integrate his roster. Publicly, Mack claimed that he "could not cross the well-known prejudices" of Commissioner Landis and, therefore, never considered integration of his team. Although Mack apologized for his policy, it was not in his nature to accept integration. For years, he fought to exclude blacks from his Germantown neighborhood.[33] This mentality followed Mack into his career in baseball. Although he respected the abilities of the finest Negro League players, he remained loyal to his segregationist policies.

While serving as owner and manager of the Athletics, Mack once told Negro League star Judy Johnson that, "it's a shame that you are a Negro." Mack contended that with so many good black players, there was not enough room for everybody in the major leagues.[34] When Mack's Athletics were to play Brooklyn in a 1946 spring training exhibition game, a reporter asked him how he would react if the Dodgers brought Robinson. He replied, "I wouldn't play him. I used to have respect for Rickey. I don't anymore."[35] Even as late as 1949, Mack felt that there lacked a significant number of qualified black players by saying, "I have been advised that there are not many Negro boys playing baseball."[36] The city's black newspapers considered Mack as one of the major league owners who "most bitterly" opposed integration. Mack preferred to maintain segregation and suffer with a mediocre team that drew fewer fans instead of integrating with the possibility of fielding a more competitive team.

While it became obvious that the major league owners of Philadelphia shied away from integration, the debate continued in the Negro Leagues. Since Ed Bolden remained a key figure in the Negro Leagues, his opinion mattered. Despite the opposition of many of his fellow owners, Bolden publicly supported integration of organized baseball. He stated that "he would never stand in the way of a player's advancement" into major league baseball. Although it could doom his control of a professional baseball team, Bolden appeared to support any opportunity to integrate. *Philadelphia Tribune* columnist and former Negro League Commissioner W. Rollo Wilson believed that the presence of integrated professional baseball would actually improve the Negro Leagues. Wilson wrote that the possibility of "big money in the major leagues will bring more and more ambitious players in the Negro loops for training and experience."[37] Unfortunately, this faithful opinion eventually came undone as major league teams eventually chose to use their own farm systems to nurture black players. The feeling of most major league teams was that such players could become better fundamental players than they would in the Negro Leagues. Therefore, the Negro Leagues did nothing more than discover players that would eventually become signed by major league teams.

Another agent of the continuation of the segregation of major league baseball in Philadelphia, interestingly enough, was Philadelphia Stars' co-owner Eddie Gottlieb. He sold Mack on the idea that "colored teams" could bring large crowds to Shibe Park. Since Mack could book yet another tenant to his ballpark, it proved in his best financial interest to do what he could to ensure the survival of the Stars. Aside from both the Phillies and Stars, Shibe Park was also used several times for the Negro Leagues World Series.[38] Therefore, the survival of the Negro Leagues definitely did not hurt Mack's bank account. Since the Stars proved a profitable business for both Mack and Gottlieb, neither was in a hurry for major league integration because it would harm this business arrangement. Therefore, Gottlieb abandoned any future attempt to enter the major leagues and Mack's club remained segregated.

Mack, however, eventually investigated the possibility of the racial integration of the Athletics after Jackie Robinson's achievement. He hired ex–Hilldale superstar and future Hall-of-Famer Judy Johnson to scout out potential Negro Leaguers who might make the jump into the majors. Johnson succeeded in finding skilled Negro League players ready to move to the major leagues. He found that the Athletics could acquire Larry Doby, Minnie Minoso, and Hank Aaron from teams in Negro Leagues. According to Johnson, the Athletics could have acquired Aaron from the Indianapolis Clowns for $3,500.[39] If these acquisitions occurred, the circumstances surrounding the relocation of the Athletics may have turned out differently. The combination of these talented players and the best of the existing Athletics would elevate the team to a higher standing in the American League. Instead, the floundering Athletics moved out of Philadelphia.

Obviously, these findings took place over several years because Aaron was only 20 years old when he broke in with the Milwaukee Braves in 1954. That year marked the last season the Athletics played in Philadelphia. Since Doby first played for the Indians in 1947 and Minoso entered the majors in 1949, one may perceive that Johnson worked for Mack for close to seven years. Doby became the first African American to play in the American

League and he enjoyed a very productive major league career, as did Minoso, who played in the major leagues for twenty years. The three of them could have become the nucleus of a pennant-winning team and the Athletics might have remained in Philadelphia. Instead, Mack rejected Johnson's proposal to sign each of them and his franchise continued to struggle. By 1950, Mack retired from managing and, after the 1953 season, his family sold the team to Chicago businessman Arnold Johnson. Soon after the sale, the new owner moved the team to Kansas City.[40] After this relocation to the Midwest, Judy Johnson no longer scouted for the Athletics.

The Phillies also added an African American scout to their payroll, former Philadelphia Stars player Bill Yancey. The Phillies, however, did not employ Yancey until 1955, several years after Judy Johnson's hiring. This hiring also occurred after the actual integration of Athletics with Bob Trice's arrival in September 1953.[41] This dragging of the feet appears indicative of the early years of the club's ownership by the Carpenter family. When Bob Carpenter bought the team in the late 1940s, he opposed the integration of the Phillies. His manager, Ben Chapman, was renowned for his intolerance, as was his General Manager, Herb Pennock. Before Jackie Robinson and the Brooklyn Dodgers first came to Philadelphia in 1947, both Pennock and Carpenter warned Dodger president Branch Rickey not to bring Robinson into Shibe Park. Needless to say, the resolve of both Rickey and Robinson overcame such intolerance and Robinson did play against the Phillies. Although Carpenter publicly said that he never opposed the integration of profes-

Shown in his playing days, Bill Yancey was a Negro League star in Philadelphia. Later, Yancey served as the advisor for the black players in the Phillies organization. (Courtesy of the National Baseball Hall of Fame)

sional baseball, he also said that he would refuse to integrate his own team merely for the sake of doing so.[42]

Carpenter's philosophy lacked sincerity because there were still many outstanding Negro League players available when he took over. During the late 1940s and early 1950s, it was possible for Carpenter to integrate the team with a player of major league ability. The Phillies owner, however, decided to avoid integration as his team showed signs of contending for the National League pennant. Conceivably, Carpenter and the rest of the Phillies management felt that integration proved unnecessary at this time. In 1950, the all-white Phillies' "Whiz Kids" won the National League pennant over the integrated Brooklyn Dodgers. This championship team was relatively young, as most of its key players were in their early to mid-twenties. Therefore, Carpenter chose not to integrate while other teams acquired most of the talented Negro League players. "We didn't win after 1950, but I think there's a reason," Whiz Kids centerfielder Richie Ashburn once said. "We were the last team to get any black ball players. The Giants, the Dodgers, the Braves were getting the good black ball players. We were still pretty good, but they were just getting better."[43] Furthermore, Carpenter quite possibly followed the lead of many major league owners who chose only to integrate with players who possessed talents "worthy of promotion." Such owners ignored a bench player or even an average performer, choosing to fill that position with a white player.[44] Only black players with superstar abilities would receive serious consideration from major league teams. A more marginal player would end up becoming a career minor league player or never get an opportunity at all. If a black player did not perform at the highest level in the major leagues, his career ended almost immediately. As owner of the Phillies, Carpenter appeared to possess this mentality.

Some of Carpenter's true feelings were reflected in his opinions of the case of Sam Jethroe. Jethroe, a black outfielder, first integrated the Boston Braves roster. The Braves purchased Jethroe's rights from the Brooklyn Dodgers and he was expected to help the Braves both on the field and in the box office. Braves owners felt that Jethroe would serve as a gate attraction to the black residents of Boston. In his first year with Boston, Jethroe appeared to tire out and play poorly in the second half of the season. Carpenter suggested that Jethroe was "lonely" and that the Braves should have taken more than one black player in order to make the situation more comfortable. Braves management denied this by saying that if Jethroe had a problem, he could always tell them so without recrimination.[45] The expression of this opinion suggests that Carpenter needed to justify his own policies through the struggles of Jethroe and

Connie Mack (left) as owner of the Athletics, and Bob Carpenter, as owner of the Phillies, were slow to accept integration of their ballclubs. Mack made money renting Shibe Park to Negro League teams and Carpenter said that he would not integrate the Phillies "merely for the sake of doing so." (Courtesy of the National Baseball Hall of Fame)

the Braves. To Carpenter, it appeared that integration was too much of a problem to deal with and he would rather remain with the *status quo*. One may argue that the failure of the Phillies to integrate possibly led to their gradual free-fall from the top of the National League standings in 1950 to a dismal last place finish by the end of the decade.

The racial attitudes displayed by both Mack and Carpenter indicates their reticence towards accepting African Americans to their teams. While most other teams explored integration, both Philadelphia teams apparently refused to do so. Many outstanding opportunities presented themselves to these owners, but they remained committed to their segregationist policies. These attitudes would contribute to the Athletics leaving Philadelphia and the Phillies' gradual fall from the top of the standings.

6

The Demise of Black Baseball

> *The important thing as I see it is that I, as a Negro, have been given a great privilege and I just wish all members of my race felt the same deep gratitude that I do. Here I am making more money than a great percentage of the men of my race. Here I am on a ballclub where I've been given every chance in the world to make good. What more could I possibly want?*
> —Harry Simpson, outfielder,
> Kansas City Athletics, 1956[1]

The end of the Negro Leagues is traced to one moment in time: Jackie Robinson's entry into the major leagues. The long struggle that Rube Foster first embarked on in the early 1900s was now complete; black players could now perform in the major leagues. Robinson's successful effort made it possible for other Negro League baseball players to enter the major leagues. Instead of being an alternative, the Negro Leagues now provided a fresh supply of talent to the major leagues. As one major league team after another began to integrate their rosters, they depleted the talent level of the Negro Leagues. Soon, teams would sell off their best players in order to remain solvent. By the mid–1950s, the Negro Leagues no longer existed as a complete entity and the surviving teams began to rely on barnstorming tours.

Despite many attempts and much campaigning, the major leagues were still not integrated during World War II. Major league rosters became tremendously depleted during the war and in order to fill the void, major league teams quietly considered integration. Such a strategy succeeded in industry and African Americans even served in the armed forces. In fact, examples existed of Negro League ballplayers who served in segregated units of the armed forces during World War II. For instance, Kansas City Monarchs outfielder Alfred "Slick" Suratt served as a bulldozer operator in the Navy. His units built airfields at Guadalcanal and other South Pacific islands.[2]

While the armed forces remained segregated, it became obvious that these units contributed to the overall success of the American war effort. Unfortunately, when Suratt and other Negro League players returned from the service, they found that the door to the major leagues remained shut. Although some owners thought of integration, they failed to act upon it. This lack of opportunity contrasted with the philosophies and goals of the American fighting force, to provide freedom for those living overseas. This contradiction made it more difficult to continue the conspiracy of excluding black players from the major leagues.[3]

Kenesaw Mountain Landis, despite of his advancing age, continued to serve as commissioner of baseball. Landis remained the major proponent of segregation in professional baseball, even during the war years. With the consistent support of major league owners, he refused to waver from his stance despite pressure from writers such as Sam Lacy of the *Baltimore Afro-American* and Wendell Smith of the *Pittsburgh Courier*. Often, such writers attempted to arrange tryouts for black players with major league teams. Although these efforts usually failed, these writers remained persistent and continued to work towards their goals.

Significant pressure also came from another source, *The Daily Worker*. The pro–Socialist publication often supported civil rights causes in the workplace and, beginning in 1941, it launched a strong campaign to integrate major league baseball. *The Daily Worker's* participation in this effort to integrate created mixed reaction from black players and newspaper writers. This campaign occurred at a time when many African Americans began to consider Communism as an alternative to American democracy. Frustrated by the failure to achieve equality amongst the races, African American personalities such as racial activist W.E.B. Du Bois and actor Paul Robeson became members of the Communist party during the 1940s and 1950s. As far as the players, many failed to take *The Daily Worker* seriously. Most black players did not feel a connection to the Communist party or the publication. But *The Daily Worker* actually became more successful in arranging potential tryouts for black players with major league teams.[4] Despite these efforts, Commissioner Landis and most major league owners remained skeptical and unimpressed.

Landis maintained this segregationist policy until his death in 1944. As Negro League player and coach Buck O'Neil explains, "Landis might have been a great man in some regards, but he did all of us a favor when he died...."[5] Landis' replacement was former Kentucky Senator Happy Chandler. Since Chandler came from the South, the *status quo* was expected in regard to the integration of major league baseball.

When he took office, however, Chandler proved a refreshing change. When asked about integration, Chandler replied, "If they can fight and die in Okinawa, Guadalcanal, in the South Pacific, they can play baseball in America." Therefore, the presence of Chandler failed to serve as an excuse for the continuance of segregation.[6] The question remained as to which club owner would stick his neck out and move towards the integration of major league baseball.

During the 1940s, rumors persisted of tryouts with major league teams. Many Negro League players were told about the arranging of tryouts with major league teams. Roy Campanella received news of the interest that the Pittsburgh Pirates had for his services. This news came from *The Daily Worker*, which still sought to integrate baseball. *The Daily Worker* contacted the Pirates' front office and received a positive response from Pirates president William Benswanger.[7] In fact, Campanella was told, "You'll receive a letter from William Benswanger, president of the Pirates. He'll tell you when to report." All Benswanger could offer was the possibility of a minor league tryout. Confident of his abilities, Campanella accepted but Benswanger did not follow through with the offer. Campanella never received the tryout.[8] Benswanger's failure to make good on his word occurred because of the intense pressure he received when news of this tryout became known. Therefore, Benswanger gracefully backed out and because he at least tried to do something, he never received serious criticism. Campanella was thankful for the efforts of *The Daily Worker* to provide him with the opportunity to play major league baseball. One may speculate, however, how baseball and civil rights history may have changed as a result of this tryout. It does prove that teams did think about integration but failed to make a stand and go through with it.[9]

Many major league owners and executives secretly wished to improve their clubs through integration but seemed afraid to do so. According to Buck Leonard, "I think they believed we could play major-league baseball, but everyone hated to be the first."[10] This reluctance probably prevented the integration of major league baseball during the war. Although new players were sought to replace those who enlisted in the military during World War II, African American players still were not invited to play on major league teams. Without the support of team owners, the best Negro League players would not get the opportunity to play in the major leagues.

On October 23, 1945, the Brooklyn Dodgers made a historic announcement: Jackie Robinson signed a contract to play for the Dodger organization. The man most responsible for this arrangement was Dodger President Branch Rickey. For years, Rickey desired to integrate the major leagues and felt that the time had come to make the move. After scouting the Negro Leagues for that potential first African American major leaguer, Rickey chose the college educated Robinson.[11] This news created great excitement throughout the Negro Leagues as players felt that progress was finally made. As Buck O'Neil explains, "This was progress. The Dodgers signing Jackie wasn't just about baseball or about opportunities for the Negro-leaguers. This was progress for the whole country. It didn't matter who was the first or which team had the courage; this was the first real step toward integration, toward equality, since maybe Reconstruction."[12] The white leadership of the major leagues refused to comment on the signing. Athletics owner Connie Mack said that he did not know of Robinson and could not comment. Obviously, the white baseball establishment attempted to downplay Robinson's signing. As far as the civil rights issue is concerned, the mere presence of Robinson meant that race could no longer be criteria for exclusion from the major leagues.

While Robinson's eventual presence in the major leagues met with the approval of African Americans everywhere, it did not receive the full support of several Negro League players. To many, Robinson signified an athlete who played baseball, not a full-blown baseball player. At UCLA, Robinson played four sports and baseball was his least favorite. Robinson also lettered in football, basketball, and track. In fact, Robinson was an All-American in both football and basketball for UCLA. During the Spring sports season, he often left in the middle of a baseball game in order to compete in an event during a track meet. Yet when he left the service in 1944, Robinson played professional baseball for the Kansas City Monarchs. As a rookie shortstop, Robinson was a decent fielder who hit well and stole many bases. But he was not considered the best player in the Negro Leagues.[13] Some black players were skeptical of the Robinson signing.

Many Negro Leaguers believed that they were a better choice. Negro League star pitcher and eventual Hall-of-Famer Satchel Paige exclaimed, "It still was me that ought to have been first!" Another star Negro League player, Jimmie Crutchfield, asked, "How would you feel seeing a rookie selected?" Another Monarch, Bennie Sorrell, was quite upset that he was not first and spent the rest of his career playing in Mexico. More tragically, many attributed the early death of Negro League slugging catcher Josh Gibson to being "brokenhearted" that he was not chosen. To most Negro League veterans, the signing and eventual success of Robinson was a bittersweet time.[14] Robinson's signing with the Dodgers, however, soon provided opportunities in the major leagues for many black ballplayers.

The choice of Robinson, however, indicated the beginning of a pattern of how major league teams integrated their rosters. Big league teams, for the most part, chose to integrate with younger, up-and-coming black ballplayers rather than established Negro League stars. Younger players such as Robinson, Monte Irvin, and Larry Doby proved more attractive than older players such as Paige, Gibson, and Crutchfield. Younger players, even today, offer more "upside" potential for less money. A veteran drawing card such as a Paige or Gibson usually would command a larger salary than a hungry newcomer eager to show his developing talent. Also, players such as Paige and Gibson would probably only last a couple of years before their skills would deteriorate. Furthermore, younger players offered less of a challenge to management while the well-known veterans of the Negro Leagues might want more special treatment. Therefore, younger black players became more desirable.[15] Although this theory is not completely foolproof, the only exceptions to this argument were Satchel Paige and Willard Brown. In 1947, the St. Louis Browns signed the 37 year old Brown and the Cleveland Indians acquired Paige in 1948. The acquisition of Paige by Indians' owner Bill Veeck became viewed more as a gate attraction rather than a move to improve the long-range fortunes of the club. Although Paige played a few seasons in the American League and even made the All-Star team, neither he nor Brown enjoyed a lengthy major league career.[16]

The best example of the reticence to hire veteran Negro League players is the case of Hall-of-Fame outfielder "Cool Papa" Bell. Bell performed with brilliance in the Negro Leagues beginning in the 1920s and by the late 1940s, Bell still excelled on the field. With age creeping up on him, Bell did not believe that he would ever get a chance to prove himself against major league competition. In his prime, Bell was the consummate leadoff hitter who possessed legendary speed. However, by the late 1940s and early 1950s, Bell's skills eroded. When Bill Veeck owned the St. Louis Browns in the early 1950s, Bell attempted to meet with him in order to receive an opportunity in the big leagues. At this time, Veeck was regarded as a soft touch on the issue of integration. Whenever Bell visited the Browns' offices, however, Veeck refused to meet with him. Bell never received an opportunity with any major league team.[17]

Another example of this policy is the case of Negro League outfielder Henry Kimbro. Kimbro began his Negro League career in 1938 and eventually became part of a star-studded lineup of the Baltimore Elite Giants. This team included such future major league stars as catcher Roy Campanella and infielder Junior Gilliam, both of whom later played with the Brooklyn Dodgers. By the time Jackie Robinson broke into professional baseball in 1946, Kimbro was in his mid-thirties and, according to typical major league policy, classified as over the hill. Despite this reputation, Kimbro played his best baseball during the early days of integration. In 1946, Kimbro hit for a lusty .376 average against still formidable Negro League competition. The next season, Kimbro continued his fine play by batting .363 and still playing a strong defensive centerfield. Although the validity of Negro League statistics remains questionable, no one could dispute Kimbro's talent. Yet, while Kimbro continued his fine play, no major league team took a chance on him. There remains little doubt that a player of Kimbro's ability could help a major league team. But a player in his mid-thirties did not fit the profile of a black player entering the major leagues in the late 1940s.[18]

Locally, players such as outfielder Gene Benson and catcher Bill Cash would not receive that opportunity from big league teams because of their age. In the case of Benson, no major league organization took a chance on him and by the 1950s, he no longer played regularly in the Negro Leagues and faded away. Cash, like many older Negro League stalwarts, joined major league organizations but never got out of the minors. Individuals such as Cash, third baseman Ray Dandridge, and first baseman Buck Leonard excelled for minor league teams but for one reason or another, never made it to the big leagues. Although those players could easily make it onto a major league roster during their primes, teams chose to go with younger talent. Even as late as 1953, Athletics General Manager Art Ehlers admitted that the majors preferred younger black players. Ehlers said that the players most prepared to jump from the Negro Leagues to the majors "became over age and lost their opportunity."[19] Either way, it appeared that the black players wanted the opportunity in the big leagues rather than continue to toil in the Negro Leagues. Unfortunately, only a limited number would receive that opportunity.

As far as former Negro League players were concerned, there remained various degrees of bitterness regarding major league integration. Josh Gibson, weakened by years of consistent alcohol abuse, became so distraught and depressed with the selection of Robinson that he began to experience nightmares. With both his mental and physical health deteriorating, Gibson died at a young age. Other players, like Bennie Sorrell, went elsewhere to play. Others refused to act bitter towards the professional baseball establishment. For example, "Slick" Suratt believes that he possessed the ability to play in the major leagues. Today, Suratt still believes that playing in the Negro Leagues "was a good life." Suratt argued that a Negro League player had a better salary than almost all other occupations held by blacks at the time.[20] Nevertheless, the arrival of Robinson to the Brooklyn Dodgers radically altered the face of organized baseball.

Despite the success of Jackie Robinson in 1947, major league teams remained quite slow to accept black players on their rosters. At the end of the 1947 season, only the Cleveland Indians and the St. Louis Browns attempted to follow the Dodgers' lead in hiring black players. While many owners, including Connie Mack, publicly praised Robinson, very few teams explored integration. Some club owners feared backlash from their own fans if a black player made it onto their own team's roster. Others feared the potentially hostile reactions from opposing fans that maintain their prejudice against black players.[21] Overall, owners remained apprehensive due both to concern for their finances and their own personal hang-ups regarding race and integration. These views reduced the opportunities for the best Negro League players to sign with major league organizations.

The lure of potentially playing for the more lucrative major leagues was too powerful for the best players of the Negro Leagues. When Veeck bought the more successful Cleveland Indians, he then signed such Negro League stars as Larry Doby, Luke Easter, and Satchel Paige, who contributed to the Indians' 1948 World Series victory. Other Negro League stars such as Monte Irvin and Hank Thompson of the New York Giants, Don Newcombe and Roy Campanella of the Brooklyn Dodgers, and Sam Jethroe of the Boston Braves experienced success when they entered the majors.[22] But this success would prove fatal to the Negro Leagues.

An example of the hard times experienced by Negro League franchises is the Newark Eagles. The Eagles attracted more than 120,000 fans in 1946. The following year, when Robinson first played for the Dodgers, attendance decreased to 57,000 and 35,000 the next. Mrs. Effa Manley, whose husband owned the Eagles but who ran the club herself, complained of the poor attendance. In response, the black press declared: "The day of loyalty to Jim Crow anything is fast passing away."[23] At first, Manley sold her best players to the major leagues and then, finally, persuaded her husband to sell her beloved team.[24]

In Philadelphia, outfielder Harry Simpson, shortstop Buzz Clarkson, and infielder Milt Smith were sold by the Stars to major league teams.

A standout outfielder for the Philadelphia Stars, Harry Simpson jumped to the American League, where he had a couple of good seasons with the Kansas City Athletics. (Courtesy of the National Baseball Hall of Fame)

Of these players, Simpson proved the most successful. He played eight seasons for several American League teams and made the AL All-Star team in 1956. Simpson, known for his hustling play, finished his career with a lifetime batting average of .266 and played for the World Champion New York Yankees team of 1957.[25] Clarkson played shortstop briefly with the Boston Braves in 1952 at the age of thirty-four, somewhat "elderly" for the typical player in the early days of integration. He was sent down to the minors after only 25 at-bats.[26] Smith did not make the big leagues until near the end of the 1955 season. The 26 year old Smith batted .196 for the Cincinnati Reds as a back-up infielder. Traded to the St. Louis Cardinals organization the following season, Smith went back to the minors, never to play in the big leagues again.[27] Without these three players, the Stars could no longer continue to operate and ceased operations in 1952. Overall, the presence of black players in the big leagues caused the decline of even the best of the Negro League clubs.

The Eastern clubs felt the decline more sharply than the Negro League teams of the Midwest. The lure of watching Jackie Robinson play for the Brooklyn Dodgers was too strong as fans abandoned their home teams and traveled to watch the Dodgers.[28] The nation's leading African American newspapers began to cover black players in the major leagues rather than seriously following the Negro League teams. Existing franchises were reduced to nothing more than showcases for the up-and-coming black players hopeful of playing in the major leagues. The *Philadelphia Tribune* chose to follow the careers of Robinson, Campanella, Willie Mays and others, turning away from covering the declining Philadelphia Stars. Furthermore, the black press attempted to convince all major league teams to integrate their rosters as resistance amongst major league clubs remained. By the early 1950s, almost half of the teams in the majors still failed to embrace integration.

While the black press and its readers celebrated the integration of the major leagues, Negro League owners actually became agents against this movement. Although many of them believed that integration of all American institutions was essential, they felt that their businesses were under siege by major league organizations. For example, Newark Eagles owner Effa Manley fought for many civil rights issues throughout her life. But when it came to the success of her team, Manley ironically opposed the integration of major league baseball. As an influential club owner, Manley feared that she would lose her best players to the majors. Major league team owners faced tough negotiations with Manley in order to acquire one of her prized players. She received much criticism for her policies from black newspapers that described her as a supporter of Jim Crow. To many, Manley became recognized as a barrier to racial progress. To the contrary, Manley merely symbolized a person whose once profitable business began to fail exponentially. With the dramatic decrease in profits, Manley also experienced a loss of status within the African American community. She no longer served as a leader for African Americans like she once did during the heyday of the Newark Eagles. Her plight became common in the lives of all Negro League club owners.[29]

Furthermore, many accused the Negro League and major league owners of cooperating to block further integration. Wendell Smith of the *Pittsburgh Courier* feared that a counter-revolution would prevent other black players from entering the big leagues. Smith charged that Negro Leagues and the majors were "working hard behind closed doors" to prevent defections from one organization to the other.[30] While there remains no proof of such an arrangement, the possibility of such potentially disallowed the opportunity for the best black players to join the major leagues. But the lure of performing against the best became too much for the finest Negro League players.

As for the remaining teams of the Negro Leagues, they were willing to try anything to remain in business. All of the Negro League teams sold their best players to major league teams in order to remain financially solvent. An example of this was the sale of Hall-of-Fame shortstop Ernie Banks from the Kansas City Monarchs to the Chicago Cubs for

$20,000 in 1953. His case serves as more of the exception rather than the rule. Often, Negro League teams sold their players out of desperation and did not receive adequate compensation for their better players. In fact, the Kansas City Monarchs did not receive any compensation for Jackie Robinson when he signed with the Dodgers in December 1945.[31] A more typical example was outfielder Sam Jethroe, who was sold from the Cleveland Buckeyes to the Dodgers for $5,000 prior to the 1949 season.[32] After Jethroe excelled at Montreal, Dodger president Branch Rickey sold him to the Boston Braves for $100,000, quite a nice profit in those days. Jethroe's fine play for the Braves earned him the National League Rookie of the Year Award for the 1950 season.[33] For major league teams willing to integrate during the early 1950s, the Negro Leagues now served as a form of farm system that provided a seemingly unlimited supply of talented ballplayers whose acquisitions came rather cheaply. However, several major league teams, including the Phillies and Athletics, refused to take part in this enterprise. These teams chose to use white players only.

Negro League teams tried assorted gimmicks to entice fans to watch their flagging franchises play. The best example occurred in 1953 when the Indianapolis Clowns signed a woman, Toni Stone, to a $12,000 contract to play second base.[34] While the Clowns publicly denied that this was a publicity stunt, it became clear that this move appeared as one of total desperation and serves as nothing more than a historical footnote. This move typified the Clowns' franchise because, at this time, they attempted to become the Harlem Globetrotters of professional baseball. Toni Stone became another example of the clowning that the Indianapolis club desired. A few of the other Negro League teams also hired women to play for them, to no avail. The Negro American League lasted until 1960, but it really ended when Jackie Robinson first put on a Dodger uniform.[35]

The demise of the Negro Leagues created other problems. The majority of the Negro League franchises were actually run by African Americans. Teams such as the Homestead Grays, Pittsburgh Crawfords, Newark Eagles, and Philadelphia Stars became quite successful under African American management. These were talented teams who maintained strong followings that provided consistent revenue for many seasons. This information clearly proves that blacks, whether African Americans or Latin Americans, proved quite capable of running their own teams. But with the integration of major league baseball, black players performed for white owners and white management. The Negro Leagues offered the opportunity for African Americans to control their own teams. They lost that ability with the breaking of the color barrier because major league organizations chose to keep blacks out of the front office.

Unfortunately, while it became important to integrate the major leagues on the playing field, other institutions were left behind. While many major league teams demonstrated a willingness to acquire the best Negro League players in order to improve their teams on the field and at the gate, little thought was given towards integrating management. Although many teams hired ex–Negro League players to serve as scouts, they symbolized the single-minded desire of clubs to find the best black players and sign them to a contract. Often, in order to make the adjustment to the major leagues easier, former Negro League players were hired by clubs to serve as a sort of mentor for black players. The Phillies hired former Stars' player Bill Yancey to shepherd the black players on the roster, ex–Hilldale star Judy Johnson did the same for the Athletics.[36] But major leagues teams had no inclination to hire black general managers, managers, or coaches throughout the 1950s. This pattern continued until the hiring of former Kansas City Monarch player and manager Buck O'Neil by the Chicago Cubs as a coach in 1962. He was, however, given little chance of ever managing the team.[37] Only two weeks before his death in 1972, Jackie Robinson addressed a World Series crowd in Cincinnati on the virtues of hiring of a black manager.[38] However, no team hired a black manager until 1975, when the Cleveland Indians hired Hall-of-Fame outfielder Frank Robinson to lead the club. Even today, the process of integrating upper management in major league baseball remains quite slow. To date, the Phillies have yet to hire a black general manager or field manager.

7

Intolerance

> *"Robinson, you're one hell of a ballplayer, but you're still a nigger."*
> —Ben Chapman, Phillies Manager,
> on meeting Jackie Robinson in 1947[1]

The failure of Philadelphia's major league teams to integrate their rosters was the beginning of many events that painted the city as intolerant towards black baseball players. Beginning with the arrival of Jackie Robinson and the Brooklyn Dodgers, the underlying racism present in Philadelphia baseball was evident in unfortunate incidents taking place over many years. These incidents range from hotels exercising policies of segregation to the hostility both the Phillies and the Athletics expressed towards integrated opposing teams. The reputation that Philadelphia is a difficult place for African Americans to play began with these incidents and continues until today.

When Robinson broke in with the Dodgers, all opposing teams took their shots at rattling him. Dodger President Branch Rickey prepared Robinson for this type of treatment when he first met him in his office. Rickey wanted to integrate major league baseball for many years and he wanted to make sure that he hired an individual who could bear the responsibility of being the first. Rickey simulated the taunts and insults Robinson could receive from opposing teams, from fans, and even from teammates. Rickey mentioned the possibility of bean-balls, take-out slides, and spiking. Rickey said that he was looking for more than results from Robinson, he wanted someone to represent the race. In other words,

Robinson could not fight back and appear as a violent individual. When Robinson asked Rickey, "Are you looking for a Negro who is afraid to fight back?" Rickey answered: "Robinson, I'm looking for a ballplayer with guts enough not to fight back." Robinson signed with the Dodgers under the provision that he could not fight back or lash out against any opposing player for three years.[2]

As anyone who knew Robinson would understand, this promise became a tough proposition. He was a very proud man whom his contemporaries considered a "Race Man."[3] While in the army during World War II, Robinson was ordered by a white bus driver to move to the rear of an army bus. He refused and believed he was within his rights because he outranked the driver. Nevertheless, the incident was reported and Robinson began to go through a court-martial. The case was eventually dropped and Robinson received a transfer to another outfit, never leaving the United States during World War II. Finally, Robinson received an honorable discharge.[4]

After leaving the army, Robinson joined the Kansas City Monarchs. The Monarchs traveled to away games on their own team bus. The bus often rode through the sparsely populated Midwest and depended on the generosity of small-town gas stations to complete their trips. One such place was Muskogee, Oklahoma, where the Monarchs always stopped to fill their gas tanks. The bus could fill its tanks but the players could not use the restrooms because they were for whites only. Previously, the Monarchs complied with the wishes of the station and only bought gas. Every time they came, the Monarchs bought 100 gallons of gas. With Robinson on the bus, however, things were different. When Robinson headed towards the restroom, the station attendant told him he could not go because it was for whites only. Robinson went to the attendant and said, "Take the hose out of the tank. Let's go, we don't want his gas." Faced with the prospect of losing a big sale, the attendant relented and the Monarchs could now use the restrooms. Prior to his signing with the Dodgers, Robinson had a reputation of having a "hair-trigger temper."[5] Nevertheless, he became Rickey's choice to break baseball's color barrier.

Aside from his playing ability, Robinson became Branch Rickey's choice for another reason. Rickey knew that Robinson would enter an all-white institution if he tried to play major league baseball. Therefore, Rickey wanted an athlete who had a background of excelling in a predominantly white environment. Robinson's career as an All-American football and basketball star at UCLA proved quite helpful towards his assimilation into major league baseball. Unlike most black athletes, Robinson excelled at a college that was primarily a white institution. This experience gave Robinson the confidence

Upon his first visit to Philadelphia as a member of the Brooklyn Dodgers, Jackie Robinson was refused entrance into the Ben Franklin Hotel. Furthermore, he endured fierce taunts from Phillies players and fans during this time. (Courtesy of the National Baseball Hall of Fame)

to succeed in an integrated situation. But nothing at UCLA could ever compare to the virulent opposition he would receive in major league baseball.[6]

The Phillies were among many National League teams that opposed Robinson's ascension into the big leagues. The club, however, became the most vocal about this reluctance. Phillies management, particularly General Manager Herb Pennock and Manager Ben Chapman, expressed the most hostile feelings. Pennock, a former Hall of Fame pitcher with the New York Yankees, called Rickey to demand that Robinson remain in Brooklyn when the Dodgers visited Philadelphia. Pennock was reported as saying, "(You) just can't bring that nigger here with the rest of the team, Branch. We're just not ready for that sort of thing yet." Rickey challenged this demand by stating that he would accept forfeit victories and allow Robinson to arrive with the rest of the Dodgers. Although no official documentation exists of this conversation, the legend that surrounds it paints the Phillies organization as resistant to integration. The debate surrounding Pennock's role in the Phillies' management's resistance to Robinson's first visit to Philadelphia haunts his memory even today. His alleged role in this fiasco provided fuel to the fire for those who opposed a statue in his honor in Kennett Square, Pennsylvania.[7]

Although Rickey thoroughly tested Robinson prior to the signing, nothing prepared Robinson for that first meeting with the Phillies on April 22, 1947. The Phils traveled to Brooklyn's Ebbets Field for a series with the Dodgers. The manager of the Phillies was former Yankee outfielder Ben Chapman, an Alabama native. As a player, Chapman was infamous for his reactions towards Yankee fans when they jeered him after he made a bad play. He would shout ethnic insults back to the fans and offended fans demanded action from Yankee management. Because of the constant complaints, the Yankees traded Chapman away.[8] This was the man who led the Phillies against the newly integrated Dodgers. The contrast between Robinson and Chapman created an explosive situation at Ebbets Field.

As the 1947 season began and it became apparent that Jackie Robinson would open the season with the Dodgers, many teams wrestled with this unprecedented situation. Some teams, such as the Pittsburgh Pirates, secretly voted on whether to go on strike instead of playing the Dodgers. The Pirates, however, were convinced by team owners and the National League to play. Other teams also voted on the issue but chose to play against Robinson and the Dodgers. One of the teams that voted on whether to play against the integrated Dodgers was the Phillies.

Seen during his playing days as a star pitcher with the New York Yankees, Herb Pennock also served as the Phillies General Manager during the 1940s. His staunch criticism of integration remains a source of controversy even to this day. (Courtesy of the National Baseball Hall of Fame)

As the voting took place, there was much debate amongst the Phillies players. Those players from the South held the strongest views against Robinson and the Dodgers. While those individuals would have preferred not to take the field against the Dodgers, the majority of the Phillies voted to play.[9] Most players and fans handled integration rather well but the resistant minority still created problems.

When it came to the Phillies, Chapman wanted to show his true feelings. He ordered all of his players to taunt Jackie Robinson whenever he took the field. As the Dodgers took the field, the Phillies deluged Robinson with so much abuse that many observers considered the worst ever given to any athlete.[10] Some of the ringleaders of the abuse were Chapman, Phillies coaches Dusty Cooke and Jim Tabor, and shortstop Skeeter Newsome. These individuals came from the South and possessed negative views towards the integration of the major leagues. Their taunts reflected their dim view of racial progress.[11] Some examples were:

> Hey, nigger, why don't you go back to the cotton field where you belong?
> They're waiting for you in the jungle, black boy!
> Hey snowflake, which one of those white boys' wives are you dating tonight?

Some of the Phillies picked up baseball bats and used them as simulated rifles aimed at Robinson. After losing to the Dodgers in the first game of the three game series, the frustrated Phillies continued to pour on the insults. In fact, they insulted the entire Dodger team because of the presence of Robinson. The anger that Robinson felt towards the Phillies almost overcame him. He believed that it was closest that he came to ruining Rickey's noble experiment because he wanted to "stride over to the Phillies dugout, grab one of those white sons of bitches and smash his teeth in with my despised black fist."[12] But Robinson was spared from replying to violence because outside agents proved quite supportive.

On the field, his insulted Dodger teammates responded to the Phillies' taunting by challenging both with their play and their replies. Second baseman Eddie Stanky yelled to the Phillies dugout, "Listen, you yellow-bellied cowards, why don't you yell at somebody who can answer back?" Other Dodger players responded by voicing their displeasure to the press. It is worth remembering that a few of the Dodgers petitioned in spring training to keep Robinson off the team, including Stanky. Now, Robinson's struggle against the displays of prejudice did more to unite the Dodger players than anything else. Both the white press and the black press responded angrily to this incident. The black press reacted instantly to Chapman's treatment of Robinson while the white press came along after listening to the complaints of Dodger players. Furthermore, fans seated near the Phillies' dugout sent letters of protest to Commissioner Chandler. Newsman Walter Winchell attacked the Phillies and Chapman on his highly rated national Sunday night radio broadcast. The public outrage against the Phillies forced Chandler to warn Phillies owner Bob Carpenter that if the harassment continued, the club would suffer punishment.[13]

Chapman defended his actions by saying that it was typical of the "bench jockeying" that existed between opposing teams. The abuse that he and his team delivered to Robinson was no different than for any Jewish, Italian, and Polish player. He hurled insults hoping to enrage the opponent and keep him from performing at this best. Chapman responded to criticism by saying, "There is not a man who has come to the big leagues since baseball has been played who has not been ridden. We will treat Robinson the same as we do Hank Greenberg of the Pirates, Clint Hartung of the Giants, Joe Garagiola of the Cardinals, Connie Ryan of the Braves or any other man who is likely to step to the plate and beat us." He said that the treatment of Robinson was not unlike that given to any other rookie. One of his players, outfielder Harry Walker, agreed with this explanation by saying that Chapman felt that "he could beat you by getting under your skin." He achieved this goal by levying ethnic insults at his opponents.[14] Chapman even went so far as to say that he gave Robinson his toughest test to make sure that the player could remain in the big leagues. Although some people, most critically Phillies management, accepted Chapman's excuse, the majority judged the manager's behavior totally unacceptable.[15]

Chapman received such heavy criticism that he apologized publicly and had his picture taken with Robinson. Despite the negative publicity, Chapman continued with his personal onslaught of Robinson. Also, Phillies players were often instructed to run at Robinson whenever he stepped on the first base bag on a groundout. Phillies outfielder Johnny Blatnick received a severe chewing out when he avoided a collision with Robinson at first base. First base coach Dusty Cooke yelled at Blatnick saying, "You could

Manager of the Phillies after the Second World War, William "Ben" Chapman's brutal taunts of Jackie Robinson created much controversy and eventually forced his dismissal. His actions still arouse much debate and criticism among baseball historians. (Courtesy of the National Baseball Hall of Fame)

have cut his Achilles' tendon and then we wouldn't have to put up with him anymore."[16] Throughout the 1947 season, Chapman and other Phillies continued their barrage against Robinson, but could not seriously rattle him.

The negative behavior of the Phillies continued beyond the 1947 season. Some Phillies players, such as pitchers "Schoolboy" Rowe and Russ "Mad Monk" Meyer, had run-ins with Robinson during the season. Meyer, in particular, became known for his intolerance of not only black players but also Jewish hitters as well. Meyer's nickname comes from his penchant for brushing back batters with high and tight fastballs. Also called "Russell the Red-necked Reindeer" by Phillies owner Bob Carpenter, Meyer frequently fired "beanballs" at members of the Dodgers. Robinson became one of his favorite targets, especially during the Phillies' 1950 pennant drive. While the Phillies and the Dodgers competed for the National League championship, Meyer's actions often caused tense moments between the two rivals. Ironically, Meyer received quite a surprise in 1953 when he ended up becoming a member of the Dodgers. Because of the number of black, Hispanic, and Jewish teammates on the Dodgers, Meyer began to refrain from his ways and became an effective addition to the pitching staff. But Meyer's actions with the Phillies certainly did not help the club's poor reputation regarding race relations.[17]

Nicknamed the "Mad Monk" for his hair-trigger temper, Russ Meyer often fired beanballs at opposing black players. (Courtesy of the National Baseball Hall of Fame)

Unlike Russ Meyer, Phillies starting pitcher Ken Raffensberger refused to get caught up in this ugliness. He had been pitching for the Phillies since 1943 and even served as the club's lone representative at the 1944 All-Star Game. The left-handed throwing Raffensberger was known as the reliable workhorse of the

7. Intolerance

Phillies pitching staff and suffered through many of the team's lean years during the war. In 1947, Raffensberger was pitching for the Phillies when Robinson joined the Dodgers. While some Phillies listened to Ben Chapman's instructions to harass and possibly injure Robinson, Raffensberger refused to follow his manager's directive. Chapman ordered Raffensberger and the other Phillies pitchers to throw at Robinson whenever there were two strikes in the count. In his own words, Raffensberger said, "I didn't go along with it, I never believed in throwing at a guy." As a result of his failure to follow Chapman's instructions, Raffensberger was traded to the Cincinnati Reds during the 1947 season. He starred for the Reds for several seasons, leading the National League in shutouts in 1949 and 1952.

One may certainly argue that the Whiz Kids of 1950 could have certainly used the steady Raffensberger, especially when they lost starting pitchers Curt Simmons (to military service) and Bubba Church (to injury) just prior to the World Series. Unfortunately, the mid-season trade of Raffensberger to the Reds in 1947 would later leave a void on the Phillies staff.

After the 1947 season, Robinson moved from first base to second base. Playing second base often proves dangerous when attempting to turn a double play. Chapman instructed his players to slide into Robinson extra hard to break up double plays. In their attempts to do so it was the Phillies players who got hurt, not Robinson. For example, starting catcher Andy Seminick hurt his shoulder when trying to collide with Robinson. Ultimately, Chapman's attempts to rattle Robinson and defeat integration proved insufficient because the

Star catcher of the Phillies during the late 1940s and early 1950s, Andy Seminick once hurt himself sliding into second in an attempt to take out Jackie Robinson in a game against the Brooklyn Dodgers. It was said that Seminick was instructed to slide hard into Robinson by Phillies Manager Ben Chapman. (Courtesy of the National Baseball Hall of Fame)

Phillies eventually fired him as manager of the club.[18] Even after Chapman lost his managerial job with the Phillies, he still consistently insulted Robinson on the field while serving as a third base coach of the Cincinnati Reds. But it was Robinson who outlasted Chapman. If Chapman hoped to enrage, it backfired because Robinson's teammates became more united. This unity ensured Robinson's survival in the big leagues and provided greater opportunities for integration.[19]

The dismissal of Chapman did not mean the end of the verbal abuse from members of the Phillies organization to black players. In addition to Robinson, the Brooklyn Dodgers acquired several black players who became key components of their National League pennant–winning teams of the late 1940s and early 1950s. Also during that time, the Phillies had a strong team that often challenged the Dodgers for league supremacy. Since the Phillies remained an all-white team, the contrast between the two clubs became obvious. Several of the Dodgers players, therefore, contend that the Phillies continued their verbal onslaught on their black teammates. Players such as Robinson, Campanella, and pitcher Don Newcombe felt that the Phillies intentionally attempted to enrage them. The target of their accusation came in the form of a Phillies first base coach named "McDonald."[20]

In a 1950 game between the Dodgers and the Phillies, this coach kept up a constant barrage of verbal insults towards the black players. For the most part, the insults were directed at Newcombe while he faced Phillies hitters. Between innings, Robinson went over to Newcombe in the Dodger dugout and asked him if he heard the insults. Newcombe replied, "You think I'm deaf, Jackie?" Robinson replied by saying, "Newk, you got to do something." When Phillies power-hitting outfielder Del Ennis came to the plate against Newcombe, the Dodger pitcher threw at him with a fastball. According to published accounts, Ennis went to McDonald and said, "Listen, you little son of a bitch, he damn near killed me and with the shit you're yelling, he's got a right to." Ennis, in his own way, told the coach to cool it before someone really got hurt.[21]

In this published account, the coach was not identified with a first name or his proper last name. The Phillies had a coach with a similar last name on staff at the time. A small man of only 5'6", this coach served as a batting practice pitcher for the club for several seasons. Some of the Phillies players remember this particular individual as a stand-up guy, which possibly disputes the previous story.[22] Nevertheless, the mere presence of such a story begs the question: Was the verbal abuse something that proved typical and expected by all members of the Phillies organization or was it an isolated incident? This story appears sincere, adding to the legacy that the Phillies of the late 1940s and early 1950s were racially intolerant. Whether true or not, one may argue that it gives detractors yet another reason to dismiss Philadelphia as a racially intolerant environment.

While much evidence accumulates against the Phillies, were their reactions towards integration any different than other major league teams? Other teams besides the Phillies voted on whether to play against the integrated Dodgers. Enos "Country" Slaughter, star outfielder of the St. Louis Cardinals, deliberately spiked Robinson at first base during the 1947 season. Other Cardinal players often attempted to do the same to Robinson during that season.[23] Despite these incidents, the Phillies still emerge as the most racially intolerant team of this era. The actions ranging from management's demand to the Dodgers not to have Robinson play against them to the constant verbal assaults towards black opponents by the Phillies players and coaches led to this reputation.

The results of this reputation, without a doubt, did more harm than good. A vengeful Robinson often had his best games against the Phillies. An example of Robinson's exceptional performances against the Phillies was witnessed on the final day of the 1951 season. While the Phillies floundered that season, the Dodgers fought the New York Giants for the National League pennant. The Dodgers were playing the Phillies and if they lost, the Giants would win the pennant. Robinson rallied his team from behind by making a diving, game-saving catch that prevented a loss and forced extra innings. In the fourteenth inning, Robinson hit a game-winning home run as the Dodgers tied the Giants to force a three-game playoff. Unfortunately for the Dodgers, they lost to the Giants in the playoff.[24]

While Robinson overcame the terrible abuse leveled by Chapman, it did not mean the end of his problems. In most cities, hotels refused to house Robinson while they would accept the rest of his teammates. This treatment became common in the Negro Leagues as players could only choose between staying at bedbug-ridden black hotels, sleeping on the bus, or outside the ballpark. Staying at the white hotels was not an option to most Negro Leaguers.[25] Although major league policy for integration was changing, the tenant policy at hotels lagged behind. For example, the Benjamin Franklin Hotel in Philadelphia, which housed the Dodgers for years, refused to admit Robinson.[26] A heated conversation between Dodger traveling secretary Harold Parrott and the manager of the Franklin Hotel concluded with the manager declaring, "And don't bring your team back here while you have any Nigras with you!" Actually, the Dodgers ended up in the plusher Warwick Hotel. Though it proved more costly to the Dodgers, the manager of the Warwick was "delighted" to house them.[27] In most cities, Robinson could not find a satisfactory place

Larry Doby first integrated the American League when he became a member of Bill Veeck's Cleveland Indians. He endured harsh treatment from Philadelphia fans. In fact, the Athletics hired a heckler to distract Doby whenever he came to bat. (Courtesy of the National Baseball Hall of Fame)

to eat because most restaurants refused to serve blacks. In most cases, he had to eat "in the back" or go somewhere else.[28] The presence of this kind of *de facto* racism existed for many years and proved as another of the more unreasonable aspects of playing in Philadelphia.

While the Phillies received severe criticism for their treatment of Robinson, the Athletics did nothing to improve the city's reputation. When Larry Doby broke the color barrier in the American League with Cleveland Indians in 1947, the Athletics hired a heckler to torment Doby. Pete Adelis, known as the "loudmouth" of Shibe Park, received a seat right behind the opponents' dugout from which he could insult Doby and other black players. In addition, Adelis was paid to trail Doby around the league and heckle him.[29] As Doby came to bat, Adelis banged on a steel German war helmet with a billy club and screamed "Hey Dopey!" Doby thought that once the Indians left Shibe Park he would not hear anything further from Adelis but the loudmouthed fan traveled to New York to continue his heckling. Doby's fine play, however, proved the best way to discourage Adelis. The following season, Adelis actually approached Doby and said, "You know, you're a good sport." By that time, Adelis focused his attentions on another black player on the Indians, Luke Easter.[30] These actions demonstrate the Athletics' views towards the presence of black players in the American League during the late 1940s.

By 1948, it became clear that the infusion of black players to the major leagues would continue. As more blacks trickled into the major leagues, fans became less resistant and more interested in watching integrated baseball. In Philadelphia, the best example of this in-terest occurred with the arrival of former Negro League pitching great Satchel Paige. Paige, then a member of the Cleveland Indians, debuted in Philadelphia as his club faced the Athletics in a July 10 twilight doubleheader. Given the prospect of seeing the legendary Paige pitch in the majors, fans flocked to Shibe Park. The doubleheader was sold out and thousands more were turned away. Since Paige pitched in relief at this latter stage of his career, there was no guarantee that he would pitch against the Athletics. But in the second game, Paige came into the game to pitch his club out of a tough situation. With two men on base in the sixth inning, Paige pitched the Indians out of trouble. Although Paige allowed the tying runs the following inning, his teammates rallied to give him his first major league win. Despite the Athletics' loss, the overflow crowd served as an example of how the presence of a charismatic black player can affect the attendance.[31] Still, both the Athletics and Phillies remained quite hesitant to include blacks onto their teams.

Since both the Phillies and Athletics were notoriously slow in the integration of their teams, it made for a potentially explosive situation because the neighborhood surrounding Shibe Park, the home field of both the Phillies and the Athletics, became predominantly black. As the twentieth century progressed, the white immigrants who settled in the area surrounding the park left to the greener pastures of the suburbs. As businesses moved to the periphery of the city, white citizens moved out of Philadelphia and into places such as Havertown and Cherry Hill. To fill the vacancies, blacks moved into the Shibe Park area. Because of the racial make-up of the neighborhood, fans from the suburbs believed that they would become victims of crime if they merely went to a baseball game. This situation meant that many white fans refused to enter the area to go to Phillies and Athletics games while African American baseball fans shunned the major league games as well. This problem existed primarily due to the club's failure to embrace integration, resulting in a dramatic increase in empty seats for Phillies games.[32] Declining attendance forced the team to explore the possibility of building a new stadium. The search for a new home field eventually led to the building of Veterans Stadium in largely white South Philadelphia.[33] There is no doubt that the racial chasm between black and white forced the removal of the Athletics and the relocation of the Phillies to a less threatening part of the city.

8

Integration of Philadelphia Baseball

Pitching in the major leagues "just wasn't fun anymore; it was work. Maybe I am crazy, as everyone says, but to me the reasons seem logical enough."

—Bob Trice, pitcher,
Philadelphia Athletics,
upon asking for a demotion
to the minors in 1954[1]

Both the Phillies and Athletics struggled to integrate their teams and gain the acceptance of their fans. This was difficult because these teams did not accept the first attempts to integrate baseball. Furthermore, while most of the first black major leaguers helped their teams, those on the Phillies were less than impressive. When Philadelphia finally hired its first black baseball superstar, the reception was far from positive.

By 1952, Philadelphia, hailed as the "City of Brotherly Love," began to lose some of its luster as a result of the failure to integrate its major league baseball teams. When asked about integration, the mayor of Philadelphia, called his city a "training ground for human understanding" without the existence of discrimination. A sportswriter challenged that claim by asking why "neither Philadelphia club has hired a Negro."[2] With morale and reputation of the city at stake, it became apparent that the city's two teams needed to commit themselves to integration.

The Athletics became the first of the two teams to integrate its roster. Towards the end of the 1953 season, the Athletics called up ex–Negro League pitcher Bob Trice. Trice, who previously pitched with the Homestead Grays, was signed by the Athletics prior to the 1952 season and sent to their Class C farm club at St. Hyacinthe. During that season, Trice won 19 games and even hit a respectable .297. In fact, Trice's hitting allowed him to become a part-time outfielder in the minor leagues. After that successful season, Trice moved on to the Athletics' Triple-A Ottawa farm club. At Ottawa, Trice led the International League with 21 victories that season and hit .283. For his stellar performance, Trice received recognition as the International League's Most Valuable Player of 1953.[3] Trice had nothing else to prove in the minor leagues and appeared ready for the big leagues. Trice's minor league success created much debate in Philadelphia: had the time come for the Athletics to integrate its roster? The city's African American community believed that the Athletics were slow in bringing Trice to the majors.

The Athletics finally brought Trice up in September 1953. His arrival was only given limited exposure in the city's white newspapers, while it was front-page news for the black *Philadelphia Tribune*.[4] This division existed within the coverage of the early days of major league integration. According to some of the white newspaper and magazine writers of the era, reporting on black players did not make good copy. Publishers became afraid that if they spent more time reporting on black players, they might lose their more lucrative white readership. Therefore, such publications chose to report more extensively on the plights of white players and barely scratch the surface covering black players.[5] Such was the case with Trice, who received more publicity from the *Tribune* than from the *Inquirer*.

Trice made his first start on September 12 against the St. Louis Browns, losing 5–2.[6] Trice, however, won his next two starts and earned a place on the roster the following season.[7] Due to his performance at the end of the 1953 season, Trice actually figured prominently in the Athletics' plans. Trice appeared to fit in with the Athletics, who were desperate for starting pitching, as a player. But as a black man, this transition proved a more daunting task. The good-natured and personable Trice merely wanted to blend in quietly into this potentially explosive situation.

According to the fans of the Athletics, Trice succeeded in blending into the organization. Former Athletics fan Rob Bonter describes the scene at Shibe Park as a "low-key" moment of integration of Philadelphia baseball. Trice was considered a "friendly, affable kind of guy" who made no waves in the clubhouse. The majority of Philadelphia fans generally wished Trice well and rooted for him. Any negative response to

Trice was relatively minimal.[8] Although the fans apparently accepted Trice, he still received taunts and brush-back pitches from opponents. Black players like Trice became used to such treatment and even expected it. Trice said that if he did not receive such harsh treatment, he felt he was not doing his job well.

Trice began the 1954 season quite strong. He won his first four starts, which included a 1–0 shutout over the World Champion New York Yankees. But the good times only lasted for the beginning of that season. Trice struggled to a season record seven wins and eight losses with an Earned Run Average of 5.60. The next season, Trice went back to the minors. He pitched briefly for the Athletics in Kansas City in 1955 but was released and never pitched in the big leagues again. To Trice, pitching in the big leagues was not an enjoyable experience. He felt that the issues of race took much of the fun out of the game. Trice eventually abandoned his quest in becoming a career major league pitcher. Overall, Trice's career numbers were 9 wins, 9 losses, with an ERA of 5.80. Although Trice's statistics proved less than stellar, further integration followed.[9]

Trice's appearance on the Athletics roster paved the way for other black players in Philadelphia. One example is Vic Power, who, in his rookie year of 1954, became a starting outfielder for the Athletics' final season in Philadelphia. Power arrived in Philadelphia in a trade with the New York Yankees. While in the Yankees organization, Power led their minor league affiliate

Bob Trice, a former Negro League pitcher, became the first black player for the Athletics late in the 1953 season. Although he was sent to the minor leagues after the 1954 season, Trice felt relieved of the pressure that he struggled under during his stay in Philadelphia. (Courtesy of the Philadelphia Athletics Historical Society)

team in Kansas City in hitting for two seasons. Despite his domination of minor league pitching, Power never received an opportunity with the Yankees, who by 1954 had yet to integrate its club.[10]

Power suffered under the racial tensions that existed in Kansas City at that time. Power, from Puerto Rico, had not experienced such difficulties prior to his arrival in the minor leagues. He often fought against the prejudice that confronted him, a rarity in the 1950s. While this reaction garners respect today in American society, Power received the reputation as an "attitude problem." This tag meant that he refused to accept the racism inherent in Yankee management easily. In particular, the Yankees objected to his relationship to a "white woman." Actually, the woman in question was his wife, a light-skinned Puerto Rican lady. Furthermore, Power became known for his flashy play, especially while playing first base. Later in his major league career, Power's ability at first base earned him the Gold Glove Award for his fine defensive play. But in the early 1950s, he received the reputation of "hot dog" or a "showboat." These misconceptions convinced the Yankees that Power appeared unsuitable to become the man who first integrated their team, which led to the trade with the Athletics.[11]

When Power arrived in Philadelphia, he moved to the outfield so that the club could get his strong bat into the lineup while starting other players at first base, his natural position. As a regular during the 1954 season, he hit only .255 but demonstrated the ability to show improvement in the future. Power did perform better, but not in Philadelphia, as the Athletics left the city prior to the 1955 season. Although Power's statistics improved when the Athletics moved to Kansas City, he probably would have preferred to remain in Philadelphia. He still held the unpleasant memories of Kansas City from his time in the Yankees chain. Power, however, eventually enjoyed a productive major league career as a first baseman during the 1950s and early 1960s. Power played twelve seasons in the majors and posted a career batting average of .284.[12] Despite this attempt to bring in new fans and improve the club, the Athletics still moved to Kansas City.

The main causes for the move to Kansas City relate to changes within the organization and a decline in attendance. By 1950, Philadelphia baseball patriarch Connie Mack retired from managing the Athletics and turned over much of the administration of the club to his sons. Mack always provided stability within the organization and as he aged, that stable environment began to crumble. The Athletics struggled financially throughout the last few years of their tenure in Philadelphia, which made the club vulnerable to takeovers from prospective owners. One intriguing

Arnold Johnson took over ownership of the Philadelphia Athletics in 1954. Although Johnson allowed integration to take place within the organization, he moved the club to Kansas City prior to the 1955 season. (Courtesy of the National Baseball Hall of Fame)

offer came from Philadelphia native Jack Kelly Sr. (father of actress Grace Kelly, who later became Princess Grace of Monaco), who would have certainly kept in Athletics in town. But the deal fell through when Jack Sr. insisted that his son, Jack Jr., receive a front office job. Eventually, Chicago businessman Arnold Johnson bought the team and then moved it to Kansas City.[13]

The more obvious cause of the Athletics' move was the sharp decline in attendance during the early 1950s. In 1949, the team drew 900,000 fans to Shibe Park. By 1953, when the Athletics first became integrated, the team drew only 362,000. This sharp decline horrified management and led to the sale of the club. In 1954, when rumors of a possible sale dominated the scene, only 300,000 fans attended Athletics home games.[14] Lack of interest made the move to Kansas City inevitable.

Critics may argue that as integration of the Athletics began, attendance fell sharply. The only fact that supports this contention is the higher attendance figures of the 1952 season. The information that opposes such an argument, however, clearly outweighs any opposition towards integration. First, in 1950, the attention of most Philadelphia baseball fans shifted towards the National League Champion Phillies club. The "Whiz Kids" captured the imagination of the city and dominated the Philadelphia baseball scene. For the first time in Philadelphia baseball history, the interest in the Phillies clearly outweighed that of the traditionally more successful Athletics. Obviously, the Phillies would draw more fans to Shibe Park (which both teams shared at this time) than the floundering Athletics.[15]

The Athletics also drew well in 1952 because of the presence of star pitcher Bobby Shantz and hot-hitting first baseman Ferris Fain. During that season, Shantz led the American League in victories with twenty-four and earned him Most Valuable Player honors. Fans would check the newspaper in order to find out when Shantz pitched again. In games that Shantz pitched, the Athletics drew more than twice as many fans as opposed to games started by other pitchers. In addition, Shantz stood only five feet, six inches tall, rather small for a baseball player. The diminutive pitcher served as an everyman who defied his smallish stature in order to succeed in the major leagues. Unfortunately, late in that 1952 season, while batting, Shantz broke his wrist when struck by a pitched ball. Not fully recovered from the injury, Shantz's numbers dipped sharply the following season.[16]

Furthermore, the Athletics also had star first baseman Fain on its team in the early 1950s. In both the 1951 and 1952 seasons, Fain led the American League in batting average, hitting .344 and .327 respectively. But since the Athletics remained in financial trouble, they traded the potentially high-salaried Fain to the Chicago White Sox prior to the 1953 season. Fain could not equal his Athletics' performance and was out of the major leagues by 1955. With Shantz ineffective and Fain in Chicago, the Athletics' performance declined, as did their attendance figures.[17]

If anything, the Athletics' hesitation to integrate their roster possibly accelerated their move from the city. If the team followed Judy Johnson's advice and acquired those players that he suggested, the Athletics would have attracted new fans. A winning club always brings an increased number of supporters to the ballpark. Furthermore, the presence of quality black ballplayers would entice the support of the city's African American and Latin American communities. Because of the Phillies' apparent reticence to integrate, the Athletics could corner the market on the very same fans that rooted for the Hilldale club or the Philadelphia Stars. The Brooklyn Dodgers and New York Giants embraced integration and received greater support from blacks than did the perennial World Champion New York Yankees. The Athletics had the opportunity to do the same in Philadelphia. Unfortunately, their reluctance cost them and eventually forced the move to Kansas City.

One positive aspect of the Athletics' delay with integration was that their management learned from the mistakes of others. An example was a mistake made by the St. Louis Browns of 1947. Shortly after the Dodgers promoted Jackie Robinson and the Indians acquired Larry Doby, the perennially dreadful Browns franchise decided to cash in on breaking the color barrier. They brought two Negro League stars onto their roster late in the season. One of them was longtime power hitter Willard Brown, nearing the end of a long and productive career. Unfortunately, Brown was no longer the player that he once was in his previous years in the Negro Leagues. His stint proved unsuccessful (batting only .179 in 21 games) and he never again appeared in the major leagues.[18]

The other player on the 1947 Browns was the athletic Hank Thompson, who previously played for the Kansas City Monarchs. Thompson possessed the ability to play either in the infield or outfield effectively. Unfortunately, Thompson's career with the Browns proved an unhappy experience for both him and the team. Playing second base for the Browns, Thompson hit .257 in 37 games. Neither happy with his performance nor situation, Thompson left the Browns to go back to the Negro Leagues for the 1948 season. Thompson eventually became a member of the New York Giants, where he enjoyed several productive years for a team that twice won the National League Championship in the early 1950s.[19]

While the Browns seemed willing to integrate, they did a poor job of following through with the venture. The front office believed that the mere presence of the two players would automatically increase attendance, especially amongst the city's African American community. However, St. Louis was not ready for integration and the Browns failed to accommodate the two players whatsoever. Both players felt alienated from the rest of the team and it affected their play. While Jackie Robinson excelled for the Brooklyn Dodgers, Brown and Thompson left the Browns after the 1947 season.[20] The Athletics attempted to avoid such failure.

In 1954, the Athletics hired Judy Johnson to assist in the transition of the black players on the team. Once a scout for the team, Johnson now assumed the task of helping these players adjust to the major leagues on the field and the trials off the field. While Johnson was certainly a qualified individual, it seemed debatable whether he could understand the plight of these players. Johnson's playing career in the Negro Leagues ended before the breaking of the major league color barrier. But at least this served as an indication of the Athletics' attempts to ease into integration.[21] But Johnson's attempts went for naught after the team's relocation the following season. Johnson left the Athletics organization prior to their move to Kansas City. Johnson eventually became a roving scout and spring training instructor for the Phillies, jobs he continued for many years.[22]

It took longer for the Phillies to admit black players to its roster. In 1957, John Kennedy broke in with the team. Kennedy came from the Kansas City Monarchs in 1956 and performed solidly in 1957, which allowed him to open the season with the Phillies.[23] His debut was met with little enthusiasm from the city's white press. The *Philadelphia Inquirer* did not mention Kennedy in its opening day issue.[24] But the *Philadelphia Tribune* treated Kennedy's arrival as big news. It became headline news because the many years of campaigning from the city's black press had finally paid off.[25] The *Tribune* optimistically predicted stardom for Kennedy, known as a shortstop with speed. Most fans, however, believed that Kennedy merely got the "monkey off the Phillies' back" through integration.[26] With every issue, the *Tribune* followed his progress in spring training and continued once the regular season started.

Near the end of spring training that same year, the Phillies also acquired a light-skinned Cuban shortstop named Chico Fernandez from the Brooklyn Dodgers. Fernandez was highly touted prospect and the Phillies hoped he would fill the void at shortstop. Obviously, Kennedy did not fit the bill at shortstop, which frustrated the local black

Regarded as the first black player to appear in a game for the Phillies, John Kennedy's career only lasted five games and consisted of two hitless at-bats. Eventually relegated to the Phillies' minor league system, Kennedy never made it back to the big leagues. (Courtesy of the National Baseball Hall of Fame)

press. The *Tribune* did not think much of Kennedy's chances of succeeding after the acquisition of Fernandez. "If the Phillies keep Kennedy he wouldn't play every day ... and most of the Negro fans would holler loud" and that the Phillies only signed Kennedy to draw black fans to the ballpark. If and when an African American does play with the Phillies, "he must be cut from the piece of stone that Jackie Robinson, Larry Doby, Hank Aaron, Ernie Banks, Don Newcombe, and etc. came from."[27] Unfortunately, Kennedy's major league career lasted exactly five games and two hitless at-bats in April 1957. An injured shoulder suffered that month did little to help his cause. Soon, the Phillies optioned Kennedy to the minor leagues and he never again appeared in the major leagues.[28] Kennedy remained in the Phillies' minor league system until the club released him in 1960. Like Trice, Kennedy appeared to enjoy the game more when freed from the spotlight. Kennedy played in a 30-and-over league in his hometown, Jacksonville, Florida, almost until his death in 1998.[29]

For his part, Fernandez's presence allowed the white press to claim that he truly integrated the Phillies. He was, however, in a state of ethnic limbo throughout his Phillies career.[30] When acquired by the Phillies, the city's African American community viewed Fernandez as a roadblock to John Kennedy's progress. The *Tribune* wrote that "Kennedy will have the job in his hip pocket by mid-June."[31] This quote suggests that the Hispanic Fernandez was not the choice of the city's African American community. On the other hand, many Phillies considered Fernandez a "white Latin player" and it did not occur to them that he was integrating the Phillies.[32] In fact, Fernandez's Phillies career began six games before Kennedy ever appeared in a major league game. Most reporters and fans, however, dismissed Fernandez as a "Cuban" and believed that he did not truly break the color line. Fernandez remained bitter towards this historical slight because he "was forced to live in the black section of town" and never received his due for his achievement.[33]

Chico Fernandez—Debate surrounds this Cuban shortstop as to whether he was the one who broke the color line for the Phillies. He feels that baseball historians who credit John Kennedy with integrating the Phillies slighted him. (Courtesy of the National Baseball Hall of Fame)

As for his playing ability, Fernandez was a highly regarded shortstop prospect for the Brooklyn Dodgers. Unfortunately, his path remained blocked by longtime great Pee Wee Reese, which necessitated the trade with the Phillies. Fernandez started at shortstop two of the next three seasons before being traded to the Detroit

Tigers. In his three seasons, Fernandez batted .248 and received recognition for his steady play in the field.[34] But Fernandez never became considered part of the city's African American community and his presence did not attract new fans to Connie Mack Stadium. Therefore, the brief careers of John Kennedy and Chico Fernandez failed to engender much enthusiasm from the city's African American community.

The presence of Kennedy and Fernandez signify the inconsistent policies of integration by the Phillies organization. In the early days of the integration of major league baseball, Carpenter maintained that the Phillies would not admit black players onto the roster merely for the sake of doing so. Although Fernandez actually started at shortstop for the Phillies, one may argue that either Carpenter lacked the sincerity in his policy or changed his mind when he suffered under the criticism from the local media. Whatever the reason, the actions of the Phillies indicated anxiety and haste as team management searched for black players to quell critics. This desperation probably contributed to the consistently poor finishes of the Phillies in the late 1950s and early 1960s. The team seemed more concerned about racial discrimination than providing a quality baseball team to the people of Philadelphia. As a result, some black players who made the Phillies had a difficult time adjusting to the city.

Aside from Kennedy and Fernandez, none of the other early examples of the integration of the Phillies thrilled the home crowd either. Such players were pitcher Hank Mason and first baseman Pancho Herrera, both of whom were acquired from the barely surviving Kansas City Monarchs, as well as catchers Valmy

Veteran Negro League pitcher Hank Mason had several strong seasons in the Phillies' minor league system. Unfortunately, Mason never managed to parlay this mastery into the big leagues. (Courtesy of the National Baseball Hall of Fame)

Thomas and Choo Choo Coleman. While their play failed to make the Phillies instant pennant contenders, each has their own story worthy of mention.

Hank Mason became part of the Phillies' first wave of recruits from the fading Negro Leagues. Mason was a twenty-four year old ex–Marine from Missouri who previously spent a couple of years with the Monarchs. The Kansas City club now became more of a touring team that played exhibitions throughout the country. Newly hired Phillies scout Bill Yancey, himself a former Negro League star, used his connections to sign Mason, as well as other Monarch players. Once signed in 1955, Mason initially received an assignment to the Phillies' Triple-A team in Syracuse. Unfortunately, after struggling at Syracuse, the Phillies sent Mason to their Double-A affiliate in Schenectady, New York. This demotion made Mason the first black player in Schenectady club history. Fortunately for Mason, his presence did not pose a problem for the home crowd. Without incident, Mason became Schenectady's leading pitcher for two seasons and then received a promotion to Triple-A, where he continued to flourish. Eventually, Mason earned a promotion to the Phillies, becoming the team's first-ever black pitcher in 1958.[35] Unfortunately, Mason pitched only four games for the Phillies with little success.

Like Kennedy and Mason, Francisco "Pancho" Herrera was signed by the Phillies from the roster of the Kansas City Monarchs. The powerfully built Cuban also was sent to Triple-A Syracuse but was demoted to Schenectady during the 1955 season. The Spanish-speaking Herrera also contended with the language barrier and the cultural differences that existed for all Latin American players.

Originally from Cuba, Pancho Herrera served as the starting first baseman for the Phillies for two seasons. He was one of many Phillies regulars from Cuba during the early 1960s. (Courtesy of the National Baseball Hall of Fame)

While Herrera often felt lonely, his hitting and amiable personality made him a favorite of the home crowd. Originally signed as an outfielder, Herrera's poor fielding led Phillies management to convert him to first base. This position switch kept him at Schenectady for another productive season.[36] His impressive hitting eventually led him to the majors in 1958. Herrera managed to play three seasons with the Phillies, starting at first base in 1960 and 1961. In these three seasons, Herrera batted a strong .271 but struck out quite often and still possessed the reputation as a liability in the field. Herrera was eventually sent back to Triple-A, never to play in the majors again.[37]

Thomas became the most forgettable of the early black Phillies, arriving in town prior to the 1959 season. Unlike Mason and Herrera, Thomas came to the team in a controversial trade with San Francisco Giants. The Phillies traded pitcher Jack Sanford, National League Rookie of Year in 1957, for a player they hoped could fill a void at catcher. While Sanford flourished with the Giants for several seasons, Thomas flopped miserably with the Phillies under the weight of heavy expectations. During the 1959 season, Thomas hit only .200 in 66 games and received his release before the next season.[38] Thomas, from the Virgin Islands, signified the Phillies' penchant for acquiring Latin American or Caribbean black players.

Coleman, however, is probably the most well known of these early black Phillies. His play for the Phillies was hardly distinguishable: he batted a horrendous .128 in 1961.[39] Coleman's claim to fame (or infamy) was his subsequent

After arriving in Philadelphia via trade with San Francisco, Valmy Thomas struggled under heavy expectations and a tough atmosphere. A native of the Virgin Islands, Thomas only lasted one season in the Phillies organization. (Courtesy of the National Baseball Hall of Fame)

career with the expansion New York Mets. The original Mets of 1962 remain the worst team of the 20th century, but were loved by fans starved for baseball after the Giants and Dodgers moved west in 1957. These fans reveled in the stunning incompetence of the Mets' performance. With this in mind, Coleman's continued ineptitude made him a popular comedic target of the crazed Met fans.[40] Needless to say, the performance of any of the first black players failed to create much confidence that integration could succeed for the Phillies. But as the civil rights movement in America raged on in the late 1950s and early 1960s, it appeared to the Philadelphia community that the Phillies resisted change.

Although he broke in with the Phillies in 1960, Clarence "Choo Choo" Coleman is best known for being a member of the original Mets. (Courtesy of the National Baseball Hall of Fame)

Meanwhile, the Phillies' performance on the field suffered badly in the late 1950s. As their woes continued, Carpenter began to look at other options for increasing the value of the franchise. While most of the popular "Whiz Kids" players faded away or traded to other teams, the club could not find adequate replacements in order to attract fans to the ballpark. This struggle occurred after the Brooklyn Dodgers and New York Giants moved to Los Angeles and San Francisco respectively. Major league owners noticed that the failure for New York to have a National League team became a serious problem. This void moved New York City Mayor Wagner to explore both the possibility of attracting a National League team and the opportunity to build a new stadium for such a team. At this time in 1959, negotiations began between representatives from Wagner's administration and Phillies management. At first, the Phillies only wanted to broadcast their games in the New York area. But, eventually, the talks turned towards the luring of the Phillies into a new ballpark constructed in the Flushing Meadows neighborhood. According to accounts from the *New York Times*, the Carpenter family seriously considered this move.[41]

Since the Phillies struggled mightily on the field and at the gate, as well as bearing the financial burden of owning crumbling Connie Mack Stadium, such a move to New York became conceivable. Also, New York baseball fans were accustomed to integrated National League teams playing in their city. Therefore, with the specter of racism gone, Carpenter could be free to integrate his team without burning under the microscope of the Philadelphia's media or fans. But the negotiations between the Phillies and New York officials eventually broke off and the club remained in Philadelphia. The talks died down after the major leagues began to explore the possibility of expanding with new teams. Since New York became a prime target for expansion, the city's attention turned towards this opportunity rather than accept the floundering Phillies franchise.[42] Therefore, Carpenter had to stay put in Philadelphia and make do. This meant that the subject of racial division in the organization would continue to plague the Phillies.

Overall, the conduct of the Phillies franchise displayed a less than inspired effort to include African Americans into the organization as a whole. By the late 1950s, the Phillies did not have a full-time African American employee within the front office. The National Association for the Advancement of Colored People (NAACP) strongly criticized owner Bob Carpenter for not hiring any minorities. In response to this criticism, Carpenter submitted a list of forty-three minority employees. On the surface, it seemed a respectable number but most of these workers performed menial tasks on the cleaning staff or as toilet attendants. Needless to say, this response failed to satisfy the NAACP and they called for the Phillies to upgrade the positions of African Americans.[43]

Others denounced the club because it appeared that hiring mediocre black players justified its opposition to integration. The Phillies attempted to answer this criticism by submitting a list of minority players in the entire system by August 1960. James T. Gallagher, the Phillies' Director of Scouts, compiled a list of 34 players. It appeared that the Phillies wanted to prove that the club actually committed itself to integration. This list included the hometowns of the players and their levels of advancement within the organization. Of this list of 34 players, seven were on the Phillies roster and the others toiled in the minors. All seven of those players were from Central American countries; no African Americans were on the big league roster.[44] Outfielder Tony Curry, from the Bahamas, serves as an example of such a player. Of the seven, four were everyday players but this does not say much since the team finished last in 1960.

Although it appeared that the Phillies initially preferred Latin American players over African Americans, they did not scout any of those players themselves. Of all of the early Latin American players on the Phillies, none came directly from the Phillies farm system. Pancho Herrera, from Cuba, initially played in the Negro Leagues. Others came from different major league organizations by way of trades or some other type of transaction. At this time, the Phillies did not seriously scout out top flight Latin American talent. As they did with African Americans, Phillies management lagged behind while teams such as the San Francisco Giants went into Latin American countries to find players to improve the team. While the Giants were finding such outstanding players as pitcher Juan Marichal, first baseman Orlando Cepeda, and the Alou brothers (Felipe, Matty, and Jesus), who played the outfield.[45] So now the Phillies experienced difficulty in not only acquiring African American players, but Latin Americans as well.

The club's inability to acquire top level African American talent during the 1950s led to its demise in the early 1960s. The club's perception, however, was that blacks from Latin America proved less threatening to management than African Americans.[46] But consecutive last place finishes in 1960 and 1961 proved that a change in policy was necessary. In fact, the Phillies set a National League record by losing 23 consecutive games in 1961.[47] Shortly thereafter, the ethnic makeup of the Phillies began to change.

By 1962, the Phillies managed to acquire several serviceable black players including African American outfielder Wes Covington, as well as infielder Tony Taylor and outfielder Tony Gonzalez, both from Cuba.[48] All three became starting players for the Phillies and helped the team to improve. Gonzalez arrived in Philadelphia from the Cincinnati Reds

A reserve outfielder in the late 1950s and early 1960s, Tony Curry was a native of the Virgin Islands. During this time, the Phillies organization seemed more inclined to integrate using players from the Caribbean. (Courtesy of the National Baseball Hall of Fame)

organization in 1960 and immediately became the starting centerfielder. A left-handed hitter with good speed, Gonzalez held the position for nine years. Known as a superb defensive centerfielder, Gonzalez became a key player on a Phillies team that would seriously contend for the National League pennant in 1964.

Like Gonzalez, Taylor came to the Phillies in a trade with the Chicago Cubs in 1960. Originally a member of the New York Giants organization, Taylor became a steadying influence on a rebuilding Phillies team. This contrasts with Taylor's early days in American professional baseball when he nearly quit the game because of homesickness. As a minor leaguer, Taylor missed Latin companionship and yearned for home.

Acquired from Cincinnati Reds, Tony Gonzalez served as the starting centerfielder for the Phillies throughout much of the 1960s. Originally from Cuba, Gonzalez and teammate Tony Taylor became the first two black players to serve the Phillies on a long-term basis. (Courtesy of the National Baseball Hall of Fame)

Taylor, however, could not afford to pay for a return trip to Havana and, as a result, remained in the United States playing minor league baseball.[49] Eventually, he made the Cubs as a starting second baseman in 1958, and two years later, became a member of the Phillies. Known for his consistent play at second base and clutch hitting, Taylor became a fan favorite. In two different tours of duty, Taylor played fourteen years for the Phillies.

Taylor's early struggles are reflective of the struggles of black Latin American players coming from their homeland to play major league baseball. Coming from Cuba, a player like Taylor was prepared well for playing professional baseball in the United States. Unfortunately, he was not

Having first arrived in Philadelphia via a trade with the Chicago Cubs, Tony Taylor played thirteen seasons in two tours of duty with the Phillies. Because of his dependability, Taylor became popular with Phillies fans during a time when the city was criticized for its treatment of black players. (Courtesy of the National Baseball Hall of Fame)

ready to handle the problems off of the field. Raised in a Spanish speaking country, Taylor had little help adjusting to this strange, new environment. The first words he learned in English were "ham and eggs," which forced him to eat that meal for some time. He developed his English acumen in an attempt to successfully order from a menu at a restaurant. However, it was often problematic for Taylor to gain entrance into a restaurant because of the color of his skin. Unlike African American players, Latin Americans never saw this type of racism in their homeland and were totally unprepared for it. Often, teammates had to go into restaurants and get food for Latin American players. Many Latin players chose to return to their homelands rather than endure this treatment. As Taylor himself said in a recent interview, "If I would have had the $82 I needed [for a flight], I would have gone back to Cuba." Phillies fans are quite fortunate that he stuck it out and excelled.[50]

Unlike Taylor and Gonzalez, Covington came from the United States and signified a change from recent black Phillies players. The acquisition of a veteran like Covington meant that the Phillies became less worried about which type of black players wore their uniform. Now the Phillies moved from merely integrating to creating a strong, pennant-contending team. As a younger player, Covington played for two pennant-winning Milwaukee Braves teams of the late 1950s. An experienced player like Covington could help the younger Phillies star players such as outfielder Johnny Callison and third baseman Dick Allen. For the first time club history, the team counted on a black player for leadership and stability. Furthermore, at the time of his arrival, Covington did not appear to represent the type of player that would challenge club management. But soon, the issue of integration would become an explosive topic at Connie Mack Stadium.

With Connie Mack Stadium located in a then predominantly African American neighborhood but using a team that would prove less attractive to the surrounding community, attendance became problematic. White fans seemed reluctant to venture into this neighborhood to watch a Phillies game. Also, with parking at a minimum, the stadium appeared antiquated and obsolete. Then, with the arrival of Dick Allen and players like him, the environment around Connie Mack Stadium appeared to take a turn for the worse.

Veteran outfielder Wes Covington joined the Phillies in 1961 and served as the leader for the few black players on the roster. (Courtesy of the National Baseball Hall of Fame)

9

Integration in the 1960s and 1970s

Integration took on a different look in September 1963 with Dick Allen's arrival in Philadelphia. Allen, originally from the western Pennsylvania town of Wampum, proved far more talented than any previous African American or dark-skinned Hispanic who played before him. Unlike many of the previous minorities on the Phillies roster, Allen was not a product of the Negro Leagues and represented the second wave of black ballplayers who signed directly into major league organizations. In his first few seasons in the Phillies farm system, he demonstrated athletic ability never before seen in the organization. His minor league hitting statistics were so prodigious and he moved so quickly through the Phillies organization that many considered Allen the finest player ever produced by the farm system.

Allen's minor league success was even more impressive considering that he broke the color barrier on the Phillies' Arkansas farm team in 1963. Only six years before, the state of Arkansas was the center of the violent struggle for the integration of public schools. Now, in 1963, Allen had to worry equally about integration as well as his play in this difficult atmosphere. Allen felt that he failed to receive the necessary support from Phillies management or from the front office of the Arkansas club. This experience in the South terrified him to the point that he soon became distrustful of the policy-makers in professional baseball.[1] This original fear explains the bizarre actions of both Allen and the Phillies' organization during the next several years. Such actions included Allen's frequent instances of lateness and even occasional failure to show up for games. Management, however, often exacerbated the situation by making excuses for Allen. But after Allen showed the boundless potential in his one-month trial at the end of the 1963 season, there was no reason to exclude him from the Phillies' roster the following year.

As 1964 spring training neared, a difficult decision faced Phillies management: Where to play Dick Allen? He played in the outfield in the minor leagues, but the Phillies were already well stocked in that position. With such players as Johnny Callison, Tony Gonzalez, and Wes Covington, the Phillies felt secure with their outfield situation. First base, a position he played later in his career, was not an option either because the Phillies had another prospect, John Herrnstein, to occupy that position. Third base, a position Allen only played sparingly, was available and therefore, appeared the best place for him. Also, in putting Allen at third base, the Phillies could trade the previous starter at that position, Don Demeter, to the Tigers before the 1964 season. In return, the Phillies received Jim Bunning, who became one of the finest pitchers in team history and an eventual Hall-of-Famer. Allen now became a regular, but third base was a foreign position for him. Management explained that a player of his athletic ability could learn to play the position quickly. While Allen's batting statistics were good enough to earn the National League's Rookie of the Year Award of 1964, his fielding often garnered criticism from the Phillies fans. Allen's reaction to this criticism provided much controversy for the next several years.[2]

Prior to Allen's ascent to stardom, black players failed to respond to criticism or abuse from the fans. This precedent was set with Branch Rickey's insistence that Jackie Robinson keep his cool while playing for the Brooklyn Dodgers. These players needed to "rise above" the insults and excel on the playing field. The mere success of integration created pride within the African American community. Fans followed the progress of black players without serious concern about the "politics" prevalent in the major leagues. But Allen represented a "second wave" of black players who never suffered prior exclusion from the major leagues. His rise to the majors was similar to that of any white player. Prejudice and discrimination suffered by a player like Dick Allen became viewed as open hostility instead of "business as usual."

With the new generation of players came a new outlook. These players did not look at major league baseball as an opportunity to advance their race; it was merely their job. They did not feel that they had to control their tempers or their statements to the press. The reactions to this new outlook, however, varied in different cities. Certain cities, such as

Chicago and Pittsburgh, accepted black players rather easily when compared to many other cities. By 1964, Philadelphia was not ready for a Dick Allen–type of player who openly challenged the baseball establishment. Athletes such as Allen became more common in the 1960s and many clubs did not look forward to dealing with them.

Conversely, Allen was ill prepared for the virulent fan reaction. Allen's presence represented the division between the white fans of the Phillies and the black neighborhood surrounding Shibe Park (now renamed Connie Mack Stadium). Many of the white fans chose not to attend Phillies games because of their desire to avoid the black neighborhood around the ballpark. Instead, many decided to just watch the games on television or listen to them on radio. Those who actually attended Phillies home games took a dim view of the surrounding area. Furthermore, the differing views provided by both the white and black press suggest that there was a racial chasm within the Philadelphia athletic community.

Unfortunately, this division between the races occurred not only because of the time but also from the historical geography. The original construction of Shibe Park took place in undeveloped section of Philadelphia north of the Pennsylvania railroad tracks. Ben Shibe, then co-owner of the Athletics, wanted to get his team out of the rickety fire-hazard known as Columbia Park and into a new concrete and steel ballpark. He chose this section of the city because the land was cheap due to its close proximity to a smallpox hospital. Obviously, that hospital made the land undesirable to homeowners and tenants. Shibe's actions were typical of other club owners; Brooklyn Dodgers owner Charles Ebbets used the same philosophy to build legendary Ebbets Field. Completed in 1908, Shibe Park made the surrounding real estate more enticing and residents began to move into the area.[3] But by the 1950s and 1960s, the area became part of the city's African American community. This shift did not please many of the white fans and by the time of Allen's first tour of duty with the Phillies, Connie Mack Stadium unwittingly became the center of racial unrest.

Allen's career occurred at a time when the attitudes of black athletes changed greatly. Previous black athletes such as Jesse Owens in track-and-field and heavyweight boxer Joe Louis were considered subdued and thankful for their opportunities. In the late 1940s, Jackie Robinson received instructions from Dodger president Branch Rickey to keep his emotions to himself in order to endure the success of integration. In the 1950s, former Philadelphia Star outfielder Harry Simpson graciously expressed his gratitude for the opportunity to play big league baseball. By the 1960s, however, the civil rights movement sought to eliminate segregation and prejudice. Therefore, successful athletes became less inclined to "go with the flow" and began to exercise greater individuality. Examples of such athletes were heavyweight boxer Muhammad Ali, who refused induction into the army at the height of his career, and professional football player Jim Brown, who organized a coalition of African American professional athletes. Allen served as yet another example of such an athlete. He did not want to merely try to blend in like Bob Trice nor did he need to learn a new language or culture like Latin American players. Allen chose to exercise his personal beliefs, which appears normal in today's sporting world. Unfortunately, Philadelphia fans proved unprepared for such an individual.

As Allen made waves as a player with the Phillies in the 1960s, the civil rights movement raged throughout America. Although places such as Alabama, Mississippi, and Arkansas serve as the historical epicenter of civil rights, racial problems existed in Philadelphia during this time as well. Most of the intense struggles revolved the issue of education. Throughout the 1960s, fierce protest centered on Girard College, a private school in Philadelphia. The all-male and all-white institution became a source of inspiration for civil rights activists who desired change. Although the United States Supreme Court ordered Girard College to follow nondiscriminatory admission policies, the school failed to do so. For the next ten years, the school became a lightning rod for both violent and nonviolent protests.[4] This racial unrest coincided with the Phillies career of Dick Allen and both issues appeared to divide the city's loyalties.

While Allen posted impressive numbers from 1964 to 1969, he never completely won the admiration of all the Phillies fans. This failure occurred for many reasons that are both the fault of the overly critical fans and of Allen himself. He immediately attracted the attention of the black press, which felt the time had finally come for a big-time African American baseball hero in Philadelphia. The white press proved a little more guarded of Allen's early success but nonetheless admitted that he was unlike any previous black Phillies player. In addition, Allen's exploits brought more black fans to Connie Mack Stadium than ever. In the 1960s, this change tended to make the white fans uncomfortable, which means that conflict between the two races proved inevitable. Despite this potentially explosive situation, inexplicably, the Phillies' play on the field improved dramatically in the early 1960s.

For most of the 1964 season, the Phillies confounded baseball experts by being in first place most of the season. But the bubble burst on the

Probably the most talented player ever to wear a Phillies uniform, Dick Allen became a lightning rod for controversy during his first tenure with the club (1963–1969). Because of his stormy relationship with management, the Phillies came to be regarded as the worst place for black players for many years. (Courtesy of the National Baseball Hall of Fame)

team in September as a fatal 10-game losing streak cost them the National League pennant and a World Series appearance.[5] The St. Louis Cardinals came from behind and took the Phillies by surprise by winning the pennant. The Cardinals eventually defeated the New York Yankees to become World's Champions. Bitterly disappointed Phillies fans looked for someone to blame and Allen seemed a likely target. Although named National League Rookie of the Year, Allen failed to receive the unconditional support of Phillies fans.

When he first broke in with the Phillies, Allen was described as a "big kid who loved baseball." But he was much deeper than that, which posed a problem to owner Bob Carpenter. But as Allen's career progressed, several controversies developed that strained relations between Allen, the Phillies organization, and the fans. For one thing, Allen's given first name was Richard and he went by "Dick." Phillies public relations and the Philadelphia press chose to call him "Richie." Allen did not like "Richie" and fought it every time he could. Allen considered it a little boy's name and refused to acknowledge it. Rather than submitting to Allen's wishes, people continued calling him "Richie." Allen received persistent criticism for his refusal to go by the name of Richie.

During the early days of integration, name changes of this kind existed primarily for Latin American players. Most of these players had long Hispanic names that proved difficult for the average American baseball fan to pronounce. Since the major leagues existed entirely in the United States at this time, little thought was given to catering to bilingual fans or attracting interest from people of other countries. It became necessary for Latin American players to learn about American culture and speak English. A part of this cultural conversion occurred with the altering of Latin names. For example, Phillies first baseman Guillermo Montanez (who played for them from 1970 to 1975) was called "Willie." Despite his opposition, the name "Willie" persisted and it was used for the rest of Montanez's career.[6] Incidentally, during his time in Philadelphia, Montanez became quite a popular player before a 1975 trade to the San Francisco Giants, which brought centerfielder Garry Maddox to the Phillies. Maddox starred for the Phillies for almost a decade, winning many Gold Gloves for his fielding prowess. But Allen was African American and it would seem that the name problem would not become an issue, but it did. As trivial as it initially appeared, the "Richie" issue remained a controversy that Allen could not seem to shake.

But it was a particular moment that caused a stir and probably began the problems that Allen later experienced. It occurred in September 1964 while the Phillies became mired in that disastrous losing streak. Jewish and African American businessmen organized an impromptu "night" for Allen prior to a game. During the early and mid–1960s, the causes of Jews and African Americans often intersected. In Philadelphia, Allen became a hero to both groups at this time and they felt it necessary to honor the player for his fine rookie season. Phillies management opposed this event because they felt that a rookie did not deserve such an honor. Nevertheless, the ceremony commenced as Allen received many expensive gifts and was presented a $1,000 scholarship for his young daughter. Meanwhile, many in the Phillies front office felt that this night distracted from the tight pennant race.[7] It also suggests that this incident began the racial division between not only baseball fans but also the Philadelphia community in general.

The frustration of the 1964 collapse was seen in the following season. Although Allen remained popular with most of his teammates, others proved problematic. Veteran outfielder Frank Thomas created most of the problems for Allen in 1965. Thomas, a white player, liked to "yank the chains" of his teammates and particularly enjoyed razzing the sensitive Allen on a regular basis. One day during batting practice, Allen had enough of Thomas' insults and punched him. Most of his teammates felt Thomas had it coming and that the punch became the culmination of problems between the two. In retaliation, Thomas picked up a bat and swung it at Allen, striking him on the shoulder. The two were separated before further hostilities ensued, but the emotional damage was done. The incident was reported to the press and most wondered what the club would do next. The Phillies brass responded by releasing Thomas from

A veteran outfielder and first baseman, Frank Thomas arrived in Philadelphia for the Phillies' stretch run of 1964. But it was Thomas' well publicized fight with Dick Allen the following season that created much controversy and led to his removal from the club. (Courtesy of the National Baseball Hall of Fame)

the team, essentially ending his career.[8] Furthermore, Allen faced the threat of a $2,000 fine from management if he discussed this matter with the press. Many white fans vehemently opposed this action because they thought the Phillies showed favoritism. They booed Allen incessantly, which created further ugliness between the slugger and the Phillies fans.[9]

Many fans called for the return of Thomas, despite the fact that he was an aging slugger at the end of his career. Those same fans attacked Allen as a spoiled superstar whose feelings superseded those of the rest of the team. Since the Phillies management placed a gag order on Allen, he could not respond to the criticism. On the other hand, the black press felt that Allen got the raw deal. *Philadelphia Tribune* sports columnist Claude E. Harrison chastised Philadelphia fans by writing that "Philadelphia is the town where a Negro star is unwanted."[10] The booing of Allen continued. He began to receive racist hate mail and his daughter received taunts at her elementary school.

While Phillies fans jeered Allen, they began to embrace other teams' black players. One such example of this conduct was Willie Mays of the San Francisco Giants. His enthusiastic and accomplished play impressed the tough-to-please Phillies fans. They began to cheer Mays, which often disappointed some of the Phillies players. "He owned our park," recalled former Phillies infielder Cookie Rojas. "Leave it to our fans. They'd ride us and cheer him."[11] Although Rojas' quote refers to Mays' brilliant performances against the Phillies and the toughness of Philadelphia fans, it also shows that those who attended the games were much more tolerant of visiting black players. A hometown player like Allen, however, found it difficult to win over the fans' affection.

When the fans turned on Allen, he retreated into a shell. He spent much time with his racehorses, drank heavily, and often showed up late for games. Management was of little assistance because they rarely confronted Allen on any issue and became, for the most part, accepting of his erratic tendencies.[12] Prior to the 1965 season, Allen said he would refuse to play unless the Phillies quadrupled his salary, which they did.[13] Therefore, fans accused Carpenter of giving Allen preferential treatment rather than dealing with the troubled slugger more harshly.

The enabling influence that the Phillies' management provided to Allen often created a division in the clubhouse. Some teammates supported Allen because they felt he received unfair criticism from the press. Other teammates, especially those who did not know Allen for long, would react angrily towards the controversy that surrounded the team. One such example came from pitcher Dick Ellsworth upon his 1968 trade to the Boston Red Sox. Ellsworth had this to say about Allen: "His behavior on and off the field has been disgusting. People would be amazed at what guys think of him. He drags us down. He couldn't carry Tony Taylor's socks as a team player—if he hit 100 home runs." It is interesting to note that Ellsworth used the dark-skinned Cuban Taylor as his example of a team player. Whether his name-dropping acted as a chance offering or was a well-chosen example remains unknown.[14]

Regardless of how well Allen performed on the field, he constantly served as the center of controversy. He suffered a mysterious wrist injury during the 1967 season. When asked about the injury, Allen explained that he injured the wrist when he was forced to push his car. As he pushed the vehicle, his hand slipped and went through his taillight.[15] While Allen's explanations became publicized in the local media, his account was not believed by all of his teammates nor by all members of the press. This situation became further exacerbated when Phillies General Manager John Quinn attempted to sign Allen to a conditional contract for the following season. Although Quinn explained that his concerns were over the wrist injury, Allen felt that the Phillies were only concerned whether he could swing a bat.[16]

Allen's relationships with his managers also became the subject of controversy. When he first joined the Phillies in September of 1963, Gene Mauch managed the team. At that time, Mauch received the reputation as the hard-driving manager of a young, up-and-coming Phillies team. During the 1964 season, Mauch's players responded to his taskmaster ways as they reached the brink of the National League pennant. Unfortunately, as the team sank into that fatal, late-season losing streak, many of the players believed that Mauch panicked, especially when it came to the use of his pitchers. Mauch overworked some of his better pitchers, who faltered during the last two weeks of the season. After that season, Mauch's respect from his players gradually began to erode. This problem became especially true in his relations with Dick Allen.

While Phillies fans hoped that Mauch and the Phillies could regroup and return to their pennant-contending form, the chasm between the manager and star player widened. While Mauch attempted to understand the moody slugger, Allen often failed to grasp the rules that he was asked to follow. But as the different, unsettling matters began to occur with great frequency during the 1965 and 1966 seasons, the relationship between Mauch and Allen became almost unbearable. Both men were headstrong individuals who rarely admitted their own errors. Mauch fined Allen for a curfew violation in 1966 and twice for showing up late for games in the 1967 season. Often, however, management did not support Mauch's actions. But the 1968 season brought the rift to a much higher level.[17]

When Allen abruptly left spring training camp in March 1968, he received the first of many fines for that season. His tardiness for an April game in New York cost Allen another fine from Mauch. But his apparent failure to hustle on the bases in a game in May caused the biggest stir of that season. Although Allen said he suffered a groin pull, some say that he conducted a "sit-down" strike.[18] This proved the final straw as Mauch was fired in June of that season and replaced by Bob Skinner. Most in the press feel that the club chose its star player over their manager. Therefore, Allen received much of the blame for Mauch's firing.[19]

Gene Mauch served as Phillies manager from 1961 to 1968. Although responsible for bringing Dick Allen into the big leagues, his battles with the talented slugger eventually led to his firing during the 1968 season. (Courtesy of the National Baseball Hall of Fame)

When Skinner took over the Phillies' managerial position in June 1968, he said he believed that he could get along with Allen. Skinner called Allen a "tremendous player" and said he would talk with him. But Skinner also said that only one set of rules would govern the members of the club. Those would prove fateful words, as Skinner would find out during the 1969 season. Meanwhile, the Phillies resisted attempts to trade Allen to other clubs and hoped that the managerial change would become the cure for their problems.[20] But the 1969 season proved otherwise as the situation worsened.

Tired of all of the turmoil, Allen requested a trade from the Phillies. By 1969, while playing first base, he often wrote messages in the dirt with his spikes. The most common was "trade me" and many of the Phillies fans hoped that he would get his wish. To make matters worse, Allen failed to show up for a game in New York that led to a 25-day suspension by the club.[21] In response, Skinner said, "Allen is not bigger than baseball, and he'll be suspended until he convinces me he can obey the same rules as the other 24 players."[22] Shortly thereafter, Skinner became the next Phillies managerial casualty. Towards the end of the 1969 season, several teams attempted to acquire Allen for their pennant drive. No teams, however, traded for Allen as Phillies management merely looked forward to the end of the season.[23] Losing the backing of the front office sealed his fate and, after the 1969 season, Allen finally was traded to the St. Louis Cardinals.

For Dick Allen, the trade meant freedom. Eventually, though, this trade launched Allen on an odyssey that took him through both leagues in the next few seasons. Allen played only the 1970 season with the Cardinals. Although he led the team in home runs and runs batted in, Allen suffered from leg injuries and was traded to the Los Angeles Dodgers.[24] He spent only one season there also and was dealt to the Chicago White Sox, where he won the American League Most Valuable Player Award for the 1972

Manager Bob Skinner experienced great difficulties with Dick Allen despite his pledge to work with him. Such poor relations cost Skinner his managerial job and caused Allen to eventually be traded to the St. Louis Cardinals. (Courtesy of the National Baseball Hall of Fame)

season. Usually such movement from team to team indicates that a problem exists and many teams took seriously Allen's reputation as having a "bad attitude." Nevertheless, after the events in Philadelphia in the 1960s, Allen felt free after the trade from the Phillies.

For Phillies fans, the tumultuous tenure of Dick Allen offers much debate. It appears that fans remain divided over whether to praise or vilify Allen. In particular, many fans blamed Allen for ruining a potentially pennant-winning Phillies team and the managerial tenure of Gene Mauch. Some portrayed Allen as a underachiever who failed to utilize his vast talents. Many experts believed that, without the persistent problems, Allen would have been the most accomplished Phillies player in club history. The failure to achieve this status left a lingering bad taste in the mouths of many fans who hoped that Allen would bring a championship to Philadelphia. But few of Allen's critics willingly accepted any counterarguments on his situation in Philadelphia.

While Allen did "mess up" during his career in Philadelphia, the front office must shoulder some of the blame for these problems. The first error probably occurred when Allen had to play in Arkansas in 1963. While the club merely promoted one their prized prospects to the highest level of the minor leagues, necessary steps were not taken to allow Allen to adjust comfortably to a potentially explosive situation. Unfortunately, this type of behavior became symptomatic of the club's failure to look after the African American and Latin American players in their farm system. Often, the Phillies put such players into difficult situations with relatively little assistance. Therefore, the team acquired the reputation as a franchise that failed to accommodate their black players. As a result, this mentality probably prevented the Phillies from signing many top prospects into their farm system.

While the situation in Arkansas adversely affected Allen, the incidents that occurred once he arrived in Philadelphia did even more damage. Many experts believed that the Phillies' mishandling of the Frank Thomas scuffle really served as the beginning of the end of the relationship between Allen and the front office. Manager Gene Mauch himself took the blame for this mishap. Mauch felt that Thomas' best playing days were behind him and that management should have released him sooner. By doing so, the fight between the two players would have never occurred. Releasing Thomas immediately after the fight opened the team to severe criticism from fans and the media. Also, the timing of Mauch's firing also put Allen in a negative light. It occurred after that 1968 road trip to the West Coast when Allen embarked on that "sit down" strike. In reality, the decision to fire Mauch came before that trip. But due to the timing of the firing and the team's failure to publicly tell the truth, Mauch became a martyr at the expense of Allen. Furthermore, this situation ruined the tenure of Mauch's successor Bob Skinner even before it began.[25]

The tragic comedy of errors between Allen and Phillies management doomed both the player and the team. Sure Allen drank heavily, showed up late for games, and failed to develop a positive relationship with either of his managers, but the team's conduct deserves criticism as well. Their poor judgment created a distrustful and uncomfortable atmosphere in which to play. Therefore, whatever possibilities the team had of winning the National League pennant became doomed by the failure to create a relaxing environment for players and fans alike. More importantly, the reputation that the Phillies were an organization intolerant of black players created future hassles that adversely affected the club. While the trade of Allen to the St. Louis Cardinals appeared to end the seemingly relentless controversy, new problems soon arose.

For other blacks that followed, playing in Philadelphia seemed like a death sentence. One of the players acquired from St. Louis for Allen was star centerfielder Curt Flood. Flood, a steady hitter and Gold Glove fielder, served as the backbone of the best Cardinal teams of the mid–1960s. He was also an African American proud of his race. Flood feared reporting to Philadelphia for two reasons: first, the treatment that Allen received from the fans and, second, the tough Philadelphia press. Prior to the trade, Flood already suffered the wrath of the white press in Philadelphia. During the 1968 World Series, Flood misplayed a fly ball into a triple that allowed the Detroit Tigers to clinch the championship. The next day, the *Philadelphia Inquirer* had this to say: "World Series goats move over, make room for Curtis Charles Flood." Both factors caused Flood to do the then-unthinkable: challenge the business of professional baseball by not reporting to the Phillies.[26]

Prior to the 1970s, players were irrevocably tied to their major league franchises by the reserve clause. This meant that if a player was traded to another team, by rule he became legally bound to report to the new team or retire from the game. A player could not attain free agent status without the permission of the team that "owned" him. Flood believed that this was unfair and, when traded to Philadelphia, he chose to fight the system through the courts rather than play for the Phillies.[27] Flood's playing career essentially ended with his refusal to report to the Phillies. Technically, Flood did not succeed in his attempt. In 1972, he lost his case in the Supreme Court but his actions encouraged revision of the reserve system. By the end of 1975, the reserve clause died as a result of an

Curt Flood's trade from the St. Louis Cardinals to the Philadelphia Phillies paved the way for change in professional sports. Because of Dick Allen's struggles in Philadelphia, Flood chose to challenge baseball's reserve clause, which bound a player to whichever team owned his contracr, rather than play for the Phillies. (Courtesy of the National Baseball Hall of Fame)

arbitrator's decision allowing free agency. Flood receives credit as the player who fostered free agency and big contracts in professional sports. As for his playing days, Flood never suited up for the Phillies and played only briefly for the Washington Senators in 1971, retiring after a few weeks.[28]

Because of the problems with Allen and Flood, the Phillies again showed a degree of reluctance to acquire black players who demonstrated independence. The organization wanted to avoid another "Dick Allen–type" of player. Scouting reports of potential Phillies players included the individual's race and "off-the-field behavior." This was done for two reasons: to continue to keep records of the percentage black players in the organization and to gauge whether a player's attitude and habits affected his play.

The scouting reports of some black players in the Phillies organization prove quite interesting. Black players such as outfielder Larry Hisle stayed in his room most of the time and did not make waves. Hisle probably understood that any black player who stepped out of line might never get a chance with the Phillies. On the other hand, outfielder Mickey Bowers was termed a problem by the scouts. He was a player who "fought for his rights" and did not like "whites pushing him around or telling him what to do." Bowers' scouting report stated that "Richie Allen, his attitude & conduct, is his idol" and that the organization should not suffer through "another such era with this young player."[29] Hisle enjoyed a productive major league career with several teams while Bowers never played a game in the big leagues. This dichotomy symbolizes the legacy of Allen and Flood, the less "difficult" black players more desirable to major league organizations during the 1960s and early 1970s.

In the early 1970s, the Phillies received much criticism over their policies towards race. This criticism arose because the team consistently finished near the bottom of the National League Eastern Division standings. After the departure of Allen and the beginning of Flood's crusade, it appeared could not attract top-flight talent. Furthermore, the black players that the Phillies let go during the 1971 season criticized team management for their policies on this issue. For example, after his trade to the Los Angeles Dodgers, former Phillies outfielder Larry Hisle had this to say: "I feel for the fellas (Negro players) who have to stay in Philadelphia." Two years later, Hisle became a steady regular for the Minnesota Twins, suggesting that the environment in Philadelphia adversely affected his performance.[30]

Always a talented outfielder, Larry Hisle had a largely unpleasant stay in Philadelphia and expressed relief after leaving the Phillies organization. He later starred in the American League for a number of seasons. (Courtesy of the National Baseball Hall of Fame)

In response to Hisle's comments, Phillies owner Bob Carpenter admitted that if black players felt this way, then the club needed to address the problem of prejudice. "We've been fretting and fuming about this for the last couple of years," Carpenter said. "Our track record hasn't been good." General Manager John Quinn defended his own actions by saying that he attempted to trade for such black stars as California Angels outfielder Alex Johnson, who won the 1970 American League batting title, and Houston Astros second baseman Joe Morgan, a future Hall-of-Famer. Neither player wound up in Philadelphia as the controversy festered.[31]

The Phillies also received criticism for their failure to sign quality young players from the Caribbean and Latin America. While many National League organizations attracted players from Puerto Rico, the Dominican Republic, and Mexico, the Phillies could not keep pace. By 1971, Carpenter vowed to address this problem. Unfortunately, the Phillies continued to experience difficulties in attracting quality young Latin American players.[32]

Overall, Carpenter believed that the failure of Phillies management to communicate effectively with black players caused this situation. "I feel it can be only one thing—the lack of communication between the front office and the black players." Carpenter accepted the blame for this problem: "This is my problem. The buck stops here." He said that the difficulties between him and Dick Allen created this reputation. He claimed that his efforts to discuss these problems with Allen went for naught, saying that his "door was always open." "Rich didn't come up," he said.[33]

These problems proved formidable for the Carpenter family, so much so that Bob Carpenter relinquished much of his power to his son, Ruly. As Ruly Carpenter took over, race relations became less of an issue. The fans became excited about some of the new players that arrived in Philadelphia during that time. The club traded for left-handed pitcher Steve Carlton and brought third baseman Mike Schmidt, outfielder Greg Luzinski, and catcher Bob Boone up from the minor leagues. The presence of these players provided the Phillies with a strong nucleus for future success. Furthermore, the Phillies' move to Veterans Stadium, away from the explosive neighborhood surrounding Connie Mack Stadium, tempered the controversy over prejudice.

Epilogue

For any viewer of televised Phillies action or anyone who attends Veterans Stadium to see the team play, it would be difficult to spot African Americans in the stands. One of the major criticisms of the Phillies organization is that it fails to attract minorities to the ballpark. The legacy of the difficult transitions from segregation to integration is quite strong and makes it difficult for the Phillies to market to African Americans and Latin Americans. It also affects the African Americans who play in the organization. While the Phillies have made strides in this department over the years, some angst about integration still remains.

After Dick Allen's trade in 1969 and Flood's refusal to report to the Phillies in 1970, it appeared that the club would never resolve its problem with integration. Some changes, however, occurred in the organization that proved successful. First, the team left the difficult atmosphere of Shibe Park for Veterans Stadium in South Philadelphia. The new home was far removed from the racially explosive atmosphere where the Phillies once played. Furthermore, Bob Carpenter, whose views of black baseball players proved questionable, turned over control of the team to his son Ruly. The younger Carpenter hired the right people for front office positions and the team began to improve. He replaced longtime General Manager John Quinn with Paul Owens and hired former Phillies pitcher Dallas Green as director of the farm system. With those individuals in place, integration became much less of an issue. One look at the rosters of the Phillies teams of the mid– to late–1970s prove that the club cared less about the color of its players and more about their abilities.

In the 1976 season, the Phillies won the National League East Division Championship. Many of the mainstays of those teams were African

Americans, including outfielders Garry Maddox, second baseman Dave Cash, and, back in a Phillies uniform, first baseman Dick Allen. Before the 1975 season, the Phillies reacquired Allen to play first base for the club. Prior to that season, the Phillies needed a power-hitting first baseman and Allen seemed like the answer. The only question became whether Allen would come back to Philadelphia after his tumultuous first tenure with the Phillies. Many current and former Phillies visited Allen's farm in western Pennsylvania to convince the player to come back to play in Philadelphia. Given the opportunity to play with a contending team, Allen decided to return to the Phillies.[1] When Allen arrived in Philadelphia, he was shocked by what he noticed.

One of the ways that the Phillies convinced Allen to play for the team was by describing of Philadelphia as a totally different place. The move to Veterans Stadium relieved much of the racial tension that became typical at Connie Mack Stadium. The confirmation of this change came when Allen received a standing ovation when he stepped up to bat for the first time in his second term with the Phillies. Finally, many of Allen's black teammates seemed more like him, talented players who spoke their mind. Allen now could express himself without serious repercussions.[2] Philadelphia seemed a totally different place and Allen's second stay with the Phillies proved far less controversial. The only problem that Allen experienced as a Phillie was a locker room scuffle with the relentlessly combative shortstop Larry Bowa in 1976. This scuffle appeared as nothing more than a dispute between two teammates and paled in comparison to the Frank Thomas debacle. Although things were better emotionally for Allen, the effectiveness of his play declined. As the Phillies began to contend for the National League Championship, Allen could not provide the much needed punch from the middle of the lineup. Because of his shoulder injury, Allen was left off of the Phillies 1976 postseason roster. As a result of this situation, the Phillies acquired longtime Pittsburgh Pirates slugger Richie Hebner to play first base and released Allen prior to the following season. He played for the Oakland Athletics in 1977, but retired before the season ended.

In a final bit of irony, Allen recently returned to the Phillies organization to serve as a roving minor league hitting instructor. Allen also counsels younger players through the difficult adjustment process of major league baseball. Allen hopes to have others avoid the problems he experienced in the past. It remains unknown whether the Phillies hope to right a previous wrong or truly believe that Allen can help the young players.[3] Nevertheless, Allen's presence on the Phillies roster in the mid-1970s and his participation in the organization at this writing reflects the changes present within the club with regard to race.

With the changes in the Phillies organization during the 1970s came success on the field. Between 1976 and 1978, the Phillies won three consecutive divisional titles and in 1980, they won their first World Championship. Among others, African American players such as Maddox and right fielder Bake McBride led the Phillies that World Championship season. Maddox had yet another Gold Glove season in centerfield and McBride was moved to the middle of the batting order, getting a career high in RBIs. With these examples as proof, it appears that racial tensions became somewhat alleviated as the Phillies fans warmed to these players. Maddox, in particular, became a leader of the community who continued to host many charitable enterprises in the Philadelphia area. Although these players received the appreciation of Phillies' fans, the legacy of racial intolerance still remained.

While the Phillies began to improve their racial situation in the 1970s, they also embraced the possibility of acquiring players from the Dominican Republic. Beginning when the San Francisco Giants brought up outfielder Felipe Alou in the late 1950s, the Dominican Republic sent hundreds of outstanding major league players to America. In the late 1970s, the expansion Toronto Blue Jays opened a baseball complex in the tiny island nation that loved the sport. The new American League franchise used this complex to eventually build their team into a contender. The first National League team to take advantage of this wealth of talent was the Philadelphia Phillies. Former Phillies shortstop Ruben Amaro opened a similar complex to attract and develop young Dominican players for the major leagues.[4]

As Amaro and the Phillies opened this complex, the team began to stockpile some fine prospects into their farm system. The player from the Dominican Republic that helped the Phillies the most was second baseman Juan Samuel. As a rookie in 1984, Samuel led the National League in triples with 19 and also stole 72 bases. Samuel served as the Phillies' regular second baseman for several seasons. In 1989, he was traded to the New York Mets for centerfielder Lenny Dykstra, who became a fixture at the top of the Phillies' lineup. In addition to Samuel, the Phillies also brought infielder Julio Franco and outfielder George Bell into their minor league system. Eventually, these two players vaulted into prominence in the American League. As a member of the Texas Rangers, Franco led the American League in hitting with a .341 average. Bell, while playing for the Toronto Blue Jays, became the first Dominican named American League Most Valuable Player. Throughout the late 1970s and early 1980s, the Phillies were the envy of major league baseball with their ability to acquire talent from the Dominican Republic. Unfortunately, this success would not last.[5]

By the mid–1980s, the Phillies began to lose their grip on this prosperity. Due to budget constraints and instability in the front office, the Phillies failed to maintain their Latin American complexes. Therefore, they could not get black Latin American players in their organization unless they acquired them from other major league organizations. About the same time that the Phillies began to neglect the possibilities in Latin America, they began to drop from contention in the National League Eastern Division. Only in 1993 could the Phillies break out of the doldrums and get to the World Series, where they lost to the Toronto Blue Jays.

Recognizing this weakness in the late 1990s, the Phillies expanded their Latin American operations. They hired Sal Artiaga as their director of Latin American operations.[6] Since then, the Phillies have once again improved their prospects in Latin America. Furthermore, the Phillies also began scouting in the newest reservoir of baseball talent, the Far East. The Phillies hoped to attract the top prospects from Japan and Korea. With these efforts, combined with an expanded attempt to acquire the finest African American players, the Phillies were recognized as an up-and-coming team in the National League. Because of the open-mindedness of Phillies' management, the team had begun to take on a much more multi-cultural look. But one may wonder if it was too late.

The history of intolerance of major league baseball in Philadelphia was relived with the 50th Anniversary of Jackie Robinson's breaking of the color barrier. The many failed attempts at integration of the Philadelphia teams and reaction towards other integrated clubs currently haunts the city. Players sometimes show an unwillingness to play in Philadelphia, as they fear the intolerance of fans and management. This reputation was earned by the previous actions of administrators of the major league teams of Philadelphia. The very fact that the Phillies became the last team in the National League to integrate its roster reflects badly on the city. Furthermore, the initial failure to embrace their own integration caused the Phillies to maintain a pattern of racial intolerance. Whenever a black player comes to Philadelphia, he has to not only overcome the opposing teams but also history itself. As then–Phillies second base prospect Marlon Anderson said of his career goals in March 1997, he looked forward to becoming the player that "takes away all the negative vibes people have about the Phillies." Anderson, an African American, refered to the reputation that Philadelphia failed to appreciate its black players.[7] A 23 year old baseball player should look forward to beginning his major league career, not carry an extra burden of race. His performance on the field should determine the contents of a man's character, not his skin color. Anderson eventually made the Phillies, where he became the starting second baseman.

While the racial situation has improved in Philadelphia baseball, there is a dearth of African Americans players available for the Phillies. Prior to Jackie Robinson's ascension to the major leagues, baseball was the top professional sport for African Americans. Whether in the cities or in the country, baseball was the most popular sport among African American youths during the first half of the 20th century. Since then, inner city fields have fallen into disrepair and public funding has disappeared. This neglect has allowed a sport like basketball to move into the forefront for African Americans. Baseball has become a "suburban" sport where better-equipped facilities are available. From an economic standpoint, it is easier for an inner city youth to get a ball and shoot it through a hoop than to organize a baseball team. Baseball requires gloves, uniforms, cleats, bats, helmets, and well-manicured fields, things that many inner city families cannot afford.[8] Therefore, fewer African American baseball players are available for the Phillies at a time when their policies towards minorities have improved.

Furthermore, the fact that African American athletes have become more dominant in football and basketball has diminished the popularity of baseball in black communities. While the number of Latin American players in major league baseball has increased over the past several decades, fewer African Americans yearn to play in the big leagues. Today, the best African American athletes rarely choose baseball as their sport. While the major leagues uses the "RBI" program to encourage the development of baseball in the inner city, the sport takes a backseat to football and basketball. As a result, fewer black players exist now than there were back in the 1950s and 1960s, when most of the best athletes chose baseball.[9] While the Phillies have acquired black players without hesitation during the last 30 years, the talent pool from which they can choose is diminishing.

By the 2001 season, some of the top players of a rapidly improving Phillies team were three African Americans: centerfielder Doug Glanville, shortstop Jimmy Rollins, and second baseman Marlon Anderson. These players are often asked about the impact of their arrival in Philadelphia. In July of 1996, the Phillies did not have a single African American on its roster. Prior to the 1998 season, it had been fifteen years since the team had two African American regular players on its roster. The success of Glanville, Rollins, and Anderson has generated interest in the Phillies from the city's African American community. While these players downplay the issue of race, they admit that they take their responsibility as role models seriously. Glanville, however, believes that he should not act as the focus of the African American community. In reacting to a letter from a young black fan, Glanville stated that "There's a lot of people, not just athletes, that he can look up to and feel proud of his ancestry and his history." To their credit, Phillies management has deflected any praise of adding minorities to the club. General Manager Ed Wade stated, "The plan was to get better.... The color of a player's skin is never an issue." For Wade, the goal was to merely field a winning team.[10] A player's ability and character should be the only criteria for a position on a major league team. Hopefully, these standards remain the only basis for judging the quality of future major leaguers.

Appendix A

Former Philadelphia Stars Who Played in the Major Leagues

The following is a list of former players of the Philadelphia Stars who later played in the major leagues. Because of the limitations and inconsistencies regarding the record keeping in the Negro Leagues, only major league statistics will be listed. Also included is a short synopsis of their playing careers.

James Buster "Buzz" Clarkson

Clarkson spent parts of eight seasons with the Philadelphia Stars prior to his entering organized baseball with the Boston Braves in 1952. As a shortstop and third baseman, Clarkson was known for his power hitting from the right-hand side of the plate. For the Stars, Clarkson hit .308 in 1936 and .308 in 1946 with 34 RBIs in only 34 games.[1] In the early 1950s, before the days of Ernie Banks playing for the Chicago Cubs, shortstops rarely possessed the ability to hit for power. However, when called up to the Boston Braves, Clarkson was 34 years old. In those days, it was rare for major league organizations to bring up former Negro League players at such an advanced age. In fact, Clarkson's age was debated to the point that some even thought he was over 40 years old. With the exception of Satchel Paige and Willard Brown, major league teams avoided the more experienced Negro League players. Nevertheless, at the time of Clarkson's call-up to the major leagues in May of 1952, it appeared that the Braves welcomed a player of his skills. But after 14 games and 25 at-bats, Clarkson was sent back to the Braves' Triple-A farm club in Milwaukee, where he finished out the season. After another season in the Texas League, Clarkson's career ended.[2]

Year	Team	G	AB	Runs	Hits	2B	3B	HR	RBI	BA
1952	Bos-N	14	25	3	5	0	0	0	1	.200

Leroy Robert "Satchel" Paige

Satchel Paige had two very brief stays with the Philadelphia Stars. His first stint came in 1946 and the second came in 1950. Paige only a pitched a couple of games in both brief tours of duty with the Stars.[3] The popularity of Paige often had him sent to franchises that needed to bolster their gate receipts. This trend would explain his two limited stays with the Stars. It is interesting to note that one of Paige's stints came prior to making the major leagues and the other came after his time with the Cleveland Indians. After 1950, St. Louis Browns owner Bill Veeck, the man responsible for bringing Paige to the Indians, again acquired Satchel to pitch for his team. Paige pitched three seasons for the Browns, even making the American League All-Star team in 1952.[4] After 1953, Paige bounced around the minor leagues and then for a few years was out of baseball until 1965. That year, in a move that was part publicity stunt and part attempt for Paige to qualify for a major league pension, Kansas City Athletics owner Charles O. Finley acquired the 59-year-old pitcher. He even gave his ageless pitcher a rocking chair to relax in during games. Paige pitched one game and three scoreless innings against Boston in September of 1965.[5] After another stint in the minor leagues, Paige finally retired for good in 1966.

Year	Team	G	IP	W–L	SV	BB	SO	ERA
1948	CLE-A	21	72.2	6–1	1	25	45	2.48
1949	CLE-A	31	83	4–7	5	33	54	3.04
1951	STL-A	23	62	3–4	5	29	48	4.79
1952	STL-A	46	138	12–10	10	57	91	3.07
1953	STL-A	57	117.1	3–9	11	39	51	3.53
1965	KC-A	1	3	0–0	0	0	1	0.00

Harry Leon Simpson

Harry Simpson was a player often burdened by high expectations. Simpson began his playing career with the Philadelphia Stars in 1946 as a platoon outfielder.[6] However, the left-handed-hitting Simpson began to hit left-hand pitching as well as right-handers. After three seasons with the Stars, Simpson began to gain the notice of major league scouts. It helped that Eddie Gottlieb, coach of the NBA's Philadelphia Warriors and part owner of the Philadelphia Stars, began to recommend Simpson to major league scouts. Gottlieb said that Simpson "has a 50-50 chance to be a second Ted Williams," which gave him an "unlimited potential" tag. But after only one tryout for Cleveland Indians general manager Hank Greenberg, Simpson was signed on the spot. The Indians' brass were so impressed by Simpson that they traded outfielder Orestes "Minnie" Minoso to the Chicago White Sox. Minoso became a long-time regular outfielder for the White Sox while Simpson was handed a regular position with the Indians. With the pressure to succeed on Simpson, the rookie only hit .229 in 122 games. Although he improved to .266 the following season with 65 RBIs in 146 games, he cooled to .227 in the 1953 campaign. With the Indians tired of waiting for Simpson to realize his vast potential, they traded him to the Kansas City Athletics. He found new life with the Athletics, hitting .300 in 1955. The following season, Simpson made the American League All-Star team by hitting .293 with 21 home runs, 105 runs batted in, and 11 triples. American League All-Star manager Casey Stengel was so taken by Simpson that he made sure that the Yankees traded for the former Stars slugger during the 1957 season. However, halfway through the 1958 season, the Yankees traded Simpson back to Kansas City. Unfortunately, Simpson could not rekindle the magic of this first tour of duty with the Athletics. After bouncing around from the Athletics to the White Sox, to the Pittsburgh Pirates, Simpson was out of the major leagues after the 1959 season.[7]

Year	Team	G	AB	Runs	Hits	2B	3B	HR	RBI	BA
1951	CLE	122	332	51	76	7	0	7	24	.229
1952	CLE	146	545	66	145	21	10	10	65	.266
1953	CLE	82	242	25	55	3	1	7	22	.227
1955	CLE	3	1	0	0	0	0	0	0	.000
	KC-A	112	396	42	119	16	7	5	52	.301
1956	KC-A	141	543	76	159	22	11	21	105	.293
1957	KC-A	50	179	24	53	9	6	6	24	.296
	NY-A	75	224	27	56	7	3	7	39	.250
1958	NY-A	24	51	1	11	2	1	0	6	.216
	KC-A	78	212	21	56	7	1	7	27	.264
1959	KC-A	8	14	0	4	0	0	0	0	.286
	CHI-A	38	75	5	14	5	1	2	13	.187
	PIT-N	9	15	4	4	2	0	1	4	.267

Milton Smith

Milt Smith played for the Philadelphia Stars from 1949 to 1951, just prior to entering the minor leagues.[8] The second baseman then played in the Cincinnati Reds organization and in 1955, Smith hit .338 with San Diego of the Pacific Coast League. That earned him an opportunity with the Reds at the end of the 1955 season, where he hit .196 in 102 at-bats in 36 games. Although the low batting average did not impress the Reds, his productivity (3 home runs) did make him a player worth acquiring. Smith was traded to the St. Louis Cardinals but failed to make the major league roster. After playing a few more seasons with a succession of Triple-A teams, Smith's career ended without making it back to the major leagues.[9]

Year	Team	G	AB	Runs	Hits	2B	3B	HR	RBI	BA
1955	Cin-N	36	102	15	20	3	1	3	8	.196

Charles White

Charlie White played for the Philadelphia Stars in 1950, primarily as a catcher and third baseman.[10] Catcher, however, was considered White's primary position as he joined the St. Louis Browns organization in 1951. The Browns were owned by Bill Veeck, who hoped to reverse the fortunes of the dismal franchise. While Veeck used many clever promotions to attract fans to the ballpark, he was forced to sell the Browns and the club moved to Baltimore. As the Baltimore Orioles began operations, White was traded to the Milwaukee Braves to serve as their backup catcher. With durable and reliable Del Crandall serving as the starting catcher, White did not receive too many opportunities to show his abilities. In 1954, White played 50 games and batted 93 times, hitting only .237 with 8 runs batted in and 4 doubles. White remained with the Braves at the beginning of the 1955 season, hitting .233 in just 30 at bats. White was sent back to the minor leagues, where he remained until his career ended in 1961. Although he had some strong seasons in Triple-A, White was unable to get a second chance to play in the majors.[11]

Year	Team	G	AB	Runs	Hits	2B	3B	HR	RBI	BA
1954	Mil-N	50	93	14	22	4	0	1	8	.237
1955	Mil-N	12	30	3	7	1	0	0	4	.233

Appendix B

Black Players with the Philadelphia Athletics

Following are the two black players who played with the Philadelphia Athletics. The statistics and comments are primarily limited to the players' time with the Athletics.

Vic Pellot Power

Power arrived in Philadelphia via a trade with the New York Yankees. Power was caught in a "numbers game" with the Yankees as they chose to go with Bill "Moose" Skowron at first base. Although Skowron went on to have a fairly successful career as the Yankees first baseman, some felt that the job should have belonged to Power. Known for his slick fielding, Power was reputed to have been the choice of Yankees manager Casey Stengel. With two impressive seasons at Triple-A Kansas City behind him, Power seemed like a shoo-in to become the first black Yankee. Originally from Puerto Rico, the outspoken Power did not seem to fit the profile. He publicly made his feelings known on such issues as his lack of opportunity with the Yankees and the fact that black players were paid less than whites. Because of the presence of Skowron and the Yankees' reluctance to integrate their team, Power was traded to the Athletics prior to the 1954 season. Instead, the Yankees integrated their roster in 1955 with catcher-outfielder Elston Howard, who played for the team for 13 seasons. Power arrived in Philadelphia claiming that he was happy just to play in the major leagues. He came to the Athletics just in time for their final, dismal season in Philadelphia.

Although best known for his fielding at first base, Power began his first season in Philadelphia playing in left field. With Lou Limmer slated to play first base for the Athletics in 1954, Power was moved to the outfield. Unable to play in New York and playing out of position, Power's numbers in his initial big league season were not up to those posted later in his career. Nevertheless, Power finished the 1954 season with a .255 batting average with 8 home runs. The following season, Power moved along with his teammates to Kansas City. In 1955, Power returned to his natural first base position and enjoyed a very productive season. Power went on to play with several American League teams before returning to Philadelphia to play with the Phillies in 1964.[1]

Year	Team	G	AB	Runs	Hits	2B	3B	HR	RBI	BA
1954	Phi-A	127	462	36	118	17	5	8	38	.255

Robert Lee "Bob" Trice

Trice arrived in Philadelphia after a very impressive season at Triple-A Ottawa, where he was named Most Valuable Player of the International League in 1953. He came up to the Athletics for a September trial in 1953, winning two of his four starts. Because of his impressive minor league statistics and the potential that he could offer to the talent-poor Athletics, Trice began the 1954 season with the big club. The move appeared successful as Trice won his first four starts, including a 1-0 shutout of the World Champion New York Yankees. But after slumping in May and June of that year, Trice asked for a demotion to Triple-A Ottawa, where he excelled the year before. Trice wanted to work out his pitching and come back to the Athletics to excel. Eventually, the Athletics complied and sent Trice back to the minors. When the Athletics moved to Kansas City for the 1955 season, Trice's contract moved with them. Trice did come back to the Athletics, but only pitched four games with an ERA of 9.00. The Athletics released Trice and he never appeared in the major leagues again.[2]

Year	Team	G	IP	W-L	SV	BB	SO	ERA
1953	Athletics	3	23	2–1	0	6	4	5.48
1954	Athletics	19	119	7–8	0	48	22	5.60

Appendix C

African American and Latin American Phillies, 1957–1979

The following is a list of the African Americans and Latin Americans who played with the Phillies between the years 1957 and 1979. The statistics and comments are primarily limited to the players' careers with the Phillies.

1957

After much delay and many excuses, the Phillies finally broke their color barrier. The presence of Chico Fernandez and John Kennedy proved historic to the once all-white franchise. The Phillies' reluctance to integrate their roster led to their freefall from the top of the standings to the second division. But now, they finally decided to "embrace" integration by bringing up Kennedy and trading for Fernandez. Although Fernandez had a fairly strong season, the Phillies remained in fifth place.

Humberto Perez "Chico" Fernandez

The Phillies acquired the Cuban born Fernandez from the Dodgers just prior to the start of the 1957 season. A highly prized shortstop prospect, Fernandez had his path to major league stardom blocked by future Hall-of-Fame Shortstop Pee Wee Reese. Although Reese was starting to show his age, he still was a mainstay for the Dodgers. His presence made Fernandez expendable, leading to the trade with the Phillies. Upon his arrival, the Phillies immediately inserted the slick-fielding Fernandez into the starting lineup, where he remained for the 1957 and 1958 seasons. Although he considered himself "black," the light-skinned Fernandez was not considered the first black player; John Kennedy received that distinction from Phillies fans. Fernandez considered this a slight, especially since he suffered from the same prejudice as other black players. Nevertheless, Fernandez had a fairly strong 1957 season, hitting .262 with 18 stolen bases. He also fielded well and showed some power with the bat. The following season, Fernandez slumped to .230 with 12 stolen bases and eventually lost his starting job to Joe Koppe. Fernandez only hit .211 in 1959 and was traded to the Detroit Tigers. Fernandez served as the Tigers' starting shortstop for the next three seasons, hitting a career high 20 home runs in 1962. A slow start at the beginning of the 1963 season led to a trade to the expansion New York Mets. After hitting just .200 in 58 games for the Mets, Fernandez's major league playing career ended at the conclusion of the season.

Year	Team	G	AB	Runs	Hits	2B	3B	HR	RBI	BA
1957	Phillies	149	500	42	131	19	5	5	51	.262
1958	Phillies	148	522	38	120	18	5	6	51	.230
1959	Phillies	45	123	15	26	5	1	0	3	.211

John Irvin Kennedy

Former Negro Leaguer John Kennedy became the first African American to play for the Phillies. He played with the Birmingham Black Barons and the Kansas City Monarchs in the Negro Leagues until 1956. After a tryout late in 1956, Kennedy was invited to spring training for the following season. Throughout spring training in 1957, the Phillies searched for a shortstop to take the place of Granny Hamner, who was being moved permanently to second base. Within the meager resources of Phillies organization, Kennedy seemed the likely choice to assume the position. Because of his speed and athletic ability, the Phillies brass seemed to gravitate toward the former Negro Leaguer. A relatively strong spring training in 1957 helped Kennedy's cause. However, they had reservations due to Kennedy's offensive limitations and lack of professional experience. As a result of their reluctance, the Phillies traded for former Brooklyn Dodger shortstop prospect Chico Fernandez. Despite the presence of Fernandez, the Phillies kept Kennedy on the major league roster for the beginning of the 1957 season. It took Kennedy a few days before he finally entered a big league game as a pinch runner. Unfortunately, an injured shoulder curtailed Kennedy's effectiveness and he was sent to the minor leagues. Although Kennedy continued to toil in the Phillies system through the 1960 season, he could not make it back onto their major league roster, finishing a brief and uneventful career.[1]

Year	Team	G	AB	Runs	Hits	2B	3B	HR	RBI	BA
1957	Phillies	5	2	1	0	0	0	0	0	.000

1958

The Phillies suffered a major free-fall from a .500 team in 1957 to a last-place team in 1958. The Phillies fired manager Mayo Smith and replaced him with Whiz Kids manager Eddie Sawyer. The change failed to ignite the Phillies and their record continued to suffer despite league leading hitting by Richie Ashburn and strong pitching from Robin Roberts, Ray Semproch, and Dick "Turk" Farrell. Declining attendance also worried the Phillies management, especially since the Athletics left town a few years earlier. As for black players, there were few. John Kennedy never made it back up to the major leagues and the only new black players was prospect Pancho Herrera, who came up for a brief trial in 1958, and former Negro League pitcher Hank Mason. Chico Fernandez continued as the Phillies' regular shortstop, but his batting average dipped to .230. In 1958, the Phillies were viewed as a team lagging behind in baseball's efforts to fully integrate the major leagues.

Juan Francisco "Pancho" Herrera

One of three former Kansas City Monarchs who played for the Phillies, Cuban-born Pancho Herrera had been in the organization since 1954. Of those three, Herrera was the best. Herrera performed brilliantly at both Schenectady and Miami before getting his first big league trial at the beginning of the 1958 season. After 11 hitless at-bats, Herrera was sent back to Miami, where he hit 20 home runs. He came back up to the Phillies later in the season and ended up hitting .270 in 63 at-bats overall. While Herrera's bat certainly earned him a regular position, it was difficult to find him one. A natural first baseman, the Phillies already had Ed Bouchee at that position. The Phillies tried Herrera at several positions in both the infield and outfield without much success. Also, prior to the 1959 season, Herrera broke his ankle in winter ball. This injury hampered his mobility at spring training and forced the Phillies to send him down to Triple-A Buffalo, where he won the International League's Triple Crown. Needless to say, Herrera was ready to play for a dismal Phillies team. Finally getting his chance in 1960, Herrera hit a strong .281 with 17 home runs and 71 RBIs while starting at first base. The following season, Herrera hit .258 with 13 home runs. Despite respectable batting numbers, Herrera suffered greatly from weaknesses in his game. He led the National League in strikeouts in 1960 with a then league record 136 in 512 at-bats. The following year, he struck out 120 times in just 400 at-bats. Furthermore, Herrera's poor fielding also hurt his chances, leading the league in errors in 1960 with 14. After the 1961 season, the Phillies demoted Herrera to Triple-A Buffalo and eventually traded him to the Pittsburgh Pirates organization. Unfortunately, Herrera never received an opportunity with Pirates or any other major league team.[2]

Year	Team	G	AB	Runs	Hits	2B	3B	HR	RBI	BA
1958	Phillies	29	63	5	17	3	0	1	6	.270
1960	Phillies	145	512	61	144	26	3	17	71	.281
1961	Phillies	126	400	56	103	17	2	13	51	.258

Henry Mason

Hank Mason came to Philadelphia for brief trials in 1958 and 1960. A former high school basketball player and star pitcher of the Kansas City Monarchs, Mason had several strong seasons in the Phillies' minor league system but could not break into the Phillies' starting rotation. He won 29 games in two seasons with Schenectady, leading the Eastern League with seven shutouts in 1956. Mason pitched only one game in 1958, going five innings and giving up six runs. After going back to the minor leagues to win 12 games in 1959, Mason returned in 1960 to pitch three games and run up a 9.53 ERA in five and two-thirds innings. The Phillies sent the 29-year-old Mason back to the minors but he never returned to major leagues.

Year	Team	G	IP	W–L	SV	BB	SO	ERA
1958	Phillies	1	5	0–0	0	2	3	10.80
1960	Phillies	3	5.2	0–0	0	5	3	9.53

1959

This Phillies team represented the end of the "Whiz Kids" era. Although Eddie Sawyer returned as manager the previous season, longtime Phillies stars ended their careers in Philadelphia. With such players as third baseman Willie Jones and second baseman Granny Hamner leaving the Phillies during season, and outfielder and fan favorite Richie Ashburn being traded to the Chicago Cubs after the season, the Phillies were in a serious rebuilding program. In addition, longtime pitcher Curt Simmons suffered through shoulder miseries and future Hall of Fame pitcher Robin Roberts was no longer as effective as he was in the early 1950s. As for black players, the massive rebuilding program did not seem to include embracing this alternative. Although they traded for catcher Valmy Thomas, outfielder Solly Drake, as well as pitchers Ruben Gomez and Humberto Robinson, none of them could contribute much to the Phillies. As a result of the turmoil, the Phillies stumbled to a disappointing last place finish.

Solomon Lewis "Solly" Drake

Once considered an outstanding outfield prospect with great speed, Solly Drake had a dislocated ankle in 1955 that adversely affected his career. After hitting a respectable .256 with 9 stolen bases in 65 games as a member of the Chicago Cubs in 1956, Drake was surprisingly sent back to the minor leagues by a talent-starved team. After leading the International League in hits in 1958, Drake made it onto the Los Angeles Dodgers' roster in 1959. Unfortunately for Drake, he was traded to the Phillies prior to experiencing the Dodgers' 1959 title run. Drake's Philadelphia career generated little enthusiasm; he hit only .145 as a reserve outfielder for a last-place club. Most distressing was the fact that during the 1959 season, Drake went 0 for 22 as a pinch-hitter, a debilitating statistic for a back-up outfielder with hopes of remaining in the major leagues. Not surprisingly, Drake's major league career ended in Philadelphia.[3]

Year	Team	G	AB	Runs	Hits	2B	3B	HR	RBI	BA
1959	Phillies	67	62	10	9	1	0	0	3	.145

Ruben Gomez

Ruben Gomez came to Philadelphia with catcher Valmy Thomas from the San Francisco Giants for pitcher Jack Sanford. Prior to the trade, Sanford won the 1957 National League Rookie of the Year Award by winning 19 games for the Phillies at age 28. After slumping to 10 victories in 1958, the Phillies felt that the 30-year-old Sanford was a flash-in-the-pan and traded him while he still had value. Gomez, from Puerto Rico, was considered an experienced starting pitcher who could stabilize the Phillies staff. Originally signed by the Yankees organization, Gomez became unsatisfied with the club's stance on promoting black players. In response to the Yankees' apparent reluctance to promote him because of his skin color, Gomez bought his freedom. He then signed with the cross-town New York Giants and won 13 games as a rookie in 1953. He followed that up with a 17-win season for the World Champion Giants of 1954 and a victory in the World Series. Known for his screwball, Gomez had a strong repertoire of pitches and an intense competitive fire. During his Giants career, Gomez developed a reputation for pitching tight to batters. He was once attacked by massive Milwaukee Braves first baseman Joe Adcock, who chased Gomez all over the outfield at the Polo Grounds. In between his seasons with the Phillies, Gomez hit outfielder Joe Christopher in the head with a pitch during a game in the Puerto Rican winter league. For that pitch, Gomez's Corvette was pelted with garbage. After slumping the following two seasons, Gomez came back to win 15 games in 1957, the Giants' final season in New York. After dropping to just 10 wins in 1958, the Giants sent Gomez to the Phillies. Despite Gomez's apparent skill and experience, he failed to help the Phillies. It appeared that years of pitching year-round and using his screwball took its toll on his arm. Gomez could only win 3 games for the 1959 Phillies with an astronomical 6.10 ERA. Relegated to the bullpen the following year, Gomez failed to win a game while sporting a mediocre 5.33 ERA. Prior to the 1961 season, the Phillies optioned Gomez to Dallas–Fort Worth in the American Association. He later surfaced with the Cleveland Indians in 1962 and then was traded to the Minnesota Twins before leaving the major leagues for five seasons. During that time, Gomez pitched primarily in the Mexican League. Then, at age 40, Gomez came back to the Phillies as reliever in 1967. After surprisingly winning a job in spring training, Gomez pitched in only 7 games for the Phillies before leaving the major leagues for good.

Year	Team	G	IP	W–L	SV	BB	SO	ERA
1959	Phillies	20	72	3–8	1	24	37	6.10
1960	Phillies	22	52	0–3	1	9	24	5.33
1967	Phillies	7	11	0–0	0	7	9	3.97

Humberto Valentino Robinson

Originally from Panama, Humberto Robinson came to Philadelphia during the 1959 season after pitching five games for the Cleveland Indians. While Robinson came to the Phillies during that season, two 1950s team icons, third baseman Willie "Puddin' Head" Jones and second baseman Granny Hamner, went to the Indians to finish their careers. In fact, the Indians received Hamner in return for Robinson. Furthermore, Robinson served as yet another example of a black player who came from Latin America or the Caribbean during the late 1950s and early 1960s. Robinson had moderate success while primarily pitching out of the Phillies' bullpen, winning two games and saving another with a decent 3.33 ERA. Robinson also sometimes acted as a spot starter for the Phillies. Robinson's claim to fame in Philadelphia came during that 1959 season when offered an opportunity by a café owner to throw a game for $1,500. Robinson rejected the offer and won the game 3–2.[4] His performance proved good enough to earn a place on the Phillies' staff for the 1960 season. Pitching primarily out of the bullpen, Robinson went 0–4 with a 3.44 ERA. Although those numbers appeared relatively respectable, Robinson did not make the team for the following season, ending his major league career at age 30.

Year	Team	G	IP	W–L	SV	BB	SO	ERA
1959	Phillies	31	73	2–4	1	24	32	3.33
1960	Phillies	33	50	0–4	0	22	31	3.42

Valmy Thomas

In each his five major league seasons, Valmy Thomas played in a different city. The Virgin Islands native came to the Phillies in what turned out as a costly trade with the San Francisco Giants. Thomas, who was a part time regular with the Giants, was expected to fill a hole at catcher for the Phillies. The previous regular catcher Stan Lopata appeared to slow down during the 1958 season and the Phillies brass decided it was time to trade for an alternative. The club sent starting pitcher Jack Sanford to the Giants for Thomas and pitcher Ruben Gomez in a trade that turned out quite badly for the Phillies. At the time, Thomas looked like he could become a major league caliber catcher. In addition, Gomez had some strong seasons with the Giants in the mid–1950s, so it looked like the Phillies received two good players for the price of one. As it turned out, Thomas could only hit .200 and got benched in favor of such luminaries as Carl Sawatski, Joe Lonnett, and aging ex–Cleveland Indians catcher Jim Hegan. After the 1959 season, the Phillies gave up on Thomas. Meanwhile, Sanford had his best years with the Giants, including winning 24 games in 1962. After leaving the Phillies, Sanford won another 107 games in the next eight years. As for Thomas, he had short stints with the Baltimore Orioles and the Cleveland Indians before his major league career ended in 1961.[5]

Year	Team	G	AB	Runs	Hits	2B	3B	HR	RBI	BA
1959	Phillies	66	140	5	28	2	0	1	7	.200

1960

The 1960 season began strangely when Manager Eddie Sawyer abruptly quit the team after an Opening Day victory. With that auspicious beginning, the Phillies tumbled to last place in the National League standings. By 1960, only pitcher Robin Roberts remained from the Whiz Kids team of a decade earlier. The team needed a major overhaul and began its rebuilding program by hiring young Gene Mauch as manager. The Phillies began to trade many of its veterans in order to acquire younger players. Of the five new black players, all of them were from either the Caribbean or Latin America. Of these players, outfielder Tony Gonzalez and infielder Tony Taylor proved the best of the bunch.

Ruben Mora Amaro

Ruben Amaro has probably done more than anyone else to improve the baseball situation for Latin Americans playing in Philadelphia. Originally from Mexico, Amaro first broke into the major leagues with the St. Louis Cardinals in 1958. After hitting only .224 in 40 games, Amaro was traded to the Phillies organization. He did not make the Phillies roster until 1960. That season, Amaro played 92 games at shortstop, hitting only .231. Despite his fairly mediocre hitting, Amaro's defensive play at shortstop kept him in the regular lineup. In 1961, Amaro pretty much served as the regular shortstop and improved his average to .257 with 9 triples. The following year, Amaro lost valuable time due to military service and lost his regular position to the slick-fielding, but even weaker-hitting, Bobby Wine. For the next three seasons, Amaro served as a utility infielder, playing all four infield positions. His versatility kept his name on the lineup card and in 1964, he enjoyed his best major league season, batting .264. Despite only playing 79 games at shortstop in 1964, Amaro's fielding ability allowed him to win the National League Gold Glove Award. Unfortunately, he slumped the following season, batting only .212 in 118 games. The Phillies then traded Amaro to the New York Yankees, presumably to replace the oft-injured and retired Tony Kubek at shortstop.[6] Prior to 1965, any player would welcome a trade to the Yankees. But injuries and age crept upon this once proud franchise and they were in a state of free fall down the American League standings. Although the Yankees finished in ninth place in 1967, Amaro served as the team's regular shortstop. But after hitting only .223, Amaro again became a utility infielder the following season. Unfortunately, Amaro could only hit a meager .122 in 1968 and was traded to the California Angels. He finished his career with a short stint with the Angels in 1969 by hitting in .222 in 27 in just at-bats.

After completing his playing career, Amaro then became an instructor for the Phillies' minor league system. Then, in the late 1970s, Amaro founded an academy for young players in the Dominican Republic. Here the Phillies began to have a presence in this small country that produces so many big league players. The Phillies found several outstanding career major league players as a result of this program and gained the team a firm presence in Latin America. This Dominican complex allowed the club to sign many fine young prospects during the late 1970s and early 1980s. This scouting complex was the envy of other major league franchises that began to establish similar institutions in the poverty stricken country.[7] After succeeding in the Dominican Republic, Amaro eventually worked his way onto the Phillies' coaching staff, where he served for several seasons. He was on the coaching staff when the Phillies won the World Championship in 1980. His son, Ruben Jr., played for the Phillies as a reserve outfielder in the 1990s and then served as the club Assistant General Manager.

Year	Team	G	AB	Runs	Hits	2B	3B	HR	RBI	BA
1960	Phillies	92	264	25	61	9	1	0	16	.231
1961	Phillies	135	381	34	98	14	9	1	32	.257
1962	Phillies	79	226	24	55	10	0	0	19	.243
1963	Phillies	115	217	25	47	9	2	2	19	.217
1964	Phillies	129	299	31	79	11	0	4	34	.264
1965	Phillies	118	184	26	39	7	0	0	15	.212

George Anthony Curry

Bahamas native Tony Curry came to Philadelphia in 1960 and received significant playing time in the outfield. Curry hit a strong .261 with 14 doubles in part-time play. At 22 years of age, it appeared that Curry had a long future in the Phillies lineup. Although he made the team the following season, he hit only .194 in just 15 games before being sent back to the minor leagues. Curry did not come back to the Phillies and it would be five years before he had a brief final stint with the Cleveland Indians in 1966.

Year	Team	G	AB	Runs	Hits	2B	3B	HR	RBI	BA
1960	Phillies	95	245	26	64	14	2	6	34	.261
1961	Phillies	15	36	3	7	2	0	0	3	.194

Andres Antonio Gonzalez

Cuban born Tony Gonzalez came to the Phillies via trade with the Cincinnati Reds for outfielder Harry Anderson. While Anderson had only 66 at-bats for the Reds, Gonzalez served as the Phillies' starting centerfielder for a decade. After hitting .299 in 78 games for the Phillies in 1960, Gonzalez became the fixture in the outfield. Known for his steady fielding and clutch hitting, Gonzalez became one of the reasons why the Phillies turned themselves into contenders by 1964. In 1962, Gonzalez hit .302 with 20 home runs, 63 runs batted in, and 17 stolen bases, the first of his three .300 seasons for the Phillies. Gonzalez hit .306 in 1963 with a career high 12 triples for the third place Phillies. Although his batting average dropped almost 30 points in 1964, he was still a major force in the Phillies' second place finish. Gonzalez's best season came in 1967 when he finished third in the National League in batting with a .339 average. After hitting .264 in the following season, Gonzalez was left exposed in the 1969 expansion draft. Selected by the San Diego Padres, Gonzalez was the club's original centerfielder but was traded to the Atlanta Braves during the season. Gonzalez helped the Braves during their stretch run to the National League West title. After another season with the Braves, Gonzalez finished his career with the California Angels in 1971. Gonzalez later served as roving instructor in the Phillies minor league system.

Year	Team	G	AB	Runs	Hits	2B	3B	HR	RBI	BA
1960	Phillies	78	241	27	72	17	5	6	33	.299
1961	Phillies	126	426	58	118	16	8	12	58	.277
1962	Phillies	118	437	76	132	16	4	20	63	.302
1963	Phillies	155	555	78	170	36	12	4	66	.306
1964	Phillies	131	421	55	117	25	3	4	40	.278
1965	Phillies	108	370	48	109	19	1	13	41	.295
1966	Phillies	132	384	53	110	20	4	6	40	.286
1967	Phillies	149	508	74	172	23	9	9	59	.339
1968	Phillies	121	416	45	110	13	4	3	38	.264

Antonio Taylor (Sanchez)

Cuban native Tony Taylor arrived in Philadelphia as a result of trade with the Chicago Cubs. The trade led to a longtime allegiance between Taylor and the Phillies organization. Taylor played 16 seasons in two tours of duty with the Phillies. Taylor later served as a minor league instructor and a first base coach for the Phillies organization. During his extensive tenure with the Phillies, Taylor (along with Ruben Amaro) probably did more to pave the way for Latin American players in Philadelphia than anyone. Because of his speed, strong fielding, clutch hitting, and enthusiasm for the game, Taylor became a popular figure in Philadelphia at a time when fans booed Dick Allen. Taylor had many fine seasons with the Phillies including hitting .281 with 102 runs scored and 10 triples in 1963, hitting .251 for the pennant-contending team of 1964, and a strong 1970 season in which he had .301 batting average with 55 runs batted in and 74 runs scored. Also, as a member of the Phillies, Taylor made baseball history when he got the first regular season hit at the Houston Astrodome.[8]

Early in the 1971 season, after a slow start, the rebuilding Phillies traded Taylor to the contending Detroit Tigers. After two and half seasons in Detroit, the Tigers released the 38-year-old Taylor. Looking for veteran leadership off the bench, the Phillies decided to sign Taylor for a second stint in Philadelphia. During this tour of duty, Taylor became a quality pinch-hitter, leading the National League with 17 pinch hits in 1974. Every time the right-handed hitting Taylor came to the plate as a pinch-hitter, the fans would come alive. More often than not, the capable Taylor came through. Taylor remained with the Phillies until an elbow injury ended his playing career in 1976. Continuing his love of the game, Taylor works at this writing as the infield coach for the Florida Marlins.⁹ Although not a Hall of Fame caliber player, Taylor was always remembered fondly by Phillies fans. Known for his hustle on the field and his class off of it, Taylor will always remain a very popular figure in Philadelphia baseball history.

Year	Team	G	AB	Runs	Hits	2B	3B	HR	RBI	BA
1960	Phillies	127	505	66	145	22	4	4	35	.287
1961	Phillies	106	400	47	100	17	3	2	26	.250
1962	Phillies	152	625	87	162	21	5	7	43	.259
1963	Phillies	157	640	102	180	20	10	5	49	.281
1964	Phillies	154	570	62	143	13	6	4	46	.251
1965	Phillies	106	323	41	74	14	3	3	27	.229
1966	Phillies	125	434	47	105	14	8	5	40	.242
1967	Phillies	132	462	55	110	16	6	2	34	.238
1968	Phillies	145	547	59	137	20	2	3	38	.250
1969	Phillies	138	557	68	146	24	5	3	30	.262
1970	Phillies	124	439	74	132	26	9	9	55	.301
1971	Phillies	36	107	9	25	2	1	1	5	.234
1974	Phillies	62	64	5	21	4	0	2	13	.328
1975	Phillies	79	103	13	25	5	1	1	17	.243
1976	Phillies	26	23	2	6	1	0	0	3	.261

1961

The 1961 Phillies team made baseball history, but certainly not in a good way. The infamous 1961 Phillies lost 23 consecutive games, setting a major league record for futility. The Phillies finished the season with just 47 wins and 107 losses, finishing last in the National League. With two expansion teams entering the National League in 1962, this was not the time for an organization to start a rebuilding program. However, the Phillies managed to find a few future standouts during the 1961 season, including outfielder Johnny Callison and pitcher Chris Short. As for new black players, the Phillies traded for well-traveled outfielder Wes Covington. The power-hitting Covington provided a left-handed bat in the Phillies lineup as they approached respectability.

Clarence Coleman

Clarence "Choo Choo" Coleman was brought up from the minor leagues to the Phillies in an effort to fill the gap at catcher. While Clay Dalrymple was a capable starting catcher, the Phillies could not find a backup at the position. In 1961, the Phillies tried Darrell Johnson, Cal Neeman, and Jimmie Coker in this role, with little success. Unfortunately, their failure to provide either strong defense or offense caused the Phillies to dip into their farm system for Coleman. But like the others, Coleman failed to fill the hole at catcher. During the 1961 season, Coleman hit only .128 in 34 games. His inability to hit major league pitching caused to Phillies to expose Coleman in the 1962 expansion draft. The fledgling New York Mets chose Coleman in the draft and kept him on their major league roster. Coleman gave the Mets his best season when he hit .250 in 55 games. Given his nickname and the Mets' own team futility, Coleman was a fan favorite. The next season, Coleman hit only .178 in 106 games. Needless to say, even the last place Mets could not endure a starting catcher with a .178 average and after 6 games the following season, the Mets sent Coleman to the minor leagues. He never again played in the major leagues.

Year	Team	G	AB	Runs	Hits	2B	3B	HR	RBI	BA
1961	Phillies	34	47	3	6	1	0	0	4	.128

John Wesley Covington

Wes Covington came to the Phillies in 1961, which was a weird season for both the team and the player. While the Phillies were finishing last in record-breaking fashion, Covington played for four teams during the season. A reliable platoon player for the Milwaukee Braves during their pennant-winning years of the late 1950s, Covington hit .330 in 1958. But by 1961, the Braves were retooling their club and traded Covington to the Chicago White Sox. After 22 games, the White Sox sent Covington to the Kansas City Athletics, who after 17 games traded the outfielder to the Phillies. For the rest of the 1961 season, Covington hit .303 in 57 games. Convinced that he could lend veteran leadership, the Phillies kept Covington for the next four seasons. Covington also served as a mentor for the young African American players that were joining the Phillies. As for his performance on the field, Covington hit well in his 4½ seasons in Philadelphia. His best full season came in 1963, when he hit .303 with 17 home runs and 64 RBIs in 119 games. In the Phillies pennant-contending 1964 season, Covington hit .280 with 13 home runs. After hitting .247 in 1965, Covington was traded to the Chicago Cubs. His career ended in 1966 with the Los Angeles Dodgers.

Year	Team	G	AB	Runs	Hits	2B	3B	HR	RBI	BA
1961	Phillies	57	165	23	60	9	0	7	26	.303
1962	Phillies	116	304	36	86	12	1	9	44	.283
1963	Phillies	119	353	46	107	24	1	17	64	.303
1964	Phillies	129	339	37	95	18	0	13	58	.280
1965	Phillies	101	235	27	58	10	1	15	45	.247

1962

Although the Phillies only finished in seventh place in the National League, they won 34 more games than they did in 1961. Furthermore, the Phillies finished with a winning record (81–80) only one season after setting a league record for consecutive defeats. They accomplished this improvement with many young players under the command of hard-driving young manager Gene Mauch. As for new black players, only Ted Savage came to Philadelphia that season. Although Savage had a respectable rookie year with the Phillies, he was traded the following season. Meanwhile, the team continued to improve and fans had reason to believe that the Phillies were now headed in the right direction.

Theodore E. Savage

Ted Savage came to the Phillies and had a fairly strong rookie season in 1962. The right-handed hitting Savage had a .266 batting average with 16 stolen bases. Savage platooned with the left-handed hitting Wes Covington and they formed a fairly productive combination in left field. Savage's fine performance in 1962 allowed the Phillies to trade him to the Pittsburgh Pirates for veteran third baseman Don Hoak. The Phillies hoped Hoak would fill the void at third base and would allow them to move slugger Don Demeter back to his natural position in left field. As it turned out, the trade failed for both teams. Hoak hit poorly for the Phillies and his major league career ended in 1963. Meanwhile, Savage hit only .195 for the Pirates and then bounced around the major leagues as a spare outfielder. His best season came with the Milwaukee Brewers in 1970, when he hit .279 with 12 home runs and 50 runs batted in for a fifth place team. Unfortunately, Savage finished his career with the Kansas City Royals in 1971 after hitting only .171.

Year	Team	G	AB	Runs	Hits	2B	3B	HR	RBI	BA
1962	Phillies	127	335	54	89	11	2	7	39	.266

1963

With the dismal 1961 season fresh in the minds of baseball experts, the Phillies shocked everyone by finishing fourth in the National League with 87 victories. Now seen as an up-and-coming team under the leadership of manager Gene Mauch, the Phillies now found themselves with a possibility of challenging for the National League pennant. With a suddenly well-developed farm system and a seemingly strong nucleus, the Phillies needed a few key acquisitions to bring it all together. As for new black players, pitcher Marcelino Lopez joined the Phillies during the season. However, he was traded to the American League, where he spent the rest of his career. But the biggest acquisition came in September when Dick Allen first arrived in town. After 10 games, it was obvious to Phillies management that they needed to find a place in the lineup for him quick.

Richard Anthony Allen

Allen came up to the Phillies in 1963 as an outfielder and he started 7 games there in September. After hitting .292 in 24 at bats, the Phillies decided that Dick Allen was ready to become a big league regular. The question was where to put him. With the outfield crowded with the likes of Johnny Callison, Tony Gonzalez, and Wes Covington, the Phillies felt that third base was the position for their prized rookie. This decision allowed the Phillies to let go veteran Don Hoak and trade Don Demeter to Detroit for starting pitcher Jim Bunning. Although playing a new position in 1964, Allen hit .313 with 29 home runs and 91 runs batted in. He convincingly won the National League Rookie of the Year Award and helped lead the Phillies to their near pennant-winning performance in 1964. Despite being involved in that fracas with Frank Thomas, Allen still hit .302 in 1965. That season, Allen hit the first regular season home run in the cavernous Houston Astrodome.[10] Allen's best season came in 1966, when he hit 40 home runs and knocked in 110 runs for the fourth place Phillies. Unfortunately, a serious wrist injury cost him the final month of the 1967 season and almost ended his career. He recovered well enough in 1968 to hit 33 home runs, but the team tumbled to seventh place. Meanwhile, the problems between Allen and club management outshone his impressive statistics. Furthermore, he never could live up to the lofty expectations of the Phillies fans, who were often left speechless with the distance of some of his home runs. With rumors of alcoholism, his penchant for smoking in the dugout during games, and his persistent troubles with management, Allen was considered a disruptive influence on the team by 1969. He was dealt away to the St. Louis Cardinals before the 1970 season, bringing outfielder Curt Flood, catcher Tim McCarver, outfielder Byron Browne, and pitcher Joe Hoerner to the Phillies. It seemed impossible that Allen would ever come back to play in Philadelphia.

In his absence, the Phillies tried in vain to rebuild the franchise. Allen drifted from the Cardinals to the Dodgers and in 1972 was traded to the Chicago White Sox for pitcher Tommy John. While playing for the White Sox for three seasons, Allen hit over .300 all three seasons, hit over 30 homers twice, and won the 1972 American League Most Valuable Player Award. But by 1974, Allen was embroiled in a contract dispute with White Sox management and even held out for part of that season. Unable to meet his demands, the White Sox traded Allen to the Atlanta Braves. Although the

Braves hoped Allen would take the place of the departed slugger Hank Aaron, Allen refused to report to Atlanta. Allen went home to western Pennsylvania and debated over whether to continue playing in the major leagues. However, after color analyst Richie Ashburn and several other Phillies players visited Allen at his home, team management was convinced to trade for the veteran slugger. Ashburn sold Allen on the idea that situation in Philadelphia was vastly different than it was in 1969.

By 1975, the Phillies moved into Veterans Stadium, Ruly Carpenter assumed control of the team from his father, and a more racially tolerant attitude surrounded the team. Furthermore, the Phillies were beginning to look like a contending team who needed one more power-hitter to truly make the lineup. Meanwhile, Atlanta gave up hope that Allen would wear a Braves uniform and wanted to unload him before he totally lost his trade value. As the 1975 season started, the Phillies decided to acquire Allen and make him their regular first baseman. In return for Allen and catcher Johnny Oates, the Phillies surrendered prospects catcher Jim Essian and outfielder Barry Bonnell. With Allen in the middle of the lineup with Mike Schmidt and Greg Luzinski, the team seemed invincible. But Allen was not in good shape and with his timing off, he struggled offensively through the rest of the season. As a result, he hit only .233 with 12 home runs. The following season, Allen hit better but a nagging shoulder injury forced him to miss significant playing time. By season's end, the Phillies won the Eastern Division and opposed the Cincinnati Reds in the League Championship series. Unfortunately for Allen, his shoulder kept him inactive for the playoffs. In addition, a locker-room scuffle with fiery shortstop Larry Bowa ruined his stay in Philadelphia. Before the 1977 season, the Phillies released Allen. Meanwhile, Essian became a serviceable catcher for the Chicago White Sox and Bonnell played several seasons with the Braves and the Toronto Blue Jays. Allen was signed by the Oakland Athletics for 1977, where ended his career prior to season's end.

Year	Team	G	AB	Runs	Hits	2B	3B	HR	RBI	BA
1963	Phillies	10	24	6	7	2	1	0	2	.292
1964	Phillies	162	632	125	201	38	13	29	91	.318
1965	Phillies	161	619	93	187	31	14	20	85	.302
1966	Phillies	141	524	112	166	25	10	40	110	.317
1967	Phillies	122	463	89	142	31	10	23	77	.307
1968	Phillies	152	521	87	137	17	9	33	90	.263
1969	Phillies	118	438	79	126	23	3	32	89	.288
1975	Phillies	119	416	54	97	21	3	12	62	.233
1976	Phillies	85	298	52	80	16	1	15	49	.268

Marcelino Pons Lopez

Like Allen, the Cuban-born Marcelino Lopez arrived in Philadelphia late in the 1963 season. When he arrived in Philadelphia, Lopez was not quite 20 years old and definitely needed more seasoning in the minor leagues. In particular, Lopez struggled with his control, walking 7 batters in just 6 innings pitched. Nevertheless, Lopez got his first major league victory as a starting pitcher in that late stint with the Phillies. He was sent to the minor leagues the following season but was not recalled by the Phillies. In 1965, Lopez was traded to the California Angels, where he joined their starting rotation and had his best season, winning 14 games with a 2.93 ERA. Unfortunately, he tailed off the following season and was eventually traded to the Baltimore Orioles. With the Orioles, he was a left-handed reliever for a team that won two divisional titles, two American League pennants, and the 1970 World Series. In 1971, Lopez was traded to the Milwaukee Brewers, where he struggled and then ended his career with the Cleveland Indians the following season.

Year	Team	G	IP	W–L	SV	BB	SO	ERA
1963	Phillies	4	6	1–0	0	7	2	6.00

1964

The Phillies' infamous tumble from first place in the last few weeks of the National League regular season is seen as one of heartbreaks in baseball history. From the end of that season, the Phillies went from being an up-and-coming team to one of unrealized potential. With the exception of Vic Power, this group of players was brought to the Phillies as up-and-coming prospects who eventually found themselves on other teams. While the Phillies began to sign talented African American and Latin American players, they were unable to inspire them to their best performances while they played in Philadelphia. While it is unclear Dick Allen and Phillies' management affected the play of other black players, it was a distraction that cast a dark cloud over the entire organization.

John Edward Briggs

The left-handed hitting outfielder from Paterson, New Jersey, made the big league roster for the 1964 season and served as a reserve outfielder for the second-place Phillies. As a 20 year old rookie, the Phillies wanted to bring Johnny Briggs along slowly. This began a 7½-year stint with the Phillies in which Briggs served as a platoon outfielder. Known for both his power and speed, Briggs never seemed to reach the high expectations that the Phillies had for him. His best season for the Phillies was in 1970, when he hit .270 with 7 triples and 47 RBIs. Unable to master hitting left-handed pitching, the Phillies never could feel confident enough to make Briggs a full-time regular during his time in Philadelphia. Finally, after a slow start at the beginning of the 1971 season, Briggs was sent to the Milwaukee Brewers, where immediately became a regular player. After three reasonably productive seasons for the cellar-dwelling Brewers, Briggs ended his major league tenure with the Minnesota Twins in 1975. Briggs eventually finished his career playing in the Japanese League.

Year	Team	G	AB	Runs	Hits	2B	3B	HR	RBI	BA
1964	Phillies	61	66	16	17	2	0	1	6	.258
1965	Phillies	93	229	47	54	9	4	4	23	.236
1966	Phillies	81	255	43	72	13	5	10	23	.282
1967	Phillies	106	332	47	77	12	4	9	30	.232
1968	Phillies	110	338	36	86	13	1	7	31	.254
1969	Phillies	124	361	51	86	20	3	12	46	.238
1970	Phillies	110	341	43	92	15	7	9	47	.270
1971	Phillies	10	22	3	4	1	0	0	3	.182

Alexander Johnson

Alex Johnson was brought up to the Phillies during the 1964 season to provide some punch from the bench. Along with Dick Allen, Johnson was known as one of the Phillies' outstanding young prospects of the early 1960s. Johnson came from an athletic family, his younger brother Ron was an All-Pro running back with the New York Giants. Capable of providing both power and speed, Johnson was expected to become a fixture in the Phillies' lineup for years. Unfortunately, Johnson was also regarded as an attitude problem that the Phillies chose not tolerate. This reputation haunted Johnson for his entire career, causing him to bounce around the majors for more than a decade. After serving as a part-time starting outfielder with the Phillies in 1965, Johnson was dealt to St. Louis Cardinals in the Bill White trade. After a poor start in the 1966 season, the Cardinals sent Johnson to the minor leagues. After struggling during the 1967 season as well, Johnson was sent to the Cincinnati Reds, where he finally began to shine. In fact, Johnson won the *Sporting News* Comeback Player of the Year in 1968. After two seasons hitting over .300 for the Reds as their regular left fielder, Johnson was then dealt to the California Angels where he won the American League Batting Title in 1970.[11] However, after suffering through a contract dispute, benchings, fines, suspension, and a bout of depression the following season, Johnson was traded to the Cleveland Indians.[12] After a mediocre season with the

Indians, Johnson bounced around the American League with several teams until ending his career with the Detroit Tigers in 1976.

Year	Team	G	AB	Runs	Hits	2B	3B	HR	RBI	BA
1964	Phillies	43	109	18	33	7	1	4	18	.303
1965	Phillies	97	262	27	77	9	3	8	28	.294

Vic Pellot Power

In 1964, Vic Power returned to the city where his big league career began, this time with the Phillies. Power was the only black player to play in Philadelphia with both the Phillies and the Athletics. He joined the club in time for its fatal stretch run of 1964, when the Phillies fell short of winning the National League pennant. In between his stints in Philadelphia, Power had many productive seasons in the American League. Known for his slick defensive work at first base, Power won several Gold Gloves during the ten years away from Philadelphia. When acquired from the Los Angeles Angels, the Phillies hoped Power would fill the hole at first base that John Herrnstein and Roy Sievers could not. But after just 18 games and 48 at-bats, Power's days with the Phillies were numbered when the club traded for veteran slugger Frank Thomas, who finished the season as the starting first baseman. Power returned to the Angels for the following season, where he eventually ended his career with in 1965.

Year	Team	G	AB	Runs	Hits	2B	3B	HR	RBI	BA
1964	Phillies	18	48	1	10	4	0	0	3	.208

Adolfo Emelio Phillips (Lopez)

Originally from Panama, Adolfo Phillips arrived in Philadelphia late in the 1964 season. Phillips was expected to add both power and speed as a spare outfielder for the Phillies' September stretch run. After 13 games in 1964, Phillips spent most of the 1965 with the Phillies, getting into 41 games and hitting .230. After starting with the Phillies in the 1966 season, Phillips was dealt with pitcher Ferguson Jenkins to the Chicago Cubs for veteran pitchers Larry Jackson and Bob Buhl. While Jackson and Buhl were expected to add veteran stability to the Phillies' staff, Jenkins and Phillips became part of the Cubs' rebuilding program. While Jackson and Buhl only lasted a couple of seasons with the Phillies, both Jenkins and Phillips became productive players during that time. While Jenkins began a long Hall of Fame career as a starting pitcher, Phillips became the Cubs' starting centerfielder. After productive seasons in 1966 and 1967, Phillips slumped in 1968 and was shipped to the expansion Montreal Expos in 1969, where illnesses and injuries hampered his performance. At the age of 30, Phillips finished his career with a short stint with the Cleveland Indians in 1971.

Year	Team	G	AB	Runs	Hits	2B	3B	HR	RBI	BA
1964	Phillies	13	13	4	3	0	0	0	0	.231
1965	Phillies	41	87	14	20	4	0	3	5	.230
1966	Phillies	2	3	0	0	0	0	0	0	.000

1965

After the crushing disappointment of 1964, the fate of the 1965 season was preordained. The failure of the previous season cast a pall over the entire team and affected their overall performance. Things got worse when the Dick Allen–Frank Thomas brawl took place. The controversy surrounding the team became such a distraction that the Phillies fell to sixth place in the National League standings. As for new players, two pitchers who had better days elsewhere came up to the Phillies in 1965. Ferguson Jenkins arrived in Philadelphia as a reliever, but became more successful as a starter with the Chicago Cubs. Grant Jackson came to the Phillies as a starter, but became better known for his relief work with the Orioles, Yankees, and Pirates.

Grant Dwight Jackson

In September of 1965, Grant Jackson first arrived in Philadelphia and received his first major league win. Although the Phillies expected big things from the young lefthander, they chose to send him back to the minors for more seasoning in 1966. Jackson stayed with the Phillies for good in 1967, pitching primarily out of the bullpen. Jackson finally made the starting rotation in 1969 and had a strong season with a fifth place team, winning 14 games with 180 strikeouts. Unfortunately, Jackson faltered to just 5 wins and an ERA of 5.28 the following season. Rather than hope for a reversal to his 1969 form, the Phillies traded Jackson to the Baltimore Orioles for then ballyhooed minor league slugger Roger Freed.[13] While Jackson provided reliable relief pitching for the American League Champion Orioles, Freed proved disappointing, hitting .221. From that time forward, Jackson had a habit of pitching with winning teams. He played for five division champions, two American League champions, and was on the 1979 World Champion Pittsburgh Pirates. Jackson's career ended with the Pirates in 1982.

Year	Team	G	IP	W–L	SV	BB	SO	ERA
1965	Phillies	6	14	1–1	0	5	15	7.24
1966	Phillies	2	2	0–0	0	3	0	5.40
1967	Phillies	43	84	2–3	1	43	83	3.84
1968	Phillies	33	61	1–6	1	20	49	2.95
1969	Phillies	38	253	14–18	1	92	180	3.34
1970	Phillies	32	150	5–15	0	61	104	5.28

Ferguson Arthur Jenkins

Chatham, Ontario, native Ferguson Jenkins arrived in Philadelphia at the end of the 1965 season. The Phillies initially envisioned the hard-throwing Jenkins as a reliever who could eventually emerge as the team's closer. In that short trial in 1965, Jenkins pitched 12 innings and struck out 10 batters. Jenkins began the following season in the Phillies' bullpen, but only pitched one game before being traded to the Cubs. The Phillies sent Jenkins and outfielder Adolfo Phillips to the Cubs for veteran pitchers Bob Buhl and Larry Jackson. Buhl and Jackson were supposed to add stability to the pitching staff and serve as the final pieces of the puzzle for the contending Phillies. It was during that 1966 season that the Cubs discovered that Jenkins could become a quality starting pitcher. The following season, Jenkins began a string of six 20-win seasons for the Cubs. Meanwhile, Buhl won only 6 games in the 1966 season and was gone the following season. Jackson managed to pitch three seasons in Philadelphia, winning 41 games before retiring prior to the 1969 season. Needless to say, based on Jenkins' performance, the Cubs got the better end of the deal. Known as one of the most durable pitchers in baseball history, Jenkins pitched in the major leagues until 1983. Jenkins won 283 games during a 19 year major league career which included stints with the Phillies, Cubs, Rangers, Red Sox, Rangers (again), and finishing with the Cubs. Of his 283 victories, only 2 of them came in a Phillies uniform. One can only imagine how the Phillies' staff would have looked with Jenkins joining Jim Bunning, Chris Short, Rick Wise, and then later on, Steve Carlton.

Year	Team	G	IP	W–L	SV	BB	SO	ERA
1965	Phillies	7	12	2–1	1	2	10	2.25
1966	Phillies	1	2	0–0	0	1	2	4.50

1966

As the shock of the 1964 collapse disappeared by 1966, the Phillies hoped to retool the club and bring a title home to Philadelphia. The team brought in first baseman Bill White and shortstop Dick Groat in a trade with the St.

Louis Cardinals in the hopes of improving their chances in the National League. While White and Groat did their jobs in 1966, the Phillies still only finished fourth and as age crept up on the team's nucleus, the team had to retool again after the season.

William Dekova White

Bill White came to the Phillies in a trade with the St. Louis Cardinals. Prior to the trade, White served with distinction as the Cardinals' starting first baseman. While at St. Louis, White regularly hit over 20 home runs and knocked in over 100 runs three times. He was a key component on the Cardinals' World Championship team of 1964, hitting .303 with 21 home runs and 102 runs batted in while playing a steady defensive first base. Meanwhile, the contending Phillies were unable to find a solid first baseman. They went through the likes of the aging Roy Sievers, the light-hitting John Herrnstein, and poor fielding Dick Stuart before trading for White in 1966. In his first season, White delivered exactly what the Phillies asked of him, hitting 22 home runs and knocking in 103 runs. He provided solid lineup support for Dick Allen, who hit a career high 40 home runs that season. Unfortunately, a nagging foot injury hampered White's effectiveness in 1967, and he hit only 8 home runs. After hitting only .239 in 1968, White was sent back to St. Louis, where he finished out his playing career. After that, however, he became a color analyst for both the New York Yankees and ABC's Monday Night baseball and later served as National League president. Known for his reliability and class as a player, announcer, and baseball executive, White did much for the advancement of African Americans in major league baseball.

Year	Team	G	AB	Runs	Hits	2B	3B	HR	RBI	BA
1966	Phillies	159	577	85	159	23	6	22	103	.276
1967	Phillies	110	308	29	77	6	2	8	33	.250
1968	Phillies	127	385	34	92	16	2	9	40	.239

1967

As the Phillies desperately tried to remain in contention for the pennant, they made several trades in order to improve their chances. However, injuries to Dick Allen, Bill White, and pitcher Chris Short dropped the Phillies to fifth place in the standings. Allen's wrist injury in particular became controversial because the true cause of the injury was under speculation. Furthermore, Allen's relationship with management and skipper Gene Mauch became such a distraction that it kept the team from performing at its peak.

Also, because of the racial climate of the neighborhood surrounding it, Connie Mack Stadium became an uninviting place for most Phillies fans. With all of this in mind, the Phillies organization now found itself in serious trouble.

Ricardo Emelindo Joseph

The Phillies brought up Rick Joseph to fill in at first base for the injured Bill White. Originally from the Dominican Republic, Joseph, who previously played for the Kansas City Athletics, batted .220 in 41 at-bats for the Phillies in 1967. Despite those fairly mediocre numbers, Joseph made the Phillies' roster as a utility infielder the following season. Joseph could play the corner infield positions as well as the outfield. After batting just .219 in 1968, Joseph hit a very respectable .273 with 15 doubles in 1969. Joseph played 53 games at third base that season and seemed like he was headed for more the following season. Unfortunately, in 1970, Joseph slumped to .227 and was let go by the Phillies, never to play again in the major leagues.

Year	Team	G	AB	Runs	Hits	2B	3B	HR	RBI	BA
1967	Phillies	17	41	4	9	2	0	1	5	.220
1968	Phillies	66	155	20	34	5	0	3	12	.219
1969	Phillies	99	264	35	72	15	0	6	37	.273
1970	Phillies	71	119	7	27	2	1	3	10	.227

1968

The Phillies ceased to remain a contender for the National League pennant in 1968, falling into a seventh place tie with the Los Angeles Dodgers with only 76 victories. Also, with expansion coming in 1969, the Phillies parted with some of their veteran players and began a rebuilding program. Unfortunately, it is often difficult to begin a rebuilding program when there are two new teams in the National League. Therefore, the rebuilding program took a very long time. The Phillies did not have their next winning season until 1975.

Roberto Ramirez Pena

Roberto Pena became the surprise of the 1968 season as he replaced the injured Bobby Wine at shortstop. Although he struggled with the Chicago Cubs in 1965 and 1966, Pena made the Phillies in spring training in 1968 and took over the shortstop position. Originally from the Dominican Republic,

Pena hit .260 while knocking 38 runs, but he was criticized for his lack of range at shortstop. Although Pena had a relatively strong 1968 season, the Phillies had both Don Money and Larry Bowa in the minor leagues. Both could play shortstop and had many years in front of them. Therefore, the Phillies left Pena unprotected in the 1969 expansion draft. Chosen by the San Diego Padres, Pena became more of a utility infielder, starting games at all four infield positions. He later played for the Oakland Athletics and finished his career with the Milwaukee Brewers after hitting .237 in 1971.

Year	Team	G	AB	Runs	Hits	2B	3B	HR	RBI	BA
1968	Phillies	138	500	56	130	13	2	1	38	.260

Larry Eugene Hisle

Considered the jewel of the Phillies farm system in 1968, Hisle came to the big leagues for a trial in September of that year. Penciled in as the starting centerfielder for the 1969, Hisle's presence allowed the Phillies to let longtime starter Tony Gonzalez go to the San Diego Padres in the expansion draft. Hisle had a very effective rookie season, hitting 20 home runs and stealing 18 bases. Since he was only 22 years old at the time, Hisle looked like a fixture in the lineup for many years to come. But while he was in the organization, Hisle was a quiet, withdrawn player who seemed unhappy with his situation. This unhappiness probably affected his performance during the 1970 season. With Dick Allen traded to the Cardinals and Curt Flood holding out, Hisle felt uncomfortable and alone playing in Philadelphia. Hisle hit only .205 with 10 home runs in 1970 and .197 in 36 games the following year. During the 1971 season, Hisle was sent down to the minor leagues and eventually traded to the Los Angeles Dodgers for first baseman Tommy Hutton. Hisle did not go quietly, criticizing the Phillies organization for their poor treatment of black players. Although Phillies management did not welcome Hisle's quotes, more of a commitment was made by the club to improve their relations with black players from that point in time. While Hisle played the 1972 season in Albuquerque, Hutton began a Phillies career that lasted until 1977. Also unable to utilize his considerable talents, the Dodgers traded Hisle to the St. Louis Cardinals, who then traded him to the Minnesota Twins, where he finally blossomed.[14] Like Oscar Gamble, Hisle had his best days in the American League. Hisle led the league in RBIs in 1977 while with the Twins and then signed with the Milwaukee Brewers as a free agent. Hisle had another strong season with the Brewers in 1978, knocking in 115 runs and leading them to their best ever record. The Brewers won 95 games the following season, but Hisle sat out most of that season with a shoulder problem that never fully healed. This injury kept Hisle out of action for much of the 1979 and 1980 seasons, never playing more than 26 games. Injuries finally forced Hisle to retire in 1982, just as the Brewers were winning their first ever American

League pennant. Nevertheless, once away from the tense environment, Hisle enjoyed a productive major league career.

Year	Team	G	AB	Runs	Hits	2B	3B	HR	RBI	BA
1968	Phillies	7	11	1	4	1	0	0	1	.364
1969	Phillies	145	482	75	128	23	5	20	56	.266
1970	Phillies	126	405	52	83	22	4	10	44	.205
1971	Phillies	36	76	7	15	3	0	0	3	.197

1969

The Phillies truly hit rock bottom in 1969. Dick Allen was suspended three times during the season, Manager Bob Skinner lost his job, and attendance dropped. Although the Phillies had many black players on its roster in 1969, the situation involving Dick Allen did not engender much enthusiasm from the African American community. With construction beginning on a new stadium in South Philadelphia, management hoped that the move would end the problems. But with only 63 wins and faced with the loss of its most marketable player, the Phillies scrambled to pick up the pieces and turn around the franchise. No new African American players joined the Phillies in 1969, but players such as Larry Hisle, Grant Jackson, Tony Taylor, and Rick Joseph enjoyed relatively productive seasons in the midst of chaos. Also, despite all of the distractions and controversy, Dick Allen still hit 32 home runs in just 118 games.

1970

This was the first year of the post–Dick Allen era in Philadelphia, but it was far from boring. The season was already sullied by Curt Flood's refusal to play in Philadelphia when another key player in that deal, catcher Tim McCarver, broke his hand and missed over 100 games of action. With the legacy of Allen and Flood combined with another dismal 5th place finish, Philadelphia became known as baseball's version of Siberia, especially for African American players. It would take some time before the Phillies managed to shake this reputation. As for the players then on the team, African American players often felt uncomfortable playing in Philadelphia.

Byron Ellis Browne

Byron Browne was a throw-in as part of the Dick Allen–Curt Flood deal. Browne was a starting left fielder for the Chicago Cubs in 1966, when he hit

16 home runs and struck out 143 times. Browne was sent to the minors the following season and bounced around the National League with Houston in 1968 and St. Louis in 1969 as a spare outfielder. Prior to the 1970 season, Browne was dealt to the Phillies as part of the Dick Allen–Curt Flood trade with the Cardinals. Presumably, Browne was to continue his role as a backup outfielder. However, with Curt Flood's refusal to play for the Phillies combined with the team's abundance of left-handed hitting outfielders and Larry Hisle's poor season, the right-handed hitting Browne played more than expected in 1970. After batting .248 with 17 doubles and 10 home runs, Browne played less the following two seasons before his major league career ended with 1972 Phillies.

Year	Team	G	AB	Runs	Hits	2B	3B	HR	RBI	BA
1970	Phillies	104	270	29	57	17	2	10	36	.248
1971	Phillies	58	68	5	14	3	0	3	5	.206
1972	Phillies	21	21	2	4	0	0	0	0	.190

Oscar Charles Gamble

Oscar Gamble came to the Phillies with relief pitcher Dick Selma from the Chicago Cubs for the aging Johnny Callison. The trade initially looked quite good as Gamble showed flashes of talent as a rookie and Selma had a very strong 1970 season out of the Phillies' bullpen. The left-handed hitting Gamble was only 20 years old when he became part of the Phillies' outfield mix. He, too, benefited from the absence of Curt Flood, which probably kept him from spending any more time in the minor leagues. Gamble became a platoon outfielder as a rookie in 1970, hitting .261 but with only one home run. In that season, hit by Gamble knocked in catcher Tim McCarver to score the winning run in the 10th inning of the final game played at Connie Mack Stadium. That run touched off a riot in which Phillies fans looted the crumbling edifice in the hopes of taking home a valuable souvenir.[15] The following season, Gamble was expected to play a major role in the outfield as the team moved to newly constructed Veterans Stadium. Unfortunately, he hit only .221 with 6 home runs. Reduced to a reserve role in 1972, Gamble hit only .237 and was dealt with outfielder Roger Freed to the Cleveland Indians for outfielder Del Unser. Once Gamble arrived in the American League, he came into his own. Although he hit 20 home runs for the Indians in 1973, Gamble became better known for the length of his hair and his marriage to a well-known singer. But Gamble continued to hit well in the American League, hitting 31 home runs with the Chicago White Sox in 1977. He also played in the World Series for the New York Yankees in 1976 and 1981. Clearly, Gamble played his best baseball after he left Philadelphia.

Year	Team	G	AB	Runs	Hits	2B	3B	HR	RBI	BA
1970	Phillies	88	275	31	72	12	4	1	19	.261
1971	Phillies	92	280	24	62	11	1	6	23	.221
1972	Phillies	74	135	17	32	5	2	1	13	.237

Guillermo Montanez (Naranjo)

Willie Montanez came to the Phillies from the Cardinals as compensation for Curt Flood's refusal to play in 1970. Although Flood was the cornerstone of the deal with the Cardinals, the Phillies probably received more productivity from Montanez. The aging Flood seemed like he had only a few seasons left to play while Montanez had 4½ productive years with the Phillies before being traded. After spending almost all of the 1970 season in the minors, the Phillies brought Montanez up for a September trial. He evidently showed enough to become the regular centerfielder in 1971. Given the chance to play every day, Montanez exploded for 30 home runs and 99 runs batted in as a rookie. Although more comfortable at first base, Montanez started in the outfield for the next 2½ seasons. After hitting those 30 home runs, he never came close to that total in his career. He did, however, lead the league in doubles in 1972 and hit a strong .304 in 1974, his first full season at first base. Montanez, a native of Puerto Rico, played the game with a certain flair that made him popular with the fans. He would twirl his bat when approaching the plate and gyrate his glove after making a play in the field. Despite his popularity and productivity, Montanez was traded to the San Francisco Giants for centerfielder Garry Maddox during the 1975 season. Although Montanez drove in 101 runs in 1975, the Giants traded him to the Atlanta Braves, where he enjoyed another two productive seasons. He then bounced around for teams in both leagues until his career ended in 1982, ironically as a pinch-hitter with the Phillies.

Year	Team	G	AB	Runs	Hits	2B	3B	HR	RBI	BA
1970	Phillies	18	25	3	6	0	0	0	3	.240
1971	Phillies	158	599	78	153	27	6	30	99	.255
1972	Phillies	147	531	60	131	39	3	13	64	.247
1973	Phillies	146	552	69	145	16	5	11	65	.263
1974	Phillies	143	527	55	160	33	1	7	79	.304
1975	Phillies	21	84	9	24	8	0	2	16	.288
1982	Phillies	18	16	0	1	0	0	0	1	.063

1971

The Phillies moved into their new home, Veterans Stadium, in 1971. Although it was one of those typical multi-purpose stadiums with Astroturf, the Phillies hoped that with the new stadium came a new attitude and a boost in attendance. Although attendance improved in 1971, the performance did not. The Phillies finished in the National League East cellar, winning only 67 games. Although no new black players came to town, Willie Montanez became one of the top rookies of 1971, slamming 30 home runs. However, many black players left town, including Tony Taylor, Johnny Briggs, and Larry Hisle.

1972

The year 1972 offered both the rock bottom and the beginning of a successful rebuilding of the Phillies franchise. The Phillies finished last in the Eastern Division with a dismal 59–97 record. What makes this record even worse is that starting pitcher Steve Carlton won 27 of those games, as well as a well-deserved Cy Young Award. After the 1972 season, the Phillies began to rapidly dismantle the team. The Phillies provided opportunities for players still looking for their niche in the major leagues. As for new black players, only Bill Robinson joined the Phillies during the 1972 season.

William Henry Robinson

After failing live up to high expectations, Bill Robinson was let go by the New York Yankees in 1969. Blessed with outstanding athleticism and a powerful bat, Robinson became an enigma who then bounced around the minor leagues until he ended up with the Phillies in 1972. The Phillies offered Robinson a new opportunity to succeed in the big leagues at a time when Philadelphia was viewed as a difficult place for African American players. Considered a retread by major league standards, the Phillies acquired Robinson in a minor league deal with the Chicago White Sox. Already 29 years old, little was expected from Robinson when brought up to the Phillies. However, since he was hitting .306 at Triple-A Eugene, the talent-starved Phillies decided to give Robinson a chance. Although he only hit a mediocre .239 in 1972, Robinson had a productive 1973 season, slamming 25 home runs. After struggling in the 1974 season, the Phillies traded Robinson to the rival Pittsburgh Pirates for pitcher Wayne Simpson. Unexpectedly, Robinson became a very productive regular for the Pirates for several seasons while Simpson only pitched 7 games for the Phillies. Robinson was a starting outfielder for the World Champion Pirates of 1979. After Robinson's many years in Pittsburgh, the Pirates dealt him back to the Phillies for outfielder Dick Davis, and Robinson ended his playing career there in 1983. Robinson later served as a coach for the New York Mets, a studio analyst for ESPN, and a manager in the Phillies' minor league system. Although Robinson had better days in Pittsburgh, his first stint with the Phillies established him as a major league player.

Year	Team	G	AB	Runs	Hits	2B	3B	HR	RBI	BA
1972	Phillies	82	188	19	45	9	1	8	21	.239
1973	Phillies	124	452	62	130	32	1	25	65	.288
1974	Phillies	100	280	32	66	14	1	5	29	.236
1982	Phillies	35	69	6	19	6	0	3	19	.261
1983	Phillies	10	7	0	1	0	0	0	2	.143

1973

Prior to the 1973 season, the Phillies made wholesale changes. The club made major trades with Cleveland, Milwaukee, and Minnesota, which brought several veteran players to Philadelphia. Furthermore, the Phillies decided to bring up several young players in order to evaluate whether they could contribute to the team in the future. Despite all of the changes, the Phillies still finished last in the Eastern Division. However, they seemed to make some progress. The two black players who were new to the Phillies were outfielder Cesar Tovar and third baseman Jose Pagan. Both were tested veterans, but both only lasted one season in Philadelphia.

Jose Antonio Pagan (Rodriguez)

Jose Pagan arrived in Philadelphia to serve as a fall back option in case of the failure of then rookie Mike Schmidt. Although Schmidt struggled mightily in 1973, the Phillies chose to stick by him rather than going to the veteran Pagan. Prior to his arrival to Veterans Stadium, Pagan was known as a steady fielder who could provide some clutch hitting. He played a key role on the 1962 National League Champion San Francisco Giants and the 1971 World Champion Pittsburgh Pirates. In fact, Pagan drove in the winning run in the eighth inning of Game 7 of the 1971 World Series.[16] Despite his experience, Pagan was at the end of his career by 1973 and could offer very little to the rebuilding Phillies. After hitting just .205 as a utility infielder, Pagan ended his major league career.

Year	Team	G	AB	Runs	Hits	2B	3B	HR	RBI	BA
1973	Phillies	46	78	4	16	5	0	0	5	.205

Cesar Leonardo Tovar (Pepito)

Always known for his durability and versatility, Cesar Tovar came to Philadelphia from the Minnesota Twins. The Phillies shipped outfielder Joe

Lis, relief pitcher Ken Sanders, and starting pitcher Ken Reynolds to the Twins in order to acquire the versatile Tovar. Since Lis and Reynolds were considered failed prospects and the veteran Sanders had yet to pitch a game for the Phillies, the trade looked pretty good on the surface. While in Minnesota, Tovar played on an American League Champion and two AL Western Division championship teams. Primarily an outfielder, Tovar once played all nine positions in a game in 1968. A regular for the Twins for many seasons, Tovar was expected to fill an outfield position for the Phillies in 1973. Plagued by knee problems throughout that season, he missed large portions of the season. Furthermore, Tovar played equal amounts of time at third base and second base as well as the outfield. Without a stable position and uncomfortable with the National League, Tovar was sold to the Texas Rangers prior to the 1974 season.[17] He finished his major league career with the New York Yankees in 1976. A few years later, Tovar attempted a comeback by playing in the newly formed Inter-American League in the early 1980s. The league folded after a short time and Tovar's playing career officially ended.

Year	Team	G	AB	Runs	Hits	2B	3B	HR	RBI	BA
1973	Phillies	97	328	49	88	18	4	1	21	.268

1974

After several dreadful seasons in Philadelphia, the Phillies finally made serious strides in 1974. Prospects such as third baseman Mike Schmidt, outfielder Greg Luzinski, shortstop Larry Bowa, and catcher Bob Boone now began to blossom as regulars. Although the team still had some weaknesses, the Phillies started to provide the first real excitement for the home crowd at newly constructed Veterans Stadium. Additions such as second baseman Dave Cash provided the first examples of the fine moves made by General Manager Paul Owens. Finally, the atmosphere around the Phillies began to resemble a more modern franchise that utilized the talents of African Americans and Latin Americans. Other new black players were relief pitcher Jesus Hernaiz and reserve outfielder Ollie Brown.

Ollie Lee Brown

Ollie Brown arrived in Philadelphia during an odyssey that also took him to San Francisco, San Diego, Oakland, Milwaukee, California, and Houston. Brown came from an athletic family; his brother Oscar played a few seasons as an outfielder with the Atlanta Braves and brother Willie was a halfback with the Los Angeles Rams and the Philadelphia Eagles. Once considered an outstanding prospect with the Giants, Ollie Brown had a few respectable seasons with the San Diego Padres before bouncing around the American League in 1972 and 1973. Blessed with an outstanding throwing arm, Brown also offered some power from the right side of the plate. In 1974, Brown began spring training with the California Angels but was sold to the Houston Astros prior to the beginning of the regular season. Then in June, Brown was sold again, this time to the Phillies. In his four years with the Phillies, Brown did a credible job as a spare outfielder and pinch hitter. After experiencing two divisional titles with the Phillies, his career ended after the 1977 season.

Year	Team	G	AB	Runs	Hits	2B	3B	HR	RBI	BA
1974	Phillies	43	99	11	24	5	2	4	13	.242
1975	Phillies	84	145	19	44	12	0	6	26	.303
1976	Phillies	92	209	30	53	10	1	5	30	.254
1977	Phillies	53	70	5	17	3	1	1	13	.243

David Cash, Jr.

By 1974, the Phillies decided to make a change at second base. After four years of the slick fielding but weak hitting Denny Doyle, the Phillies were in need of a leadoff hitter who could play a decent second base. With Dave Cash, the Phillies found their man. Cash began his career with the Pittsburgh Pirates when he succeeded the legendary Hall of Famer Bill Mazeroski. Cash also was the Pirates' starting second baseman when they won the 1971 World Series. However, by the end of the 1973 season, the Pirates decided that Rennie Stennett would play second base in the future. Stuck with two good players at the same position, the Pirates sent the very marketable Cash to the Phillies for pitcher Ken Brett. Although Brett had a good 1973 season for the Phillies, acquiring Cash filled an absolute necessity. Given the chance to play every day without competition, Cash flourished in his three seasons with the Phillies while Brett only played two seasons with the Pirates. Known as a contact hitter, Cash hit over .300 twice and played a steady second base. A very durable player, Cash only missed two games in his three years with the Phillies. In 1975, he led the National League in hits with 213 and set a league record for at-bats. Cash also led the league's second basemen in double plays in both 1974 and 1975. He also helped create a winning atmosphere in Philadelphia and (along with Larry Bowa and Mike Schmidt) inspired the "Yes We Can" slogan that helped motivate the contending Phillies. For the first time, an African American player could inspire the city's baseball fans to come to the ballpark with optimism. This upbeat attitude worked because in his final season in Philadelphia in 1976, Cash hit leadoff for the Eastern Division champions. Unfortunately, Cash chose to utilize his newly realized free agency rights and signed with the Montreal Expos. The move probably hurt Cash more than it affected the Phillies. After a productive 1977 season for the Expos, Cash slumped in 1978 and by the end of the 1980 campaign, he ended his career with the San Diego Padres. Meanwhile, the Phillies won three more divisional titles and a World Championship. It was clear that Cash's best days were spent in a Phillies uniform.

Year	Team	G	AB	Runs	Hits	2B	3B	HR	RBI	BA
1974	Phillies	162	687	89	206	26	11	2	58	.300
1975	Phillies	162	699	111	213	40	3	4	57	.305
1976	Phillies	160	666	92	189	14	12	1	56	.284

Jesus Rafael Hernaiz (Chuito)

During the 1974 season, the Phillies looked for help in their bullpen and found Puerto Rican native Jesus Hernaiz in their farm system. Hernaiz was signed as a free agent by the Phillies after being released by the Chicago Cubs organization. Hernaiz slowly worked his way up the Phillies chain until 1974. Although he began the 1974 campaign in Triple-A Toledo, Hernaiz was simply unhittable, winning five games with a 0.94 ERA in 20 relief appearances. This sterling performance inspired the Phillies to bring Hernaiz up to the major leagues. Although Hernaiz finished the season with the Phillies, he could not assume a significant role in the bullpen. Plagued by a lack of control, Hernaiz was sent back to Toledo, never again pitching in the majors.[18]

Year	Team	G	IP	W–L	SV	BB	SO	ERA
1974	Phillies	27	41	2–3	1	25	16	5.93

1975

The 1975 season provided baseball fans a glimpse into the future success of the Phillies. The club even spent a few days in first place in July before finishing second in the Eastern Division to the Pittsburgh Pirates. Already blessed with some homegrown products from the farm system, the Phillies now found themselves in the position of trying to make the right acquisitions in order to bring a championship to Philadelphia. Some of those players were African American and Latin American, meaning that the face of success in Philadelphia now had a multi-cultural look.

Garry Lee Maddox

Early in the 1975 season, Garry Maddox came to the Phillies in a trade with the San Francisco Giants. General Manager Paul Owens brought Maddox to Philadelphia to become the club's starting centerfielder. Unfortunately, it took Phillies fans some time to warm up to Maddox, since he came to Philadelphia at the expense of popular first baseman Willie Montanez. However, once fans saw the graceful Maddox roam centerfield in Veterans Stadium, they soon forgot all about Montanez. Despite a knee injury, Maddox played a strong centerfield and hit .291 for the rest of the 1975 season. His performance coincided with the Phillies' strong second place finish, giving them hope for winning the National League Eastern Division title in 1976. Their hopes became reality as the Phillies won the title in 1976, led in part by Maddox hitting a lusty .330 and playing an excellent center field. The 1976 season established Maddox as a solid fixture in the Phillies lineup for another nine seasons. During his time in Philadelphia, Maddox won several Gold Gloves and hit consistently well. "Two thirds of the world is covered by water," lamented Mets broadcaster Ralph Kiner, "The other third is covered by Garry Maddox."[19] Not coincidently, the Phillies won five Eastern Division titles, two National League Championships, and their first ever World Series title during Maddox's tenure. Furthermore, Maddox also became a leader in the Philadelphia community, taking part in many area charitable enterprises. After suffering through some knee injuries, he finished his career with the Phillies. He also served as a color analyst for Phillies telecasts and radio broadcasts. During his time with the Phillies, Maddox probably did more than anyone to improve the situation for black players in Philadelphia.

Year	Team	G	AB	Runs	Hits	2B	3B	HR	RBI	BA
1975	Phillies	99	374	50	109	25	8	4	46	.291
1976	Phillies	146	531	75	175	37	6	6	68	.330
1977	Phillies	139	571	85	167	27	10	14	74	.292
1978	Phillies	155	568	62	172	34	3	11	68	.288
1979	Phillies	148	548	70	154	28	6	13	61	.281
1980	Phillies	143	549	59	142	31	3	11	73	.259
1981	Phillies	94	323	37	85	7	1	5	40	.263
1982	Phillies	119	412	39	117	27	2	8	61	.284
1983	Phillies	97	324	27	89	14	2	4	32	.275
1984	Phillies	77	241	29	68	11	0	5	19	.282

Wayne Kirby Simpson

Wayne Simpson came to the Phillies late in the 1975 season. He was attempting to come back from arm and shoulder injuries that robbed him of much of his velocity. As a rookie, Simpson had an outstanding 1970 season for the National League Champion Cincinnati Reds in which he won 14 games and lost only three. Unfortunately, towards the end of that season Simpson suffered arm injuries and never was the same again. After bouncing around from the Reds to the Kansas City Royals to the Pittsburgh Pirates, the Phillies received Simpson in a trade for outfielder Bill Robinson. After a successful minor league season at Triple-A Toledo, winning 12 games with a 2.17 ERA, the Phillies gave Simpson a September trial. Although Simpson pitched reasonably well for the Phillies in 1975, he found himself buried behind Steve Carlton, Jim Lonborg, Larry Christenson, and Tom Underwood. In addition, the Phillies traded for veteran ace Jim Kaat, who won 20 games for the Chicago White Sox in 1975. As a result, the Phillies sold Simpson to the California Angels prior to the 1976 season. Simpson finished his career with the Angels in 1977.

Year	Team	G	IP	W–L	SV	BB	SO	ERA
1975	Phillies	7	31	1–0	0	11	19	3.19

1976

In the nation's bicentennial year, the Phillies looked like they put it all together for the first time in more than a decade, with solid starting pitching led by Steve Carlton and Jim Lonborg, fine hitters in Mike Schmidt and Greg Luzinski, and excellent fielding led by catcher Bob Boone, shortstop Larry Bowa, and centerfielder Garry Maddox. This was also the first winning team that depended on the contributions of African American players such as Maddox, second baseman Dave Cash, and first baseman Dick Allen. As for new black players, the Phillies added Bobby Tolan for bench strength and second base prospect Fred Andrews for a September trial. When the season ended, the Phillies won their first of three consecutive Eastern Division titles.

Fred Andrews

As the Phillies headed for the top of the National League standings, the farm system headed by Dallas Green still produced some top flight talent. The continued success of the farm system gave management flexibility to make trades in order to improve the team. Some of these prospects eventually made it to the Phillies, others were traded to different organizations, but the rest of them never really made it in the big leagues. Fred Andrews falls into that final category. After being touted as the second baseman of the future, Andrews was brought up to the Phillies in September of 1976. When the Phillies lost Dave Cash to free agency, the Phillies had a choice to make: go with the rookie Andrews or trade for a veteran to fill the void at second base. After some deliberation, the Phillies acquired veteran second baseman Ted Sizemore from the Dodgers to play the position regularly. Although Andrews began the 1977 season with the Phillies, he was sent back to the minor leagues after only 23 at-bats. The Phillies were never convinced that Andrews could consistently hit major league pitching. Although he was later traded to the New York Mets organization, Andrews never again appeared in the major leagues.

Year	Team	G	AB	Runs	Hits	2B	3B	HR	RBI	BA
1976	Phillies	4	6	1	4	0	0	0	0	.667
1977	Phillies	12	23	3	4	0	1	0	2	.174

Robert Tolan

Veteran outfielder Bobby Tolan joined the Phillies in 1976 as a free agent after gaining his release from the San Diego Padres.[20] Tolan came to Philadelphia after some excellent seasons with the Cincinnati Reds in the late 1960s and early 1970s. He also came with a history of knee problems, sitting out the entire 1971 campaign and part of the 1974 season. Tolan was expected to serve as fourth outfielder and provide punch from the left-hand side of the plate. Tolan did both fairly well in 1976, hitting .261 and stealing 10 bases. He began the 1977 season with Phillies, but after a slow start he was sent to Pittsburgh Pirates. Tolan finished out his career with a second stint with the San Diego Padres in 1979.

Year	Team	G	AB	Runs	Hits	2B	3B	HR	RBI	BA
1976	Phillies	110	272	32	71	7	0	5	35	.261
1977	Phillies	15	16	1	2	0	0	0	1	.125

1977

Although the Phillies won the Eastern Division title in 1976, they still had some holes to fill if they hoped to win a World Championship. They had to fill needs at first base to replace the waived Dick Allen and second base to replace free agent Dave Cash. In addition, the Phillies wanted to improve their depth and overall team speed. Furthermore, Cash's departure left the Phillies without a leadoff hitter. After Garry Maddox failed to feel comfortable batting leadoff, the team traded with St. Louis for speedy outfielder Bake McBride. Although the team appeared to take shape by winning the Eastern Division title again, they could not overcome the Los Angeles Dodgers in the League Championship series.

Arnold Ray "Bake" McBride

Known for his blazing speed, Bake McBride came to the Phillies in a trade with the St. Louis Cardinals, who received pitcher Tom Underwood. While McBride became a fixture in the Phillies' lineup, Underwood wound up pitching for the Toronto Blue Jays the following season. McBride actually filled two holes for the Phillies, one as a leadoff hitter and also as the starting right fielder. The Phillies began the season with Garry Maddox as the leadoff hitter. But despite his speed, Maddox grew increasingly uncomfortable with the role. With the presence of McBride, Maddox could move down in the lineup where he was better suited. Although he never played right field before, he filled the position quite nicely. In just 280 at-bats, McBride hit .339 with 11 home runs and 27 stolen bases. His acquisition catapulted the Phillies toward the 1977 Eastern Division Championship. After that season, McBride became a popular fixture in the Phillies' lineup. He could provide speed and power for a team in need of both. Unfortunately, McBride often suffered from nagging injuries that limited his availability. This was especially true during the 1978 season, when he missed 40 games. However, by 1980, McBride temporarily solved his injury problems and he enjoyed his best all around season (batting .309 and driving in 87 runs), helping the Phillies to their first ever World Championship. The following season, McBride suffered through knee injuries that limited his effectiveness. Prior to the 1982 season, McBride was traded to the Cleveland Indians. After a blistering start, McBride suffered a season-ending knee injury. In 1983, a shoulder injury ended his season early. Weary of his injury problems, the Indians let McBride go after the 1983 season, ending his career.

Year	Team	G	AB	Runs	Hits	2B	3B	HR	RBI	BA
1977	Phillies	85	280	55	95	20	5	11	41	.339
1978	Phillies	122	472	68	127	20	4	10	49	.269
1979	Phillies	147	582	82	163	16	12	12	60	.280
1980	Phillies	137	554	68	171	33	10	9	87	.309
1981	Phillies	58	221	26	60	17	1	2	21	.271

1978

Phillies fans looked forward to the 1978 season because now their team became an established National League powerhouse. They had won two consecutive Eastern Division titles and lost two consecutive National League

Championship series. Fans believed that the time had come for the team to win the National League pennant and play in their first World Series since 1950. In order to reach this goal, the Phillies made some roster adjustments to improve their chances. During the season, the Phillies improved their pitching by acquiring starter Dick Ruthven, who proved himself as a valuable addition to the staff. The Phillies also attempted to improve their bench strength by acquiring veteran outfielder Jose Cardenal from the Chicago Cubs. This bench strength helped the Phillies win the National League Eastern Divisional title for the third straight year. This title was won despite some nagging injuries to key personnel such as third baseman Mike Schmidt, second baseman Ted Sizemore, and outfielder Bake McBride. Because of these injuries, a veteran like Cardenal proved invaluable. Unfortunately, the Phillies suffered yet another setback in the League Championship series, losing to the Los Angeles Dodgers. Another black player who made an impression was young outfield prospect Lonnie Smith, who came up for a September trial. Although Smith did not make the major league roster for good until 1980, he was highly regarded by the Phillies organization.

Jose Domec Cardenal

Originally from Cuba, Jose Cardenal came to the Phillies for the 1978 season to add bench strength as a reserve outfielder. Cardenal was among the last generation of fine Cuban players who left their homeland to play major league baseball. Shortly after Cardenal's migration to North America, all future Cuban players remained in the Communist nation. Known for both power and speed, Cardenal had many productive seasons in both leagues but never played for a winner until he arrived in Philadelphia. Prior to joining the Phillies, Cardenal was primarily an outfielder, only rarely playing in the infield. But with the Phillies, Cardenal was counted on to act as the right-handed platoon at first base to the left-handed hitting Richie Hebner. Although Cardenal had played second base, shortstop, and third base, first base was a new position for him. Nevertheless, he held his own at the position while hitting .249 with 12 doubles. At 34 years of age, Cardenal began to lose the speed that allowed him to steal as many as 40 bases in a season. With the Phillies in 1978, Cardenal only stole 2 bases in 87 games. Cardenal began the next season with the Phillies, playing in 29 games before being traded to the New York Mets. After beginning the 1980 season with the Mets, Cardenal caught on with the Kansas City Royals. During the World Series, Cardenal started in right field against the Phillies in Games Two and Six.

Year	Team	G	AB	Runs	Hits	2B	3B	HR	RBI	BA
1978	Phillies	87	201	27	50	12	0	4	33	.249
1979	Phillies	29	48	4	10	3	0	0	9	.208

Lonnie Smith

Originally from Chicago, Smith was one of the Phillies' better prospects of the late 1970s. Smith, along with catcher Keith Moreland and infielder Jim Morrison, gave the Phillies the option of retaining their talents or using them to trade for other needs. With Smith, the Phillies chose to keep the speedy outfielder in the hopes that he could blossom into their leadoff man. By 1980, Smith made the Phillies roster after a couple strong seasons in Triple-A. With Bake McBride, Garry Maddox, and Greg Luzinski starting in the outfield, the Phillies had three accomplished veterans with experience. In 1980, Lonnie Smith was going to have to wait his turn until an opportunity came his way. With his speed on the bases, Smith could serve as a spare outfielder who could come in as pinch runner. But when Luzinski went down with chronic knee injuries, Smith was ready to step in, hitting .339 in 298 at-bats with 14 doubles and 33 stolen bases. Smith's strong rookie season helped propel the Phillies towards the 1980 World Championship. Because the Phillies could use the designated hitter, Smith started all six games of the 1980 World Series. With Luzinski's struggles during the 1980 season, the Phillies traded the slugging left-fielder to the Chicago White Sox. It was assumed that Smith would play left-field in Luzinski's place. But because of Smith's lack of power and poor fielding, the Phillies chose to trade with the Atlanta Braves for veteran Gary Matthews instead. Smith remained with the Phillies as a fourth outfielder for the strike-shortened 1981 season, hitting .324. But Smith's clumsiness in the field caused the Phillies to trade the speedster to the St. Louis Cardinals in a three-way trade that brought catcher Bo Diaz from the Cleveland Indians to Philadelphia. While Diaz had a couple of strong seasons with the Phillies, Smith exploded with a Cardinals team that won the 1982 World Championship. With the Cardinals that season, Smith hit .307 with a league leading 120 runs scored and 68 stolen bases. While it appeared that Smith was riding high, a drug suspension the following season tainted his stay with St. Louis. He then went to the Kansas City Royals for a couple of seasons before surfacing with the Atlanta Braves. With the Braves, Smith experienced a sort of rebirth, leading them to the 1991 World Series, where they lost to the Minnesota Twins in a classic seven game series. Smith ended his career with the Braves as younger outfielders such as David Justice and Ryan Klesko took regular positions in the outfield.

Year	Team	G	AB	Runs	Hits	2B	3B	HR	RBI	BA
1978	Phillies	17	4	6	0	0	0	0	0	.000
1979	Phillies	17	30	4	5	2	0	0	3	.167
1980	Phillies	100	298	69	101	14	4	3	20	.339
1981	Phillies	62	176	40	57	14	3	2	11	.324

1979

This was the year that the Phillies were supposed to win it all. In addition to the already fine nucleus, the Phillies acquired Pete Rose to play first base and slick fielding Manny Trillo to play second base. Also, Nino Espinosa was brought in from the Mets to bolster the Phillies' starting staff. Despite these transactions, the Phillies faltered to a disappointing fourth place finish. However, these moves set the table for the Phillies' World Championship season of 1980.

Nino Amulfo Espinosa (Acevedo)

Nino Espinosa was traded to the Phillies by the Mets for infielder Richie Hebner prior to the 1979 season. Originally from Puerto Rico, Espinosa was expected to fill a key role in the Phillies' starting rotation. During the 1979 season, Espinosa did just that, winning 14 games as the Phillies' number 2 starting pitcher. Espinosa began the following season strongly, but then suffered a shoulder injury that hastened the end of his career. He failed to finish the 1980 season, unable to compete in the Phillies' World Series victory. He started the following season in the Phillies' rotation, but his sore shoulder rendered his performances ineffective. The Phillies eventually released Espinosa and his career ended with the Toronto Blue Jays in 1982.

Year	Team	G	IP	W–L	SV	BB	SO	ERA
1979	Phillies	33	212	14–12	0	65	88	3.65
1980	Phillies	12	76	3–5	0	19	13	3.79
1981	Phillies	14	74	2–5	0	24	22	6.08

Notes

Preface

1. *Baseball*, dir. Ken Burns.
2. Salisbury, Jim, "Robinson in '47: Victory Over Viciousness," *The Philadelphia Inquirer*, 1 April 1997; pp. F6–F7.
3. Flood, Curt, and Richard Carter, *The Way It Is* (New York: Trident Press, 1970), p. 188.
4. The Carpenter Collection, available at the Hagley Museum, Wilmington, Delaware.
5. Early, Gerald, "Performance and Reality: Race, Sports and the Modern World," *The Nation*, August 10–17, 1998, pp. 11–20.
6. Clark, Dick, and Larry Lester ed., *The Negro Leagues Book* (Cleveland: Society for American Baseball Research, 1994), pp. 74–154.
7. *Ibid.*, pp. 160–5.
8. Burns, Ken and Geoffrey C. Ward, *Baseball* (New York: Alfred A. Knopf, 1994), p. 291.
9. Tygiel, Jules, *Baseball's Great Experiment* (New York: Oxford University Press, 1983), p. 9.

1—The Early Days

1. Burns, p. 87.
2. "Fleet" Walker's brother Welday also played briefly as an outfielder for Toledo in 1884. Peterson, Robert, *Only the Ball Was White* (New York: McGraw-Hill, 1970), p. 44. Riley, James A., "88 Years Before Jackie Robinson," *The Diamond*, January/February 1994, pp. 42–45.
3. Neil Lanctot, *Fair Dealing and Clean Playing: The Hilldale Club and the Development of Black Professional Baseball 1910–1932* (Jefferson, NC: McFarland, 1994), p. 11.
4. Weigley, Russell E. et al., *Philadelphia: A 300 Year History* (New York: W.W. Norton Co., 1982), p. 415.
5. *Ibid.*, p. 438.
6. Sullivan, Dean A., *Early Innings: A Documentary History of Baseball, 1825–1908* (Lincoln: University of Nebraska Press, 1995), pp. 32–33.
7. Lanctot, p. 12.
8. Weigley et al., p. 438. Du Bois, W.E.B, *The Philadelphia Negro: A Social Study* (Philadelphia: University of Pennsylvania Press, 1996), pp. 39–43. First published in 1898.
9. Enright, Jim, *Baseball's Great Teams: Chicago Cubs* (New York: Collier Books, 1975), pp. 116–119.
10. Sullivan, Dean A., pp. 150–152.
11. Tygiel, *Baseball's Great Experiment*, p. 14.
12. Rader, Benjamin G., *Baseball: A History of America's Game* (Urbana: University of Illinois Press, 1992), pp. 51–52. Tygiel, *Baseball's Great Experiment*, p. 14. DiClerico, James M., and Barry J. Pavelic, *The Jersey Game* (New Brunswick, NJ: Rutgers University Press, 1991), p. 137.

13. Lanctot, pp. 12–13.
14. Husman, John R., "Major League Baseball First for Toledo," *Metropolitan*, July–August 1988, p. 57. Zang, David W., *Fleet Walker's Divided Heart* (Lincoln: University of Nebraska Press, 1995), p. 96.
15. Peterson, pp. 18–24.
16. Alexander, Charles C., *John McGraw* (Lincoln: University of Nebraska Press, 1988), pp. 76–77. Lanctot, pp. 168–169.
17. Peterson, p. 56.
18. Regalado, Samuel O., *Viva Baseball!* (Urbana: University of Illinois Press, 1998), p. 19.
19. Jordan, David M., *The Athletics of Philadelphia* (Jefferson, NC: McFarland and Company, Inc., 1999), pp. 21–23. Neft, p. 16.
20. Jordan, p. 24.
21. Regalado, pp. 19–20.
22. White, C. Edward, *Creating the National Pastime* (Princeton, NJ: Princeton University Press, 1996), p. 129. Early, Gerald, "Performance and Reality: Race, Sports and the Modern World," *The Nation*, August 10–17, 1998, pp. 11–20.
23. Kaplan, Jim, *Lefty Grove: American Original* (Cleveland: The Society for American Baseball Research, 2000), pp. 120–121.
24. Stump, Al, *Cobb* (Chapel Hill, NC: Algonquin Books, 1994), pp. 199–200.
25. *Ibid.* p. 200.
26. Weigley et al., pp. 529–531.
27. Lanctot, p. 14.
28. White, Sol, *History of Colored Baseball* (Lincoln: University of Nebraska Press, 1995), p. 5.
29. Lanctot, p. 14.
30. Holway, John, *Blackball Stars* (Westport, CT: Meckler Books, 1988), pp. 36–47.
31. Sullivan, Neil J., *The Minors* (New York: St. Martin's Press, 1990), p. 189.
32. Peterson, pp. 68–69. Holway, *Blackball Stars*, pp. 8–20.
33. Holway, *Blackball Stars*, p. 13
34. Peterson, p. 72.
35. At this time, there were several professional black teams named the "Giants." This fact often creates confusion to those who study the early days of professional baseball. Sol White, pp. 31–51.
36. Lanctot, p. 15.
37. Lanctot, p. 14–15. Peterson, p. 76. Holway, *Blackball Stars*, pp. 6–7.
38. Peterson, p. 80.
39. Lanctot, p. 181.
40. Peterson, p. 66.
41. Holway, *Blackball Stars*, pp. 61–78.
42. *Ibid.*, p. 82.
43. Weigley et al., pp. 530–531.
44. Peterson, p. 37.
45. *Ibid.*, pp. 62–63.
46. Holway, *Blackball Stars*, p. 11–12.

2 — Hilldale

1. Lanctot, p. 14–16.
2. *Ibid.*, pp. 15–16.
3. *Ibid.*, p. 15.
4. *Ibid.*, pp. 16–17.
5. *Ibid.*, pp. 17–19.
6. Holway, *Blackball Stars*, p. 150–165.
7. Holway, *Blackball Stars*, p. 150–165.
8. *Ibid.*, p. 154.
9. *Ibid.*, p. 217–235.
10. Peterson, p. 86 and Clark, p. 160.
11. Peterson, p. 86.
12. *Ibid.*, pp. 86–87.
13. Kaplan, pp. 120–121.
14. Kuklick, Bruce, *To Every Thing a Season* (Princeton: Princeton University Press, 1991), pp. 49–51. Also seen in Lanctot, p. 55.
15. Neft, David S. and Richard M. Cohen, *The Sports Encyclopedia of Baseball* (New York: St. Martin's/Marek, 1985), pp. 73–87.
16. Lanctot, p. 55.
17. Lanctot, Neil (nlanctot@udel.edu), "Re: Hilldale's White Following," e-mail sent to Christopher Threston (threston@clam.rutgers.edu), 16 October 1997.
18. Holway, *Blackball Stars*, p. 154.
19. Lanctot, pp. 56–63.

3 — Ed Bolden

1. Ward, Geoffrey C., and Ken Burns, "Game Time," *U.S. News and World Report*, Sept. 5, 1994, pp. 451–452.

2. Early, Gerald, "Performance and Reality: Race, Sports and the Modern World," *The Nation*, August 10–17, 1998, pp. 11–20.
3. Lanctot, p. 17.
4. Peterson, p. 86.
5. Lanctot, pp. 93–94.
6. Peterson, p. 87.
7. White, Sol, p. 109.
8. Peterson, pp. 87–88.
9. Holway, John B., *Blackball Stars* (Westport, CT: Meckler Books, 1988), pp. 31–32.
10. Lanctot, p. 96.
11. Clark, p. 162.
12. Holway, Blackball Stars, p. 332.
13. Lanctot, p. 112–113.
14. O'Neil, Buck, *I Was Right On Time* (New York: Fireside, 1996), p. 81.
15. Lanctot, pp. 112–113.
16. Lanctot, Neil (nlanctot@udel.edu), "Loose Ends", e-mail to Christopher Threston (threston@clam.rutgers.edu), 17 August 1997. Carchidi, Sam, "A Bit of the Past," *The Philadelphia Inquirer*, August 5, 2000, p. E1+.
17. Lanctot, p. 187.
18. *Ibid.*, pp. 190–192.
19. *Ibid.*, pp. 190–193.
20. *Ibid.*, pp. 192–194.
21. *Ibid.*, pp. 193–195.
22. *Ibid.*, pp. 203–204.
23. Clark, p. 164.
24. "Leader," Philadelphia Tribune, April 7, 1932.
25. "Another Setback for Darby Phantoms," Philadelphia Tribune, June 9, 1932.

4—Here Come the Stars

1. Clark, pp. 160–163.
2. Jordan, p. 1.
3. Dixon, Randy, "Wilson Named 'Landis' of Negro Baseball," *Philadelphia Tribune*, March 15, 1934, p. 10.
4. Clark, pp. 114–115.
5. Tygiel, p. 32.
6. Jordan, p. 2.
7. *Ibid.*, pp. 1–2.
8. *Ibid.*, p. 2.
9. *Ibid.*, p. 3

10. For example, during the 1996 season, Baltimore Orioles second baseman Roberto Alomar spit in the face of American League umpire John Hirschbeck during a dispute at home plate. Although Alomar was allowed to play in the American League playoffs that season, he was suspended for seven games without pay at the beginning of the 1997 season.
11. Harris, Ed R., "Stars Clip Giant (*sic*) For Two Runs To Clinch Title," *Philadelphia Tribune*, October 4, 1934, p. 11.
12. Harris, "To Be or Not To Be," *Philadelphia Tribune*, October 4, 1934, p. 11.
13. Jordan, p. 5.
14. Holway, *Black Diamonds* (Westport, CT: Meckler Books, 1989), p. 79.
15. Tygiel, *Baseball's Great Experiment*, pp. 43–45.
16. *Ibid.*, pp. 43–45. "Boston Red Sox Try Out Two," *Philadelphia Tribune*, April 21, 1945, p. 12.
17. E-mail conversation with Neil Lanctot, July 9, 1999.
18. Clark, p. 309.
19. Riley, Jim, "Gene Benson: Baseball Pioneer," *Oldtyme Baseball News*, Spring 1990, pp. 6–7.
20. Kelley, Brent, *Voices from the Negro Leagues* (Jefferson, NC: McFarland & Company, Inc., 1998), pp. 144–153.
21. *Ibid.*, pp. 154–160.
22. *Ibid.*, pp. 199–205.
23. Clark, p. 328.
24. *Ibid.*, p. 301.
25. Clark, pp. 273–274. Moffi, Larry, and Jonathan Kronstadt, *Crossing the Line* (Jefferson, NC: McFarland, 1994) pp. 75–76.
26. Clark, p. 302.
27. Moffi, pp. 140–141.
28. Clark, p. 308. Moffi, p. 123.
29. Lanctot, p. 227.
30. Clark, p. 163.

5—Attempted Integration of Philadelphia Baseball

1. Salisbury, "Robinson in '47," p. F6.
2. Lanctot, p. 15.

3. *Ibid.*, p. 168–169.
4. Peterson, pp. 185–186.
5. Smith, Red, "Remembrances of Eddie Gottlieb," *New York Times,* January 30, 1980.
6. Kuklick, Bruce, *To Every Thing a Season,* (Princeton, NJ: Princeton University Press, 1991), p. 146.
7. Smith, Red, "Remembrances of Eddie Gottlieb," *New York Times,* January 30, 1980.
8. Kuklick, p. 146.
9. Jordan, David M., Larry R. Gerlach, and John Rossi, "A Baseball Myth Exploded," *The National Pastime,* Number 18, 1998, pp. 5–6.
10. Enright, p. 18.
11. Veeck, Bill and Ed Linn, *Veeck as in Wreck* (New York: Putnam, 1962), pp. 171–172.
12. Jordan et al., p. 11.
13. Veeck, pp. 171–172.
14. This is questionable because Easter had yet to play in the Negro Leagues in 1943. Veeck probably chose to include Easter because the slugger later played for the Indians, which he owned.
15. Veeck pp. 171–172.
16. *Ibid.*, pp. 171–172.
17. O'Neil, p. 166.
18. Peterson, p. 152.
19. Bruce, Janet, *The Kansas City Monarchs: Champions of Black Baseball* (Lawrence: University of Kansas Press, 1985), p. 109.
20. Veeck, p. 171–172.
21. O'Neil, p. 166
22. Jordan et al., pp. 5–6.
23. *Ibid.*, pp. 10–11
24. Moore, Joseph Thomas, *Pride Against Prejudice: The Biography of Larry Doby* (New York: Praeger Publishers, 1988), p. 39.
25. Dickey, Glenn, *The History of American League Baseball Since 1901* (New York: Stein and Day, 1980), p. 171.
26. Moffi, pp. 15–41.
27. Jordan et al., p. 11.
28. Campanella, Roy, *It's Good to Be Alive* (Lincoln: University of Nebraska Press, 1959), pp. 98–99.
29. Campanella, pp. 98–100. "Campanella and Newsome Get Chance," *Philadelphia Tribune,* April 13, 1946, p. 11.
30. Westcott, Rich and Frank Bilovsky, *The New Phillies Encyclopedia* (Philadelphia: Temple University Press, 1993), p. 671.
31. Campanella, pp. 98–100.
32. Roberts, Robin, and Paul Rogers III, *The Whiz Kids and the 1950 Pennant* (Philadelphia: Temple University Press, 1996), p. 671.
33. Kuklick, p. 146.
34. Holway, *Blackball Stars,* p. 163.
35. Tygiel, *Baseball's Great Experiment,* p. 109.
36. *Ibid.*, p. 243.
37. "Through the Eyes of W. Rollo Wilson," *Philadelphia Tribune,* November 3, 1945, p. 12.
38. Kuklick, pp. 146–147.
39. Holway, *Blackball Stars,* p. 163.
40. Kuklick, p. 147.
41. "Phillies Payroll Records for 1955," The Carpenter Collection.
42. Kuklick, pp. 147–149.
43. Westcott and Bilovsky, p. 671.
44. Tygiel, *Baseball's Great Experiment,* p. 287.
45. Moffi, p. 51.

6—The Demise of Black Baseball

1. Moffi, p. 67
2. Vincent, Fay, "Black ballplayer harbors no bitterness: 'We loved the game,'" *The Philadelphia Inquirer,* July 9, 1999, p. D1+.
3. Vincent, p. D1+.
4. Gallagher, Tom, "Lester Rodney, *The Daily Worker,* and the Integration of Baseball," *The National Pastime,* Number 19, 1999, pp. 77–80.
5. O'Neil, pp. 165–166.
6. *Ibid.*, p. 166.
7. Gallagher, pp. 77–80.
8. Campanella, pp. 96–98.
9. Gallagher, pp. 77–80.
10. Holway, John, *Voices from the Great Black Baseball Leagues* (New York: DeCapo Press, 1992).
11. Robinson, Jackie, *I Never Had It*

Made (Hopewell, NJ: Ecco Press, 1996), pp. 25–26.
    12. O'Neil, p. 165.
    13. *Ibid.*, p. 163.
    14. Bruce, Janet, *The Kansas City Monarchs* (Lawrence: University of Kansas Press, 1985), pp. 112–113.
    15. White, G. Edward, *Creating the National Pastime*, p. 154.
    16. Moffi, pp. 13–36.
    17. Honig, Donald, *Baseball When the Grass Was Real* (Lincoln: University of Nebraska Press, 1975), pp. 164–177.
    18. Fimrite, Ron, "A Slugger Hidden in Shadow," *Sports Illustrated*, July 26, 1999, p. 34.
    19. Tygiel, *Baseball's Great Experiment*, p. 258.
    20. Vincent, pp. D1+.
    21. Tygiel, *Baseball's Great Experiment*, p. 161.
    22. Clark, p. 255.
    23. Bruce , p. 116.
    24. Holway, *Voices from the Great Black Baseball Leagues*, pp. 324–325.
    25. Moffi, pp. 65–67.
    26. *Ibid.*, pp. 75–76.
    27. *Ibid.*, pp. 140–141.
    28. Bruce, p. 116.
    29. White, G. Edward, *Creating the National Pastime*, pp. 152–153.
    30. Tygiel, *Baseball's Great Experiment*, p. 161.
    31. *Ibid.*, p. 112.
    32. Moffi, pp. 49–52.
    33. *Ibid.*, p. 9.
    34. It is interesting to note that the All-American Girls Professional Baseball League, which existed from 1944 to 1953, was not integrated at any time.
    35. Moffi, p. 9.
    36. Kuklick, p. 147.
    37. O'Neil, p. 214–215.
    38. *Baseball*, dir. Ken Burns.

7—Intolerance

    1. Roberts, Robin, and C. Paul Rogers III, *The Whiz Kids and the 1950 Pennant* (Philadelphia: Temple University Press, 1996), p. 52.
    2. Robinson, pp. 33–34.
    3. Burns, p. 285.
    4. Robinson, pp. 18–23. Also seen in the article from
    Woolley, Bryan, "Remembering the 761st," *The Dallas Morning News,* July 17, 1994, pp. 1F+.
    5. O'Neil, p. 163–164.
    6. Early, Gerald, "Performance and Reality: Race, Sports and the Modern World," *The Nation,* August 10–17, 1998, pp. 11–20.
    7. Manasso, John, "Racial issues tarnish Hall of Famer tribute," *Philadelphia Inquirer,* July 8, 1998, p. A18. Also seen in Jules Tygiel's *Baseball's Great Experiment.*
    8. Orodenker, Richard, *The Phillies Reader* (Philadelphia: Temple University Press, 1996), pp. 56–57.
    9. Roberts, pp. 48–49.
    10. Tygiel, *Baseball's Great Experiment*, p. 182.
    11. Roberts, p. 49.
    12. Robinson, p. 59.
    13. *Ibid.*, p. 60–61.
    14. Tygiel, *Baseball's Great Experiment*, p. 181–182.
    15. Roberts, p. 49–50.
    16. Tygiel, *Baseball's Great Experiment*, p. 183.
    17. Roberts, pp. 51–52.
    18. Prince, Carl E., *Brooklyn's Dodgers: The Bums, the Borough, and the Best of Baseball* (New York: Oxford University Press, 1996), pp. 17–18. K. Raffensberger, Phils pitcher, *Philadelphia Inquirer* November 12, 2002, B11.
    19. Roberts, pp. 52–54.
    20. Robinson, pp. 61–63.
    21. Halberstam, David, *Summer of '49* (New York: Penguin Group, 1993), p. 277.
    22. Roberts, pp. 133–134.
    23. Tygiel, *Baseball's Great Experiment*, pp. 202–203.
    24. Lundquist, Carl, "Drama in Philadelphia," *Baseball Research Journal,* Number 26, 1997, pp. 3–4.
    25. Tygiel, *Baseball's Great Experiment*, p. 18.
    26. Robinson, p. 64.
    27. Tygiel, Jules, ed., *The Jackie Robinson Reader* (New York: Dutton, 1997), pp. 137–138.

28. Robinson, p. 24.
29. Kuklick, p. 147.
30. Moore, p. 90.
31. Tygiel, *Baseball's Great Experiment*, p. 231.
32. Kuklick, pp. 148–150.
33. The Carpenter Collection.

8—Integration of Philadelphia Baseball

1. Moffi, p. 103.
2. Tygiel, *Baseball's Great Experiment*, p. 291.
3. Moffi, p. 103.
4. "Trice Gets Hello From A's Today [sic]," *The Philadelphia Tribune*, September 12, 1953, pp. 1–2.
5. Kahn, Roger, *Memories of Summer* (New York: Hyperion, 1997), p. 209.
6. Morrow, Art, "A's, Browns Divide; Byrd Takes 2d, 2–0," *The Philadelphia Inquirer*, September 14, 1953, p. 29.
7. Clark, p. 333. Moffi, p. 104.
8. Rob Bonter Interview, June 25, 1998.
9. Moffi, p. 103–104.
10. Regalado, pp. 73–75.
11. Regalado, pp. 73–75. Jordan, p. 182.
12. Moffi, p. 119.
13. Caroulis, John, "When the A's Said Goodbye to Philly," *Baseball Digest*, October 1994, pp. 60–61.
14. *Ibid.*, pp. 59–61.
15. *Ibid.*, pp. 59–61.
16. *Ibid.*, p. 61.
17. Fagan, Herb, "Ferris Fain: Few Played The Game Any Better," *Oldtyme Baseball News*, Volume 7, Issue 5, pp. 28–29.
18. Moffi, pp. 13–25.
19. Moffi, pp. 13–25.
20. *Ibid.*, pp. 13–25.
21. *Ibid.*, p. 103.
22. Holway, pp. 163–164.
23. Clark, p. 288.
24. Lewis, Allen, "Roberts Seeks Fourth Inaugural Victory Over Brooks in Phils' 1st Game," *Philadelphia Inquirer*, April 16, 1957, p. 28.
25. Harrison, Claude E., "City Hails Phils' Negro Players," *Philadelphia Tribune*, April 16, 1957, pp. 1 and 13.
26. Bonter Interview.
27. Harrison, Claude E., "People in Sports," *Philadelphia Tribune*, April 13, 1957, p. 13.
28. Clark, p. 288.
29. John Kennedy's Obituary, *The Philadelphia Inquirer*, April 30, 1998.
30. Lewis, Allen, "Roberts Seeks Fourth Inaugural Victory Over Brooks in Phils' 1st Game," *Philadelphia Inquirer*, April 16, 1957, p. 28.
31. Harrison, Cluade E., "NL Champions, Brooklyn Dodgers, Open Season Tonight Against Phillies," *Philadelphia Tribune*, April 16, 1957, p. 12.
32. Bonter Interview.
33. Bjarkman, Peter C., "History's Many Shades," *Primera Fila*, October 1997, pp. 12–13.
34. Moffi, p. 149.
35. Keetz, Frank, *They, Too, Were the Boys of Summer* (Schenectady, NY: 1993), pp. 87–88.
36. *Ibid.*, p. 93–94.
37. Moffi, pp. 188–189.
38. Neft, p. 321.
39. *Ibid.*, p. 350.
40. Boyd, Brendan C., and Fred C. Harris, *The Great American Baseball Card Flipping, Trading, and Bubble Gum Book* (New York: Ticknor & Fields, 1994), p. 37.
41. From the Bob Carpenter clipping file, Baseball Hall of Fame, Cooperstown, New York.
42. *Ibid.*
43. Kuklick, p. 148.
44. The Carpenter Collection.
45. Miller, Glenn, "Dominican Gold: Mining For Superstars," *News-Press*, March 19, 2000, pp. 1A+.
46. Kuklick, p. 148.
47. Neft, p. 346.
48. From the Carpenter Collection.
49. Regalado, pp. 95–96. Brioso, Cesar, "Major League Beisbol," *Sun-Sentinel*, July 30, 2000, pp. 1C+.
50. Brioso, pp. 1C+.

9—Integration in the 1960s and 1970s

1. Allen, Dick and Tim Whitaker, *Crash* (New York: Ticknor and Fields, 1989), pp. 19–24.
2. *Ibid.*, p. 53.
3. White, Edward G., pp. 19–22. Kuklick, pp. 18–19.
4. Weigley, et al., p. 662.
5. Kuklick, pp. 156–160.
6. Regalado, p. 127.
7. Allen, p. 56.
8. Thomas bounced around with the Houston Astros, Milwaukee Braves, and Chicago Cubs before ending his career early in the 1966 season.
9. *Ibid.*, pp. 1–10.
10. Harrison, Claude E., "Phila. Is Where Roy Was Barred; Rich Allen Booed," *Philadelphia Tribune*, July 13, 1965, p. 12.
11. Smith, Curt, *Storied Stadiums: Baseball's History Through Its Ballparks* (New York: Carroll and Graf Publishers, 2001), p. 187.
12. Kuklick, pp. 156–60.
13. Bouton, Jim, *Ball Four* (New York: Macmillan & Co., 1990), p. 229.
14. From the Dick Allen clipping file, Baseball Hall of Fame, Cooperstown, NY.
15. Allen, pp. 53–81.
16. Conlin, Bill, "Richie is beautiful, he don't give a damn for nobody," *Jock*, January 1970, pp. 88–94.
17. *Ibid.*, pp. 88–94.
18. *Ibid.*, 88–94.
19. Lewis, Allen, "Allen Rift Called 'Factor' in Mauch Firing," *The Sporting News*, June 29, 1968, p. 7.
20. Lewis, Allen, "'Many Pilots Would Like Rich, I'm One of 'Em'—Skinner," *The Sporting News*, June 29, 1968, p. 7.
21. Allen, pp. 53–81.
22. Conlin, p. 90.
23. Bouton, p. 352.
24. Neft, p. 395.
25. Conlin, pp. 91–2.
26. Gutman, Dan, *Baseball's Greatest Bloopers* (New York: Viking, 1993), pp. 127–29.
27. Flood, pp. 187–206.
28. Moffi, p. 151.
29. The Carpenter Collection.
30. Lewis, Allen, "Phils Attack Old Policies of Handling Negro Players," *The Sporting News*, Nov. 20, 1971, p. 48.
31. *Ibid.*, p. 48.
32. *Ibid.*, p. 48.
33. *Ibid.*, p. 48.

Epilogue

1. Allen, pp. 153–162.
2. *Ibid.*, pp. 159–160.
3. King, Kelley, "Dick Allen, Baseball's Bad Boy," *Sports Illustrated*, p. 19.
4. Miller, Glenn, "Dominican Gold: Mining for Superstars," *News-Press*, March 19, 2000, pp. 1A+.
5. Miller, p. 1A+.
6. Brioso, Cesar, "Major League Beisbol," *Sun-Sentinel*, July 30, 2000, pp. 1C+.
7. Salisbury, Jim, "The Kid," *Philadelphia Inquirer*, April 1, 1997, F5.
8. Joseph, Dave, "Fading From The Fields," *Sun-Sentinel*, July 31, 2000, pp. 1C+.
9. Joseph, pp. 1C+.
10. Salisbury, Jim, "Relaford and Glanville changing Phils' history," *Philadelphia Inquirer*, June 12, 1998, pp. D4+.

Appendix A—Former Philadelphia Stars Who Played in the Major Leagues

1. Clark, pp. 273–274.
2. Moffi, pp. 75–76.
3. Clark, p. 328.
4. Moffi, pp. 32–36.
5. Smith, pp. 244–246.
6. Clark, p. 301
7. Moffi pp. 65–67.
8. Clark, p. 302.
9. Moffi, pp. 140–141.

10. Clark, p. 308.
11. Moffi, p. 123.

Appendix B—Black Players with the Philadelphia Athletics

1. Moffi, pp. 117-119.
2. Moffi, pp. 103-104.

Appendix C—African American and Latin American Phillies, 1957–1979

1. Moffi, p. 167.
2. Moffi, pp. 187–188.
3. Moffi, p. 147.
4. Moffi, p. 140.
5. Moffi, p. 175.
6. Moffi, p. 180.
7. Brioso, Cesar, "Major League Beisbol," *Sun-Sentinel*, July 30, 2000, pp. 1C+.
8. Smith, p. 313.
9. Brioso, pp. 1C+.
10. Smith, p. 313.
11. Douchant, Mike and Joe Marcin ed., *The Sporting News Official Baseball Register* (St. Louis: The Sporting News Publishing Company, 1976), p. 176.
12. Smith p. 325.
13. Douchant, p. 172
14. Douchant, p. 159.
15. Smith, Curt, *Storied Stadiums* (New York: Carroll and Graf Publishers, 2001), p. 248.
16. Moffi, p. 218.
17. Douchant, pp. 361–362.
18. Douchant, pp. 153–154.
19. Smith, Curt, *Storied Stadiums* (New York: Carroll and Graf Publishers, 2001), p. 360.
20. Douchant, pp. 357–358.

Bibliography

The notes provided in the text reveal what is documented and what I have interpreted. The documentation, however, needs further explanation. Because I attempted to piece together quite a number of different types of source material, some of the research referenced may exist in other sources. I did not intentionally exclude such material and would certainly credit the authors of such works if necessary. Very rarely could one source do an adequate job of telling all sides of a particular issue or provide enough detail to fully examine any subject. Furthermore, instead of handling the subject of integration of professional sports on a national basis, I chose to do it on a regional basis. This approach meant that the use of many "local" sources became necessary. Some of these local sources may be biased in their reporting or, again, only tell a particular side of the story. Furthermore, as Bruce Kuklick says in his book *To Every Thing a Season* (page 197), "The best history of Shibe Park emphasizes what went on in people's heads."[1] The same can be said about examining the integration of Philadelphia baseball. I have tolerated these shortcomings and attempted to deliver the most historically accurate work possible. But if any inaccuracies exist or if something is neglected within this work, please inform me (via the publisher). In my mind, this effort will always be a work in progress.

Various collections proved quite useful to this project. In particular, it was my graduate school buddy Jeff Anderson who uncovered a great collection of Phillies material at the Hagley Museum in Wilmington, Delaware. This collection comes from the Carpenter family, who provided a plethora of different types of material that greatly assisted this project. From scouting reports of black players to the plans for building a new stadium, this collection supplied me with much information that I could utilize.

Some terrific material came from the newspaper archives at the Free Library of Philadelphia. I successfully accessed articles from both the *Philadelphia Inquirer* and the *Philadelphia Tribune*. The ability to get both sides of the issues from both the city's white and black newspapers proved very interesting and helpful. The views I read in the *Tribune*, in some cases, definitely proved eye-opening.

On a couple of occasions, I received some very useful information from fellow baseball historians. It was Latin American baseball expert Peter Bjarkman who sent me his article on Chico Fernandez. Frank Keetz sent me his work on the baseball history of Schenectady, which gave valuable information on "Pancho" Herrera and Hank Mason. Unfortunately, Mr. Keetz does not have his own works published in a marketable format. Philadelphia native Rob Bonter called me from his Portland, Oregon, home to provide his views of the integration of the Philadelphia Athletics. The notes I took from this phone call were used to give a fan's perspective of this era. Finally, I could always go to Philadelphia Negro League historian and author Neil Lanctot for answers to just about any of my questions. Whether it was by phone or e-mail, Neil always provided the pertinent information.

I also found useful information from some unusual places. First, from my own baseball card collection, I managed to find useful tidbits about pitcher Hank Mason. Since Mason had such a brief major league career, it was difficult to get quality material on the first-ever black Phillies pitcher. But since Mason began the 1960 season on the major league roster, he had a TOPPS baseball card. The bio on the back allowed me to add some interesting information to his profile, but a bibliographical reference for this source is problematic.

Player information and statistics came from such resources as *The Sports Encyclopedia of Baseball* by David S. Neft and Richard M. Cohen, *The Sporting News' Official 1976 Baseball Register*, and Dick Clark and Larry Lester's *The Negro Leagues Book*. The completeness of these works proved exceedingly helpful. They allowed me to analyze statistics and facts successfully. Furthermore, details from specific games could be found in newspaper box scores and accompanying stories.

A final collection that I would like to make a note of is the clipping files of the National Baseball Hall of Fame located in Cooperstown, New York. Their collection is so vast and complete that I could find newspaper or magazine clippings on just about every player, manager, or executive, no matter how obscure. I believe that I only scratched the surface of this collection, but the research that I did manage to conduct proved incredibly useful. Sometimes, however, some clippings did not have complete bibliographical information and this problem should be noticeable in the notes.

Newspapers

The Evening Bulletin
New York Daily News
New York Herald Tribune
New York Times
Philadelphia Daily News

Philadelphia Inquirer
Philadelphia Public Ledger
Philadelphia Tribune
Pittsburgh Courier

Periodicals

Baseball Digest
Baseball Magazine
Baseball Weekly
The Diamond
Life
The National Pastime
Newsweek
Oldtyme Baseball News
Sport
The Sporting News
Sports Collector's Digest
Sports Illustrated
Time
U.S. News and World Report

Collections

The Carpenter Family Philadelphia Phillies Collection at the Hagley Museum, Wilmington, Delaware.
Clipping Files from the National Baseball Hall of Fame, Cooperstown, New York.
Research Library from the Society of Baseball Research (SABR).

Films

Baseball (Director Ken Burns)
When It Was A Game
When It Was A Game II
When It Was A Game III

Books

Aaron, Hank, and Lonnie Wheeler. *If I Had a Hammer: The Hank Aaron Story*. New York: Harper Collins, 1991.
Adelson, Bruce. *Brushing Back Jim Crow*. Charlottesville: University Press of Virginia, 1999.
Alexander, Charles C. *John McGraw*. Lincoln: University of Nebraska Press, 1988.
Allen, Dick, and Tim Whitaker. *Crash*. New York: Ticknor & Fields, 1989.
Barber, Red. *1947: When All Hell Broke Loose in Baseball*. Garden City, NY: Doubleday, 1982.
Berlage, Gai Ingham. *Women in Baseball: The Forgotten History*. Westport, CT: Praeger, 1994.
Billet, Bret L., and Lance J. Formwalt. *America's National Pastime*. Westport, CT: Praeger, 1995.
Bouton, Jim. *Ball Four*. New York: Macmillan, 1990.
Boyd, Brendan C., and Fred C. Harris. *The Great American Baseball Card Flipping, Trading, and Bubble Gum Book*. New York: Ticknor & Fields, 1994.
Brashler, William. *The Story of Negro League Baseball*. New York: Ticknor & Fields, 1994.
Bruce, Janet. *The Kansas City Monarchs: Champions of Black Baseball*. Lawrence: University of Kansas Press, 1985.
Burns, Ken, and Geoffrey C. Ward. *Baseball*. New York: Alfred A. Knopf, 1994.
Campanella, Roy. *It's Good to Be Alive*. Lincoln: University of Nebraska Press, 1959.
Cataneo, David. *Peanuts and Crackerjack: A Treasury of Baseball Legends and Lore*. San Diego: Harcourt Brace, 1991.
Chadwick, Bruce. *When the Game Was Black and White*. New York: Abbeville Press, 1992.

Clark, Dick, and Larry Lester. *The Negro Leagues Book*. Cleveland: Society for American Baseball Research, 1994.
Craft, David. *The Negro Leagues*. New York: Crescent Books, 1993.
Debono, Paul. *The Indianapolis ABCs*. Jefferson, NC: McFarland, 1999.
Dickey, Glenn. *The History of American League Baseball Since 1901*. New York: Stein and Day, 1980.
DiClerico, James M., and Barry J. Pavelic. *The Jersey Game: The History of Modern Baseball from Its Birth to the Big Leagues in the Garden State*. New Brunswick, NJ: Rutgers University Press, 1991.
Douchant, Mike, and Joe Marcin. *Official 1976 Baseball Register*. St. Louis: The Sporting News Publishing Company, 1976.
Du Bois, W.E.B. *The Philadelphia Negro: A Social Study*. Philadelphia: University of Pennsylvania Press, 1996.
Dykes, Jimmie, and Charles O. Dexter. *You Can't Steal First Base*. Philadelphia: J.B. Lippincott, 1967.
Echevarria, Roberto Gonzalez. *The Pride of Havana: A History of Cuban Baseball*. New York: Oxford University Press, 1999.
Enright, Jim. *Baseball's Great Teams: Chicago Cubs*. New York: Collier Books, 1975.
Eskenazi, Gerald. *Bill Veeck: A Baseball Legend*. New York: McGraw-Hill, 1988.
Flood, Curt, and Richard Carter. *The Way It Is*. New York: Trident Press, 1970.
Gibson, Bob, and Lonnie Wheeler. *Stranger to the Game*. New York: Penguin, 1994.
Good, Howard. *Diamonds in the Dark*. Lanham, MD: Scarecrow Press, 1987.
Gregorich, Barbara. *Women at Play*. San Diego: Harcourt Brace, 1993.
Gutman, Dan. *Baseball's Biggest Bloopers*. New York: Penguin Group, 1993.
Halberstam, David. *Summer of '49*. New York: Penguin Group, 1993.
Helyar, John. *Lords of the Realm*. New York: Villard Books, 1994.
Holway, John B. *Black Diamonds*. Westport, CT: Meckler Books, 1989.
_____. *Blackball Stars: Negro League Pioneers*. Westport, CT: Meckler Books, 1988.
_____. *Voices from the Great Black Negro Leagues*. New York: Da Capo Press, 1992.
Holtzman, Jerome. *The Commissioners: Baseball's Midlife Crisis*. New York: Total Sports, 1998.
Honig, Donald. *Baseball When the Grass Was Real*. Lincoln: University of Nebraska Press, 1975.
Jackson, Kenneth T. *Crabgrass Frontier*. New York: Oxford University Press, 1985.
Jordan, David M. *The Athletics of Philadelphia: Connie Mack's White Elephants, 1901–1954*. Jefferson, NC: McFarland, 1999.
Kahn, Roger. *The Era*. New York: Ticknor & Fields, 1993.
_____. *Memories of Summer: When Baseball Was an Art, and Writing about It a Game*. New York: Hyperion, 1997.
Kaplan, Jim. *Lefty Grove: American Original*. Cleveland: Society for American Baseball Research, 2000.
Kelley, Brent. *Voices from the Negro Leagues: Conversations with 52 Baseball Standouts*. Jefferson, NC: McFarland, 1998.
Kuklick, Bruce. *To Every Thing a Season: Shibe Park and Urban Philadelphia 1909–1976*. Princeton, NJ: Princeton University Press, 1991.
Lanctot, Neil. *Fair Dealing and Clean Playing: The Hilldale Club and the Development of Black Professional Baseball, 1910–1932*. Jefferson, NC: McFarland, 1994.
Leonard, Buck, and James A. Riley. *Buck Leonard; The Black Lou Gehrig: An Autobiography*. New York: Carroll & Graf, 1995.
Marshall, William. *Baseball's Pivotal Era 1945–1951*. Lexington: University Press of Kentucky, 1999.
Moffi, Larry, and Jonathan Kronstadt. *Crossing the Line: Black Major Leaguers, 1947–1959*. Jefferson, NC: McFarland, 1994.
Moore, Joseph Thomas. *Pride Against Prejudice: The Biography of Larry Doby*. New York: Praeger, 1988.

Nasaw, David. *Going Out.* New York: Basic Books, 1993.
Nash, Bruce, and Allen Zullo. *The Baseball Hall of Shame.* New York: Pocket Books, 1985.
Neft, David S., and Richard M. Cohen. *The Sports Encyclopedia of Baseball.* New York: St. Martin's/Marek, 1985.
O'Neil, Buck. *I Was Right On Time.* New York: Fireside, 1996.
Orodenker, Richard. *The Phillies Reader.* Philadelphia: Temple University Press, 1996.
Overmyer, James. *Queen of the Negro Leagues: Effa Manley and the Newark Eagles.* Lanham, MD: Scarecrow Press, 1998.
Paige, Satchel. *Maybe I'll Pitch Forever.* New York: Bison Books, 1993.
Peterson, Robert. *Only the Ball Was White.* New York: McGraw-Hill, 1970.
Plimpton, George, et al. *Sports Illustrated Baseball.* Birmingham, AL: Oxmoor Books, 1993.
Porter, David L. *Biographical Dictionary of American Sports.* New York: Greenwood Press, 1987.
Prince, Carl E. *Brooklyn's Dodgers: The Bums, the Borough, and the Best of Baseball.* New York: Oxford University Press, 1996.
Rader, Benjamin G. *Baseball: A History of America's Game.* Urbana: University of Illinois Press, 1992.
Rampersad, Arnold. *Jackie Robinson: A Biography.* New York: Ballantine Books, 1997.
Regalado, Samuel O. *Viva Baseball! Latin Major Leaguers and Their Special Hunger.* Urbana: University of Illinois Press, 1998.
Ribowsky, Mark. *A Complete History of the Negro Leagues.* Secaucus, NJ: Carol Publishing Group, 1995.
_____. *The Power and the Darkness: The Life of Josh Gibson in the Shadows of the Game.* New York: Simon and Schuster, 1996.
Riess, Steven A. *Touching Base: Professional Baseball and American Culture in the Progressive Era.* Westport, CT: Greenwood Press, 1980.
Roberts, Robin, and C. Paul Rogers III. *The Whiz Kids and the 1950 Pennant.* Philadelphia: Temple University Press, 1996.
Robinson, Jackie. *Baseball Has Done It.* Philadelphia: J.B. Lippincott, 1964.
_____. *I Never Had It Made.* Hopewell, NJ: Ecco Press, 1996.
Robinson, Sharon. *Stealing Home.* New York: HarperCollins, 1996.
Rogosin, Donn. *Invisible Men: Life in Baseball's Negro Leagues.* New York: Atheneum, 1987.
Ryczek, William J. *When Johnny Came Sliding Home.* Jefferson, NC: McFarland, 1998.
Scheinin, Richard. *Field of Screams.* New York: W.W. Norton, 1994.
Seymour, Harold. *Baseball.* New York: Oxford University Press, 1960.
Smith, Curt. *Storied Stadiums: Baseball's History Through Its Ballparks.* New York: Carroll and Graf, 2001.
Stump, Al. *Cobb: A Biography.* Chapel Hill, NC: Algonquin Books, 1994.
Sullivan, Dean A. *Early Innings: A Documentary History of Baseball, 1825–1908.* Lincoln: University of Nebraska Press, 1995.
Sullivan, Neil J. *The Minors.* New York: St. Martin's Press, 1990.
Tygiel, Jules. *Baseball's Great Experiment: Jackie Robinson and His Legacy.* New York: Oxford Press, 1983.
_____. *Past Time: Baseball As History.* New York: Oxford University Press, 2000.
_____, ed. *The Jackie Robinson Reader: Perspectives of an American Hero.* New York: Dutton, 1997.
Veeck, Bill, and Ed Linn. *Veeck as in Wreck.* New York: Putnam, 1962.
Voigt, David Q. *America Through Baseball.* Chicago: Nelson-Hall, 1976.
_____. *American Baseball.* Norman: University of Oklahoma Press, 1966.
Wallan, Peter, et al. *The Ol' Ball Game.* New York: Barnes and Noble Books, 1990.
Wallop, Douglas. *Baseball: An Informal History.* New York: Norton, 1969.
Weigley, Russell E., et al. *Philadelphia: A 300 Year History.* New York: W.W. Norton, 1982.
Werber, Bill, and C. Paul Rogers III. *Memoirs of a Ballplayer: Bill Werber and Baseball in the 1930s.* Cleveland: Society of American Baseball Research, 2001.

Westcott, Rich. *Philadelphia's Old Ballparks.* Philadelphia: Temple University Press, 1996.
_____, and Frank Bilovsky. *The New Phillies Encyclopedia.* Philadelphia: Temple University Press, 1993.
White, C. Edward. *Creating the National Pastime: Baseball Transforms Itself, 1903-1953,* Princeton, NJ: Princeton University Press, 1996.
White, Sol. *Sol White's History of Colored Baseball.* Lincoln: University of Nebraska Press, 1995.
Zang, David W. *Fleet Walker's Divided Heart: The Life of Baseball's First Black Major Leaguer.* Lincoln: University of Nebraska Press, 1995.

Articles

Albaugh, David. "Ben Chapman: Jackie Robinson's Worst Nightmare." *Sports Collectors Digest.* September 26, 1997, pp. 146-7.
"Another Setback for Darby Phantoms." *Philadelphia Tribune.* June 9, 1932, p. 11.
Bennett, Charles. "Baseball and Race: The Final Frontier—Baseball's Black Ranks Dwindling." *Times-Picayune.* May 22, 1994, pp. C1+.
_____. "Baseball and Race: The Final Frontier—The Legacy Is Dying." *Times-Picayune.* May 24, 1994, pp. E1+.
Bjarkman, Peter C. "History's Many Shades." *Primera Fila.* October 1997, pp. 12-13.
"Boston Red Sox Try Out Two." *Philadelphia Tribune.* April 21, 1945, p. 12.
Brioso, Cesar. "Major League Beisbol." *Sun-Sentinel.* July 30, 2000, pp. 1C+.
"Campanella and Newsome Get Chance." *Philadelphia Tribune.* April 13, 1946, p. 11
Carlton, Bob. "For the Love of the Game." *Birmingham News.* Feb. 5, 1995, pp. 1E+.
Caroulis, John. "When the A's Said Goodbye to Philly." *Baseball Digest.* October 1994, pp. 59-62.
Charchidi, Sam. "A Bit of the Past." *The Philadelphia Inquirer.* August 5, 2000, p. E1+.
Cohn, Bob. "Jackie Robinson's Breakthrough." *Arizona Republic.* March 30, 1997, pp. A1+.
Conlin, Bill. "Richie Is Beautiful. He Don't Give a Damn for Nobody." *Jock.* January 1970, pp. 88-94.
Conrads, David, and Steve DiMeglio. "Striking a Blow for Equality." *Baseball Weekly.* January 9-15, 2002, p. 7.
"Dick Allen: 'Still My Own Man.'" *Newsweek.* August 21, 1972, pp. 83-4.
Dixon, Randy. "Wilson Named 'Landis' of Negro Baseball." *Philadelphia Tribune.* March 15, 1934, p. 10.
Drebinger, John. "Rickey to Cancel Atlanta Games if Negro Stars Are Banned from the Field." *New York Times.* January 15, 1949, p. 12.
Early, Gerald. "Performance and Reality: Race, Sports and the Modern World." *The Nation.* August 10-17, 1998, pp. 11-20.
Fagan, Herb. "Ferris Fain: Few Played the Game Any Better." *Oldtyme Baseball News.* Volume 7, Issue 5, pp. 28-29.
Fenster, Kenneth R. "Notice on Nat Peeples." *The Baseball Research Journal.* SABR Production Number 27, 1998, p. 94.
Fimrite, Ron. "His Own Biggest Fan." *Sports Illustrated.* pp. 76-80.
_____. "A Slugger Hidden in Shadow." *Sports Illustrated.* July 26, 1999, p. 34.
Ford, John. "The End of an Era." *Baseball Magazine.* March 1955, pp. 232-241.
Fullwood, Sam, III. "Pa. Town Ponders Honor for Local Hero Accused of Racism." *The Boston Sunday Globe.* August 30, 1998, p. A11.
Gallagher, Tom. "Lester Rodney, *The Daily Worker* and Integration." *The National Pastime,* Number 19, 1999, pp. 77-80.
Gregorian, Vahe. "Summer of '47: Breaking the Barriers." *St. Louis Post Dispatch.* May 18, 1997, pp. 1B+.

Griffin, Richard. "Jackie Robinson: A Portrait in Courage." *Toronto Star.* June 1, 1996, pp. B5+.
Guss, Greg. "Skin Games." *Sport.* May 1997, pp. 52–6.
Harris, Ed R. "Stars Clip Giant [sic] for Two Runs to Clinch Title." *Philadelphia Tribune.* October 4, 1934, p. 11.
_____. "To Be or Not To Be." *Philadelphia Tribune.* October 4, 1934, p. 11.
Harrison, Claude E. "City Hails Phils' Negro Players." *Philadelphia Tribune.* April 16, 1957, pp. 1 and 13.
_____. "NL Champions, Brooklyn Dodgers, Open Season Tonight Against Phillies." *Philadelphia Tribune.* April 16, 1957, p. 12.
_____. "People in Sports." *Philadelphia Tribune.* April 13, 1957, p. 13.
_____. "Phila. Is Where Roy Was Barred; Rich Allen Booed." *Philadelphia Tribune.* July 13, 1965, p. 12.
Hepp, Christopher K. "Fans Fondly Recall Connie Mack Stadium." *Philadelphia Inquirer.* August 5, 1999, pp. E1+.
Husman, John R. "Major League Baseball First for Toledo." *Metropolitan.* July–August 1988, 54–57.
Hyman, Stanley Edgar. "The Other Jackie Robinson." *The New Leader.* April 21, 1997, pp. 8–16.
Jerome, Richard. "Man on Fire." *People Weekly.* April 28, 1997, pp. 71–4.
Jordan, David M., Larry R. Gerlach, and John P. Rossi. "A Baseball Myth Exploded." *The National Pastime.* Society of American Baseball Research, Number 18, 1998.
Joseph, Dave. "Fading from the Fields." *Sun-Sentinel.* July 31, 2000, pp. 1C+.
King, Kelley. "Catching up with: Dick Allen, Baseball's Bad Boy." *Sports Illustrated.* p. 19.
Lamb, Chris. "L'Affaire Jake Powell: The Minority Press Goes to Bat Against Segregated Baseball." *Journalism and Mass Communication Quarterly.* Spring 1999, Vol. 76, No. 1, pp. 21–34.
"Leader." *Philadelphia Tribune.* April 7, 1932, p. 11.
Leavy, Walter. "50 Years of Blacks in Baseball." *Ebony.* June 1995, pp. 38+.
Lewis, Allen. "Allen Rift Called 'Factor' in Mauch Firing." *The Sporting News.* June 29, 1968, p. 7.
_____. "'Many Pilots Would Like Rich, I'm One of 'Em'—Skinner." *The Sporting News.* June 29, 1968, p. 7.
_____. "Phils Attack Old Policies of Handling Negro Players." *The Sporting News.* Nov. 20, 1971, p. 48.
_____. "Roberts Seeks Fourth Inaugural Victory Over Brooks in Phils' 1st Game." *Philadelphia Inquirer.* April 16, 1957, p. 28.
Lundquist, Carl. "Drama in Philadelphia." *The Baseball Research Journal.* Society of American Baseball Research, Number 26, 1997.
Manasso, John. "Racial Issues Tarnish Hall of Famer Tribute." *The Philadelphia Inquirer.* July 8, 1998, pp. A1+.
Mann, Arthur. "The Truth About the Jackie Robinson Case." *The Saturday Evening Post.* 2 parts: May 13 & 20, 1950.
Marazzi, Rich. "The Yankees Passed on the Slick-Fielding Vic Power." *Sports Collectors Digest.* January 15, 1999, pp. 76–7.
Miller, Glenn. "Dominican Gold: Mining for Superstars." *News-Press.* March 19, 2000, pp. 1A+.
Morrow, Art. "A's, Browns Divide; Byrd Takes 2d, 2–0." *Philadelphia Inquirer.* Sept. 14, 1953, p. 29.
Norwood, Stephen H. "Going to Bat for Jackie Robinson: The Jewish Role in Breaking Baseball's Color Line." *Journal of Sports History.* Spring 1999, pp. 115–141.
Odom, Maida. "Philadelphia Story: A Three Part Series." *Philadelphia Inquirer.* February 23, 1999, p. D1+.
Peary, Danny. "Vic Power Remembers His Playing Days." *Sports Collectors Digest.* March 9, 1990, pp. 200–5.

Proceedings from "Philadelphia's Baseball History." The Historical Society of Pennsylvania, Symposium. February 24, 1990.
Proceedings from "When Trenton Baseball Roared Like Thunder." The History of Pro Ball in Trenton, Trenton City Museum Symposia, May 7, 1995.
Reese, Pee Wee. "What Jackie Robinson Meant to an Old Friend." *New York Times*. July 17, 1977, Sports.
Riley, James A. "88 Years Before Jackie Robinson." *The Diamond*. January/February 1994, pp. 42–45.
Riley, Jim. "Gene Benson: Baseball Pioneer." *Oldtyme Baseball News*. Spring 1990, pp. 6–7.
Robinson, Jackie. "Negro Apathy Hit." *New York Times*. October 26, 1960, Sports.
Robinson, Ray. "The Life and Death of an Enemy Within." *The Sporting News*. October 31, 1994, p. 9.
Rogers, C. Paul, III. "6/2/49: The Day the Phillies Came of Age." *The National Pastime*. Number 19, 1999, pp. 31–33.
Sailor, Steve. "How Jackie Robinson Desegregated America." *National Review*. April 8, 1996, pp. 38–41.
Salisbury, Jim. "The Kid." *Philadelphia Inquirer*. 1 April 1997, F5.
_____. "Relaford and Glanville Changing Phils' History." *Philadelphia Inquirer*. 12 June 1998.
_____. "Robinson in '47: Victory Over Viciousness." *Philadelphia Inquirer*. 1 April 1997. p. F6.
Shecter, Leonard. "Vic Power's New Wonderful World." *Sport*, May 1962, pp. 65–71.
Smith, Red. "Remembrances of Eddie Gottlieb." *New York Times*. January 30, 1980.
"Through the Eyes of W. Rollo Wilson." *Philadelphia Tribune*. November 3, 1945, p. 12.
"Trice Gets Hello from A's To-day." *Philadelphia Tribune*. Sept. 12, 1953, pp. 1–2.
Trussel, C.P. "Jackie Robinson Terms Stand of Robeson on Negroes False." *New York Times*. July 19, 1949, Sports.
Vass, George. "Problem Players' Have Always Been on Big League Scene." *Baseball Digest*. September 1996, pp. 25–30.
Vincent, Fay. "Black Ballplayer Harbors No Bitterness: 'We Loved the Game'." *Philadelphia Inquirer*. July 9, 1999, pp. D1+.
Ward, Geoffrey C., and Ken Burns. "Game Time." *U.S. News and World Report*. September 5, 1994, pp. 60+.
Westcott, Rich. "History of Phillies Spiced by Odd Characters, Events." *Baseball Digest*. July 1988, pp. 50–58.
White, G. Edward. "A Diary of the Negro Leagues." *The National Pastime*. The Society of American Baseball Research, Number 17, 1997, pp. 25–29.
Wolf, David. "Let's Everybody Boo Rich Allen." *Life*, August 1969, pp. 50–4.
Woolley, Bryan. "Remembering the 761st." *Dallas Morning News*. July 17, 1994, pp. 1F+.

Unpublished Works

Jordan, David M. "Another Philadelphia Champion—1934 Stars." Paper.
Keetz, Frank M. *They Too Were "Boys of Summer": A Case Study of the Schenectady Blue Jays in the Eastern League 1951–1957*. 1993.
Lamb, Chris. "Making a Pitch for Equality: Wendell Smith and His Crusade to Integrate Baseball." Paper, History Division, 1999 AEJMC national conference, New Orleans, August, 1999.
Rogers, James. "Connie Mack and the Cult of Responsibility." Paper, American Conference for Irish Studies at Villanova University, April 17, 1993.

Index

Aaron, Hank 55, 89, 141
Adcock, Joe 132
Adelis, Pete 80
Albuquerque (Dodgers farm team) 149
Alexander, Grover 21, 29
Ali, Muhammad 103
All-America Girls Professional Baseball League 49
Allen, Dick 1, 2, 98–112, 114–116, 136, 140, 142, 143, 145, 147, 149–151, 159, 160
Alou, Felipe 96, 117
Alou, Jesus 96
Alou, "Matty" 96
Amaro, Ruben, Jr. 135
Amaro, Ruben, Sr. 117, 134, 136
American Association 44, 132
American Broadcasting Company 147
American League 11, 13, 51, 55, 66, 79, 87, 109, 113, 117, 140, 143, 145, 149, 155
American Negro League 33–35
Anderson, Harry 135
Anderson, Marlon 118, 119
Andrews, Fred 159, 160
Anson, Cap 10, 15
Arkansas (Phillies farm team) 110
Artiaga, Sal 118
Ashburn, Rickie 53, 57, 129, 130, 141
Atlantic City Race Track 47

Bacharach Giants 26, 28, 32, 38
Baker, Frank "Home Run" 28
Baker Bowl 25, 33, 37, 40
Baltimore Afro-American 60
Baltimore Elite Giants 52, 64

Baltimore Orioles (early 1900s) 11, 18, 46; (1954–present) 124, 133, 141, 145
Banks, Ernie 67, 89, 121
Bell, "Cool Papa" 63
Bell, George 117
Bender, Chief 21
Benjamin Franklin Hotel 79
Benson, Gene 21, 40, 41, 42, 64
Benswanger, William 61
Birmingham Black Barons 128
Blatnick, Johnny 75
Bolden, Ed 25, 26, 30–38, 45, 54
Bonnell, Barry 141
Boone, Bob 114, 155, 159
Boston Braves 41, 55, 57, 65, 68, 75, 98, 121, 122, 124, 131, 138; *see also* Atlanta Braves; Milwaukee Braves
Boston Red Sox 40, 41, 107, 122, 146
Bouchee, Ed 129
Bowa, Larry 116, 141, 149, 155, 159
Bowers, Mickey 112
Brett, Ken 156
Briggs, Johnny 142, 143, 153
Brooklyn Dodgers 1, 4, 27, 30, 41, 49–51, 53, 56, 57, 62, 63, 65, 66, 68, 70, 72–74, 76–79, 87–90, 94, 101, 102, 109, 113, 127, 128, 131, 138, 149, 159, 162; *see also* Los Angeles Dodgers
Brooklyn Royal Giants 32
Brooks, Emile 39
Brown, Jim 103
Brown, Ollie 155, 156
Brown, Oscar 155
Brown, Willard 63, 88, 121
Brown, Willie 155
Brown v. Board of Education 4

181

Browne, Byron 140, 150, 151
Buffalo (Phillies farm club) 129, 130
Buhl, Bob 144, 146
Bunning, Jim 101, 140, 146
Burns, Ken 1

Caballero, Putsy 53
Callison, Johnny 98, 101, 137, 140, 151
Campanella, Roy 27, 49, 52, 53, 61, 64, 65, 67, 78
Campanis, Al 30
Cardenal, Jose 162
Carlton, Steve 114, 146, 153, 159
Carpenter, Bob 56–58, 74, 76, 94, 95, 104, 113–115
Carpenter, Ruly 114, 115, 141
Cash, Bill 40–43, 45, 64
Cash, Dave 116, 155–157, 159, 160
Castro, Luis "Jud" 13, 14
Catto, Octavius 8, 9
Central Post Office 31
Cepeda, Orlando 96
Chandler, Happy 61, 74
Chapman, Ben 1, 53, 56, 70, 72–78, 79
Charleston, Oscar 4, 43
Chicago American Giants 20, 23
Chicago Cubs 29, 48, 67, 69, 97, 98, 121, 130, 131, 136, 138, 144–146, 148, 150, 162
Chicago White Sox 12, 41, 48, 87, 109, 123, 138, 140, 141, 151, 153, 159
Chicago White Stockings 10
Christenson, Larry 159
Christopher, Joe 132
Cincinnati Reds 14, 66, 77, 78, 96, 124, 135, 141, 143, 159, 160
Civil War 8
Clarkson, Buzz 44, 65, 66, 121, 122
Cleveland Buckeyes 40, 68
Cleveland Indians 4, 13, 44, 48, 49, 51, 63, 65, 68, 69, 80, 87, 122, 123, 132, 133, 135, 142, 143, 151, 154, 161, 163
Cobb, Ty 15–17, 19
Cochrane, Mickey 27
Cockrell, Phil 26–28, 38
Coker, Jimmie 138
Coleman, Choo Choo 92–94, 137, 138
Cole's American Giants 39
Collins, Eddie 28
Columbia Park 102
Comiskey, Charlie 12
Cooke, Dusty 74, 75
Covington, Wes 96, 98, 99, 101, 137–140
Cox, William 51

Crandall, Del 124
Crutchfield, Jimmie 62, 63
Cuban Giants 10, 11, 22
Cuban X Giants 17–19, 23
Curry, Tony 95, 96, 135

The Daily Worker 60, 61
Dalrymple, Clay 137
Dandridge, Ray 64
Darby Phantoms 35
Davis, Dick 153
Dean, Dizzy 22, 38
Dean, Jimmy 42–44
Demeter, Don 101, 139, 140
Detroit Tigers 15, 16, 90, 91, 101, 111, 128, 136, 144
Diaz, Bo 163
Dihigo, Martin 4
Doby, Larry 51, 52, 55, 63, 65, 80, 87, 89
Doyle, Denny 156
Drake, Solly 131
Drew, John 35
DuBois, W.E.B. 7, 60
Duckett, Mahlon 42, 44
Durocher, Leo 50
Dykstra, Lenny 117

Earl Mack All-Stars 15, 21
East Coast League 22
East-West League 35
Easter, Luke 49, 52, 65, 80
Eastern Colored League 32, 34
Eastern League 130
Ebbets, Charles 102
Ebbets Field 72, 73, 102
Ehlers, Art 64
Ellis, Rocky 39
Ellsworth, Dick 107
Ennis, Del 78
Espinosa, Nino 164
ESPN 153
Essian, Jim 141

Fain, Ferris 87
Farrell, Dick "Turk" 129
Federal League 29
Fenway Park 40
Fernandez, Chico 89–91, 127–129
Flood, Curt 2, 111, 112, 115, 140, 149–152
Florida Marlins 137
Foster, Andrew "Rube" 7, 18, 19, 23, 31, 32, 59
Fowler, "Bud" 11

Franco, Julio 117
Freed, Roger 145, 151
Frick, Ford 47, 48

Gallagher, James T. 95
Gamble, Oscar 149, 151
Garagiola, Joe 75
Gibson, Josh 7, 27, 63, 64
Gilliam, Junior 64
Girard College 103
Glanville, Doug 119
Glenn, Stanley 42–45
Gomez, Ruben 131–133
Gonzalez, Tony 96–98, 101, 134–136, 140, 149
Gottlieb, Eddie 17, 30, 33, 35–38, 47, 48, 55, 123
Grant, Charlie 11, 12, 18, 46
Gray, Pete 49
Great Black Migration 2, 16, 25
Great Depression 26, 42
Green, Dallas 115
Greenberg, Hank 75, 123
Greentree, Gus 26, 34
Groat, Dick 146, 147
Grove, Lefty 15, 16

Hamner, Granny 53, 128, 130, 132
Harlem Globetrotters 68
Harris, Ed R. 40
Harrison, Claude E. 106
Hartung, Clint 75
Havana Stars 23
Hebner, Richie 116, 164
Hebrew All-Stars 37
Hegan, Jim 133
Hernaiz, Jesus 155, 157
Herrera, Pancho 91–93, 96, 129, 130
Herrnstein, John 101, 144, 147
Hilldale Club of Darby, Pa. 4, 20, 24–27, 30–33, 35–37, 68, 69, 87
Hilldale Park 29
Hisle, Larry 112, 113, 149–151, 153
Hoak, Don 139, 140
Hoerner, Joe 140
Homestead Grays 7, 28, 33, 34, 43, 68, 93
Houston Astrodome 136, 140
Houston Astros 113, 155, 156
Howard, Elston 125
Hoyt, Waite 21
Hutton, Tommy 149

Indianapolis Clowns 55, 68
Inter-American League 155

International League 10, 83, 131
International League of Independent Base Ball Clubs 22
Irvin, Monte 49, 63, 65

Jackson, Grant 145, 150
Jackson, Larry 144, 146
Japanese Leagues 143
Jenkins, Ferguson 144–146
Jethroe, Sam 40, 57, 65, 68
Jim Crow Laws 1, 5, 7, 67
John, Tommy 140
John Bartram High School 43
Johnson, Alex 113, 143, 144
Johnson, Arnold 56, 86
Johnson, Darrell 138
Johnson, Judy 4, 26, 27, 35, 54–56, 69, 88
Johnson, Ron 143
Johnson, Walter 21
Jones, Louis 51
Jones, Stuart "Slim" 38
Jones, Willie 130, 132
Joseph, Rick 148, 150
Justice, David 163

Kaat, Jim 159
Kansas City (Yankees farm team) 125
Kansas City Athletics 56, 59, 84, 95, 88, 122, 123, 126, 138, 141, 148, 149, 155; *see also* Oakland Athletics
Kansas City Monarchs 7, 32, 33, 40, 60, 62, 67, 69, 71, 88, 91, 92, 128–130
Kansas City Royals 139, 159, 162, 163
Kelly, Grace 86
Kelly, Jack, Jr. 86
Kelly, Jack, Sr. 86
Kennedy, John 88–91, 127–129
Keystone Athletics 11
Kimbro, Henry 64
Kiner, Ralph 158
Klesko, Ryan 163
Koppe, Joe 128
Koppel, Ted 30
Kubek, Tony 134

Lacy, Sam 60
Lajoie, Napoleon 13
Lanctot, Neil 24, 25, 29
Landis, Kenesaw Mountain 39, 50–52, 54, 60, 61
League of Colored Base Ball Clubs 22
Leland Giants 20, 21
Leonard, Buck 50, 61, 64

Index

Levy, Ike 47
Levy, Leon 47
Limmer, Lou 126
Lis, Joe 155
Lloyd, John "Pop" 16, 18, 19
Lobert, Hans 52, 53
Lonborg, Jim 159, 160
Lonnett, Joe 133
Lopata, Stan 133
Lopez, Marcelino 140, 142
Los Angeles Angels 113, 134, 136, 141, 143, 144, 155, 156, 159; *see also* California Angels
Los Angeles Rams 156
Louis, Joe 3, 102
Luzinski, Greg 114, 141, 155, 163

Mack, Connie 13, 14, 18, 28, 38, 54–56, 58, 62, 65, 85
Mackey, Biz 26, 27, 38, 45
Maddox, Garry 105, 116, 117, 152, 158–161, 163
Madison Giants 26
Malarcher, David 39
Manley, Effa 65, 67
Manush, Heinie 28
Marichal, Juan 96
Marquard, Rube 21
Mason, Hank 91–93, 129, 130
Mathewson, Christy 23
Matthews, Gary 163
Mauch, Gene 107, 108, 110, 133, 139, 147
Mays, Willie 41, 67, 106
Mazeroski, Bill 156
McBride, Arnold "Bake" 117, 160–163
McCarver, Tim 140, 150, 151
McClellan, Danny 18, 19
McDonald, Webster 38
McGraw, John 11, 23, 46
McInnis, Stuffy 28
Meyer, Russ "Mad Monk" 76
Miami (Phillies farm club) 129
Milwaukee Brewers (American Association) 44, 48, 49, 52; (American League) 139, 142, 143, 149, 155
Minnesota Twins 113, 132, 143, 149, 154, 155, 163
Minoso, Minnie 52, 55, 123
Money, Don 149
Montanez, Guillermo "Willie" 105, 152, 153, 158
Montreal Expos 157
Montreal Royals 68
Moreland, Keith 163
Morgan, Joe 113
Morrison, Jim 163
Muchnick, Isadore 40
Murphy, Danny 13

Nashua, NH (Dodgers farm club) 53
National Association for the Advancement of Colored People 95
National Association of Base Ball Players (NABBP) 9
National Association of Colored Professional Baseball Clubs 28, 30, 31
National Basketball Association 37, 47
National Football League 42
National League 2, 10, 11, 21, 23, 46–48, 53, 58, 68, 72, 73, 76–78, 93, 97, 104, 107, 113, 115, 116, 118, 131, 133, 134, 137, 139, 140, 142, 146–148, 153–155, 157–159, 161, 162
Neeman, Cal 138
Negro National League 23, 26, 28, 31, 32, 37–40
New York Cubans 43
New York Giants (baseball) 4, 11–13, 23, 49, 57, 65, 75, 79, 87, 88, 93, 94, 96, 97, 105, 106, 117, 118, 131, 133, 152, 154–157; *see also* San Francisco Giants
New York Giants (National Football League) 143
New York Mets 94, 117, 128, 138, 153, 157, 159, 162, 164
New York Times 94
New York Yankees 66, 72, 73, 84, 85, 87, 104, 123, 125, 126, 131, 134, 145, 147, 151, 153, 154
Newark (International League) 10
Newark Eagles 51, 65, 67, 68
Newcombe, Don 65, 78, 89
Newsome, Skeeter 74
Norristown Colored Elks 43
Notre Dame University 10
Nugent, Gerry 48, 51, 53

Oates, Johnny 141
O'Neil, Buck 61, 62, 69
Ottawa (A's farm team) 83, 126
Overbrook (Pa.) High School 42
Owens, Jesse 3, 102
Owens, Paul 115, 155, 158

Pacific League Coast 41
Pagan, Jose 154
Paige, Leroy "Satchel" 4, 7, 22, 44, 49, 52, 62, 63, 65, 81, 121, 122

Parrott, Harold 79
Passon Field 33, 38, 45; *see also* Elks Field
Pena, Roberto 148, 149
Pennock, Herb 56, 72, 73
Pennsylvania Supreme Court 13
Peterson, Robert 19
Philadelphia Athletics 2, 4, 5, 13–19, 27, 28, 38, 46, 54, 55, 58, 62, 63, 68, 70, 80–83, 85, 86, 88, 125, 126, 129, 144
Philadelphia Eagles 156
Philadelphia Excelsiors 8
Philadelphia Giants 17–20, 23, 24, 46
Philadelphia Inquirer 83, 88, 111
Philadelphia Item 17
Philadelphia Mutuals 11
Philadelphia Orions 11
Philadelphia Phillies 2, 4, 5, 13, 15, 19, 21, 27, 28, 33, 38, 46, 47, 49, 51–53, 56–58, 68, 70, 72–82, 86, 88–164
Philadelphia Pythians 8, 9, 46
Philadelphia Stars 4, 20, 30, 35, 37, 42, 44, 47, 56, 65, 68, 87, 102, 121–124
Philadelphia Tigers 33
Philadelphia Tribune 8, 17, 24, 25, 30, 37, 40, 45, 54, 67, 83, 89, 90, 106
Philadelphia Warriors 36, 47, 123
Phillies Cigar Company 51
Phillies Park 32
Phillips, Adolfo 144–146
Pittsburgh Courier 8, 60, 67
Pittsburgh Crawfords 7, 26, 34, 35, 68
Pittsburgh Pirates 23, 61, 73, 75, 116, 123, 130, 139, 145, 153, 154, 156, 157, 160
Plank, Eddie 28
Poles, Spotswood 19
Polo Grounds 131
Posey, Cumberland 34
Power, Vic 84, 85, 125, 126, 142, 144

Quaker Giants 23
Quinn, John 107, 113, 115

Raffensberger, Ken 76, 77
Reese, Pee Wee 90, 127
Reynolds, Ken 155
Rickey, Branch 46, 51, 56, 62, 68, 70, 71, 74, 101, 102
Roberts, Robin 129, 130, 133
Robeson, Paul 60
Robinson, Bill 153, 159
Robinson, Frank 69
Robinson, Humberto 131–133

Robinson, Jackie 1, 3, 4, 14, 40–42, 45, 54–56, 59, 62–65, 67–79, 87, 88, 101, 118, 119
Rojas, Octavio "Cookie" 106
Rollins, Jimmy 119
Roosevelt, Franklin 40
Rose, Pete 164
Rowe, "Schoolboy" 76
Ruth, Babe 19
Ruthven, Dick 162
Ryan, Connie 75

St. Hyancinthe (A's farm team) 83
St. Louis Browns 10, 13, 48, 49, 63, 65, 83, 87, 88, 122, 124
St. Louis Cardinals 22, 26, 75, 79, 104, 109, 111, 124, 134, 140, 143, 147, 149, 151, 152, 160, 161, 163
Samuel, Juan 117
San Diego (Pacific Coast League Team) 124
San Diego Padres 136, 149, 155–157, 160
Sanders, Ken 155
Sanford, Jack 93, 131, 133
Savage, Ted 139
Sawatski, Carl 133
Sawyer, Eddie 129, 130, 133
Schlichter, Walter "Slick" 17, 19
Schmidt, Mike 114, 141, 154, 155, 159, 162
Seminick, Andy 53, 77
Semproch, Ray 129
Shantz, Bobby 87
Shibe, Ben 102
Shibe Park 25, 37, 43, 45, 55, 56, 80–81, 83, 86, 91, 95, 98, 102, 103, 115, 116, 147, 151; *see also* Connie Mack Stadium
Short, Chris 137, 146, 147
Sievers, Roy 144, 147
Simmons, Curt 77, 130
Simpson, Harry 44, 59, 65, 66, 102, 122, 123
Simpson, Wayne 153, 158, 159
Sizemore, Ted 160, 162
Skinner, Bob 108, 109, 111, 150
Skowron, Bill 125
Slaughter, Enos 79
Smith, Harry 17
Smith, Lonnie 162, 163
Smith, Mayo 129
Smith, Milt 44, 45, 65, 66, 123, 124
Smith, Wendell 40, 60, 67
Sorrell, Bennie 62, 64
Stanky, Eddie 74

Stengel, Casey 123, 125
Stennett, Rennie 156
Stephens, Paul "Jake" 38
Stone, Toni 68
Stovey, George 10
Strong, Nat 17, 33, 34
Stuart, Dick 147
Suratt, Alfred "Slick" 60, 64, 65
Syracuse (Phillies farm team) 92, 129, 130

Tabor, Jim 74
Taylor, Tony 96–98, 107, 134, 136, 137, 150, 153
Texas Rangers 117, 146
Thomas, Frank 105, 106, 110, 140, 144, 145
Thomas, Valmy 91, 92, 93, 131–133
Thompson, A.D. 25
Thompson, Hank 65, 88
Thompson, Lloyd 35
Thorn, John 4
Tolan, Bobby 159, 160
Toledo (Phillies farm team) 157, 159
Toledo Blue Stockings 7, 11
Toronto Blue Jays 117, 118, 141, 161, 164
Tovar, Cesar 154, 155
Trice, Bob 56, 82–84, 103, 126
Trillo, Manny 164
Tygiel, Jules 4, 5

Underwood, Tom 159
United States Supreme Court 103, 111
University of California at Los Angeles (UCLA) 62, 71
Unser, Del 151

Veeck, Bill 48, 49, 51, 52, 63, 65, 122, 124
Venezuelan Winter League 41
Veterans Stadium 81, 113, 115, 116, 141, 151, 154, 155

Waddell, Rube 18
Wade, Ed 120
Wagner, Honus 18, 23
Wagner, Richard 94
Walker, Harry 75
Walker, Moses Fleetwood 7, 11
Warwick Hotel 79
Washington Senators 112
White, Bill 143, 146, 147
White, Chaney 38
White, Charlie 44, 45, 124
White, Sol 17, 19, 23, 30, 34
Wilkes-Barre Barons 44
Wilkinson, J.L. 17, 32
Williams, Joe 21, 22
Williams, Marvin 40–42
Williams, Ted 123
Wilmington Giants 23
Wilson, Jud 39
Wilson, W. Rollo 37–40, 54
Winchell, Walter 74
Wine, Bobby 134, 148
Wise, Rick 146
World War I 2, 3, 16, 25, 29
World War II 40, 43, 49, 71, 75

Yancey, Bill 56, 69
YMCA 24

www.ingramcontent.com/pod-product-compliance
Ingram Content Group UK Ltd.
Pitfield, Milton Keynes, MK11 3LW, UK
UKHW042012140426
5217IPUK00015B/1119